Violence in Society

Violence in Society

Edited by
Pamela J. Taylor

Head of Medical Services,
Special Hospitals Service Authority, London
and
Honorary Senior Lecturer,
Department of Forensic Psychiatry,
Institute of Psychiatry, London

1993

ROYAL COLLEGE OF PHYSICIANS OF LONDON

Publisher's acknowledgement

The Royal College of Physicians is grateful to National Power PLC for their grant towards the publication of this book.

Royal College of Physicians of London
11 St Andrews Place, London NW1 4LE

Registered Charity No. 210508

Copyright © 1993 Royal College of Physicians of London
ISBN 1 873240 47 3

Typeset by Bath Typesetting Ltd, Bath, Avon
Printed in Great Britain by The Lavenham Press Ltd
Lavenham, Sudbury, Suffolk

Foreword

By Anthony W. Clare

Clinical Professor of Psychiatry, Trinity College, Dublin

Contemporary society yearns for simple solutions to complicated problems. The seemingly inexorable rise in violence—sexual, family, marital, urban, terrorist, international—has provoked a widespread demand for an answer to what Freud called 'the greatest hindrance to civilization', namely the tendency of human beings to indulge in physically destructive or damaging behaviour. The fate of complicated questions in our increasingly impatient world is to provoke simplistic answers. Thus there are powerful and influential biological voices insisting that man's genetic endowment holds the key whereas others with a comparable stridency insist that the roots of our disaster lie deep within the social environments we create. Medicine, as befits a domain straddling the great nature–nurture divide, has tended to avoid confronting the issue of human aggression head-on, preferring instead to consider its impact in selected areas of immediate clinical relevance such as psychiatry, forensic pathology, accident and emergency medicine and paediatrics. Not surprisingly such fastidiousness has not been without its critics.

This is a timely volume. The perception is widespread, whether soundly based or not, that contemporary society is becoming increasingly violent and there must be a reason. Psychiatrists, psychologists, physicians, sociologists, ethologists, lawyers, philosophers are all represented within these pages for the simple reason that notwithstanding the yearning for the simple answer there is none. This is not because of some dry academic delight in complexity or Socratic enquiry but because the tendency to blur the differences between the various categories of human aggression, to ignore obvious and subtle distinctions of circumstances and settings, personality and provocation, gender and sex, meaning and autonomy, culture and belief and seek a unifying and all-embracing answer is itself a major obstacle to our understanding of this most troublesome of behaviours.

The conference and this volume do not pretend to be all-inclusive. Many aspects of human violence for reasons of time and space and other considerations too have had to remain unconsidered. Some topics such as the language and the morality of violence are not central to medical consideration. Others, such as the role of doctors in interrogation and punishment, aggression in the context of the doctor–patient relationship, violence and scientific research, and the relationship between individual and institutional violence most decidedly are. As with the best conferences, this one served to remind us of how extensive and far-reaching is the topic under consideration.

Underpinning this volume and running through the various contributions is what Medawar has described as 'scientific meliorism'. A meliorist is one who believes that the world can be made a better place not through a massive revolutionary reordering of priorities and realities but through painstaking, even plodding effort. None of the participants in the conference that led to this book was under any illusion concerning human violence, not least the fact that it is not a scientific problem nor does it admit of a scientific solution. If human violence is ever tamed it will not be merely because we have learned more about its origins, purposes, intents and effects but because in addition we have become willing and able to solve the subsequent political, cultural, administrative and educational problems involved in exploiting such knowledge for the benefit of individuals and societies. But the scientific meliorist is moved by the conviction that science has a major role to play in dispelling myth and obfuscation and establishing a more substantial understanding upon which politicians and legislators can operate. The extent to which in the area of human violence this is a reasonable conviction can be judged by the contributions to this book.

July 1993

Preface

This book is more than a simple record of the proceedings of the conference, but nonetheless heavily based on it. Material has been updated as necessary and as far as possible any key pointers to arise in discussion have been incorporated and pursued, although no attempt was made to record verbatim. I have added short sections which aim to set the chapters in something of their wider context.

Credit for the lead in identifying the value of a new multi-disciplinarily informed review of violence in society must rest with the Royal College of Physicians. With the encouragement and support of the then President, Dame Margaret Turner-Warwick, the Assistant Registrar, Carol Seymour, first approached Anthony Clare to consider the development of such a project, and ideas escalated from there. Anthony consulted with me, and I consulted first with others in the Department of Forensic Psychiatry at the Institute of Psychiatry, London, and especially with John Gunn who gave much wise advice on the programme and enthusiastic support throughout.

The conference, from which this book was developed, was that of a joint effort on the part of the Royal College of Physicians and the Institute of Psychiatry, although on the conference days we were delighted that the Royal College of Psychiatrists was officially represented by its then President, Andrew Sims. We were delighted too to welcome Chris Nuttall, whose presence as chairman of a session underscored Home Office interest, and similarly John Reed, from the Department of Health, whose subsequent commitment to the field has been tested and proved through his two-year chairmanship of the Department of Health and Home Office Review of Health and Social Services for Mentally Disordered Offenders and Others Requiring Similar Services. My employing authority—the Special Hospitals Service Authority—has been unfailingly helpful in allowing me time and support for both conference and book. Without these people and their generosity, neither the conference nor what follows would have been possible. Most of the speakers at the meeting have been persuaded into print; their chapters stand as testimony to the value of their work. A few had to limit themselves to presentation, and reference is made in the following text to the importance of their contributions to the field. The delegates pressed us all forward.

All that applies to the conference applies also to the book, but in addition I must express tremendous personal gratitude to Diana Beaven in the publications office of the Royal College of Physicians.

Without her constant, cheerful encouragement, guidance and sheer hard work the book would never have happened. Nor would I have been able to bring it together without my splendid, patient secretaries—Denise Formosa and Nengi Charles.

Pamela J. Taylor

July 1993

Contributors

R. Blackburn, *Professor of Clinical and Forensic Psychological Studies, Liverpool University, and Honorary Consultant Clinical Psychologist, Ashworth Hospital, Parkbourn, Maghull, Merseyside L31 1HW*

D. M. Forshaw, *Senior Registrar in General Psychiatry, Maudsley Hospital, Denmark Hill, London SE5 8AZ*

J. C. Gunn, *Professor of Forensic Psychiatry, Department of Forensic Psychiatry, Institute of Psychiatry, Denmark Hill, London SE5 8AF*

R. A. Hinde, *M.R.C. Group on the Development and Integration of Behaviour, Madingley, Cambridge CB3 8AA*

J. E. Hodge, *Director of Psychological Services, Rampton Hospital, Retford, Nottinghamshire DN22 0PD*

C. R. Hollin, *Senior Lecturer in Psychology, School of Psychology, University of Birmingham, Edgbaston B15 2TT; and Glenthorne Youth Treatment Centre, Birmingham*

A. Maden, *Senior Lecturer in Forensic Psychiatry, Department of Forensic Psychiatry, Institute of Psychiatry, Denmark Hill, London SE5 8AF*

G. Robertson, *Department of Forensic Psychiatry, Institute of Psychiatry, Denmark Hill, London SE5 8AF*

E. A. Stanko, *Director, Graduate Studies and Research, Department of Law, Brunel University, Uxbridge, Middlesex UB8 3PH*

J. Strang, *Getty Senior Lecturer in the Addictions, National Addiction Centre, Institute of Psychiatry/Maudsley Hospital, Denmark Hill, London SE5 8AZ*

E. Taylor, *Reader in Developmental Neuropsychiatry, M.R.C. Child Psychiatry Unit, Institute of Psychiatry, Denmark Hill, London SE5 8AF*

P. J. Taylor, *Head of Medical Services, Special Hospitals Service Authority, Charles House, 375 Kensington High Street, London W14 8QH*

B. Webb, *Detective Superintendent, National Criminal Intelligence Service, PO Box 8000, London SE11 5EH*

W. Yule, *Professor of Psychology, Department of Psychology, Institute of Psychiatry, Denmark Hill, London SE5 8AF*

Contents

                                                                    Page

Acknowledgements   ii
Foreword *by Anthony Clare*   iii
Preface   v
List of contributors.   vii

Violence as a health issue
Editor's introduction   1

Part 1: The origins and causes of violence
Editorial   7

1   Human violence: a biological perspective
by John Gunn   11
Concepts   11
Social functions   12
Functions of social living   13
Hierarchies and sanctions   14
Excess violence   15
Theories of violence   16
    Social dominance theory   19
    Psychiatry and psychology   20
    Criminal and group violence   21
    Domestic violence   22
    Warfare   22
Evolution of co-operation   25
Conclusion   26

**2   Aggression at different levels of social
      complexity**
by Robert A. Hinde   31
Introduction   31
Individual aggression   32
    Factors giving rise to aggression   32
Aggression between groups   33
International war   33
    Factors maintaining the institution of war . . .   34
Conclusion   34

3 The roots and role of violence in development
  by Eric Taylor   37
  Introduction   37
  Normal development   37
  Types of aggression   38
    Tantrums   38
    Rough-and-tumble play   39
    Instrumental violence   40
    Aggression in family interactions   40
    Classification of types of aggression   41
  Developmental consequences of aggression   41
    Benefits of aggression   41
    Risks of aggression   42
  Individual differences   43
  Aetiology of high aggressiveness   45
    Other psychological problems   45
    Constitutional factors   46
      Genetic inheritance   46
      Gender differences   47
      Altered neuropsychological processes   48
      Social processing   49
    Environmental factors   49
      Family relationships   49
      Maudsley Hospital family study   50
      Environmental toxins   51
  Conclusions   52

**4 Contemporary psychological research into
    violence: an overview**
  by Clive R. Hollin   55
  Introduction   55
  Conceptual bases of violent behaviour   55
  Situational analysis   56
    Physical factors   57
    Social factors   58
  The person   58
    Background   58
    Response: cognition   59
    Response: emotion   60
    Response: action   61
  Impact of violent behaviour   62
    Role of the victim   62
    Violence towards women and children   63
  Reducing violence   63

Prevention 64
Treatment . . . . . : 65
Context 66
Closing remark 67

5   **Women as violent offenders and violent patients**
by Tony Maden 69
Gender differences in offending 69
Causes of gender differences 70
Growth of feminism 71
Provocation in domestic killings 71
Female violence and psychiatric disorder 72
Psychiatric disposal 72
Reasons for different sentencing practices . . . 73
Surveys of violent offenders 74
Violence by women within prisons 74
Self-injury 75
Violent women in hospital 76
Conclusions 78

Part 2: Mental disorder and violence
Editorial 81

6   **Mental illness and violence**
by Pamela J. Taylor 85
Frequency of coincidence of violence and mental illness 86
Psychosis as a factor in causing violence 87
Symptomatic triggers of violence 87
Violence and illness careers 89
Impact of psychosis on general life-style 90
Psychosis and violence as a product of other primary pathology 91
Mentally ill and violent patients within the health service 92

7   **Personality and violence**
by Ronald Blackburn 99
Introduction 99
Aggression and personality 99
Acts and dispositions 99
Consistency of aggression 101
Individual differences and aggression 102

A cognitive-interpersonal model of personality . . .   106
    Aggression and the interpersonal circle   106
    Interpersonal style, cognition and the persistence of
        interpersonal style   108
Conclusion   110

8 Drugs, aggression and violence
    by David M. Forshaw and John Strang   113
Introduction   113
Extent of illicit drug use   113
Drugs and crime   114
Drugs and violence   115
Roles of drug use in violence   115
Nature of the relationship between drugs and crime   .   117
    Result of the sought-after effect   118
    Secondary to intoxication   118
    Secondary to an induced mental disorder   119
    Secondary to a withdrawal state   120
    Secondary to personality changes   120
    Secondary to adopted life-style   121
Drugs groups   122
    Stimulants   122
    Sedatives   122
    Opiates   123
    Hallucinogens   123
Influence of route of drug use   123
Conclusion   123

9 Alcohol and violence
    by John E. Hodge   127
Introduction   127
Alcohol and crime   128
Alcohol and violent crime   129
    Assault   129
    Homicide   129
    Rape   129
    Domestic violence   130
    Victims of violence   130
Types of relationship   130
Natural experiments   131
Violent incidents in relation to alcohol consumed   .   131
Theoretical perspectives   132
    Moral theory   132
    Disinhibition theory   132

Stimulation theory 133
Other factors which may explain the relationship
between alcohol and violence 134
Predisposing factors 135
Individual differences 135
Conclusion 136

Part 3: Victims and survivors: shifting the focus of concern

Editorial 139

10 Managing disasters and stress in police officers involved in the aftermath

by Barry Webb 147
Introduction 147
Experiences at the crash scene 147
The need for immediate debriefing of officers . . . 148
Involvement in mortuary procedures 149
Compulsory counselling 149
Support to the bereaved 149
Stress suffered by officers engaged in the support
process 151
Conclusion 152

11 Children as victims and survivors

by William Yule 153
Introduction 153
Violence within the family 153
Physical abuse 154
Munchausen syndrome by proxy 154
Child sexual abuse 155
Transgenerational transmission 156
Child witnesses of violence 158
Post-traumatic stress disorder and children 160
Common stress reactions in children 160
Studies on post-traumatic stress disorder 162
Treatment of post-traumatic stress disorder 163
Examples of treatment 164
Conclusions 165

12 Everyday violence and experience of crime

by Elizabeth A. Stanko 169
Defining public violence 169
The danger 171

Women, violence and danger   173
Men, violence and danger   175
Physicians' work and everyday violence   177
   Sexually intrusive situations   177
   Physical danger within the home   177
   Violence against men   178
   Racial or homophobic violence   178
   Post-traumatic stress disorder   178
Conclusions   178

Part 4: Evaluation of the clinician's role

Editorial   181

13 Reconviction: a measure of psychiatric efficacy?

by Graham Robertson   183
Introduction   183
The mentally ill and mentally handicapped . . .   183
   The mentally ill offender   184
   The mentally handicapped offender   185
Follow-up study of mentally disordered offenders . 185
Case histories   187
Value of reconviction data to the clinician 188
Comparison of people with psychosis and people
   with personality disorder   189
   Psychotic disorders   189
   Psychopathic disorders   189
Psychotherapy and Grendon Prison   189
   Follow-up study of reconviction: experimental design 190
   The criterion measure of reconviction 192
Case histories from Grendon Prison   193
Reconviction as a criterion of therapeutic success . . 195
Conclusion   196

14 Furthering medical and psychological understand-ing of violence

by Pamela J. Taylor   197

Violence as a health issue

Pamela J. Taylor
Head of Medical Services, Special Hospitals Service Authority, London

Doctors and their colleagues in most parts of the health service encounter violence or its consequences as part of their duties—probably more frequently than is generally realised. Violence is therefore an issue that affects them not only as members of society as a whole, but also as clinicians. A range of specific clinical issues thus has to be addressed within the professions. These include:

- definition and recognition of pathological violence
- prevention of violence
- treatment of those who perpetrate pathological violence
- recognition and correct attribution of physical and psychological sequelae of any violence
- for a few groups, such as the police, the military, emergency services personnel and health service staff themselves, who know they must face violence from time to time, the prevention and limitation of consequent physical and psychological damage
- prevention and limitation of long-term physical and psychological damage among victims of violence
- medico-legal work that is required both for perpetrators and victims
- service planning to take account of the full range of need—from general assistance to highly specialist treatments; from individuals to substantial groups such as those who are victims of terrorist acts or major disasters; for acute provision and for very long term treatment and care of both victims and mentally disordered perpetrators of violence.

As recognition grows of the full extent of the health problems to be addressed, and thus the qualitative and quantitative challenges to medicine as a whole, the conjunction of physical and psychological medicine, as led by the Royal College of Physicians and the Institute of Psychiatry in sponsoring the conference on which this book is based, could not have been more timely.

Many discussions of violence seem to follow from an assumption that it is easily recognisable, and that the reader or listener will have concepts of violence that are necessarily shared with the writer or speaker. With increasing sophistication, however, in understanding human and other animal behaviour, the concept of violence creates as much confusion as related concepts such as anger, aggression and hostility. 'Violence' is the term generally reserved for physically destructive or damaging activity. At its extreme, it is easy to recognise; for example, there is little doubt that homicide is a violent act. Killing another person may or may not be a lawful act, or an understandable act, or an act rooted in pathology, but it is certainly violent. Most would now view non-consensual sexual activity also as a form of violence. It is more difficult to use such a simple approach to classification of those activities where consent is impossible, for example, because one participant is incapable of consent, but some would judge the disregard of consent as itself a form of violence. Similarly, uncomplicated burglary or theft of various kinds would not usually be regarded as 'violent activities' in classifying the perpetrators, but the victims of such acts often feel gravely 'violated'.[1] Further, those who witness or are threatened with serious violence may develop problems almost indistinguishable from those who experience the physical blows.

'Aggression' has generally been used as a broader term, but is now so broad that not only may it be regarded as describing an unprovoked attack or assault—not necessarily physical—but also almost as a positive trait, not far removed from the notion of assertiveness. Paradoxically, professional observers may have compounded the problem in their efforts to tighten definition and measurements. As more than one person has somewhat cynically observed—aggression can be a phenomenon defined merely by answers to questionnaires completed by psychology students.

The term 'anger' is used for an explicitly emotional arousal state rather than an act or enduring trait. The differences in concepts of anger nevertheless again cause dilemmas—from anger as a positive, energising, empowering phenomenon to anger as a central determinant of individual or collective violence.[2]

'Hostility' describes the more enduring mental set of individuals who are ever ready, even over-ready, to respond to other people or situations antagonistically. At least as measured by rating scales, however, hostility, like anger or aggression, is far from necessarily correlated with violence (e.g. ref. 3).

Generally throughout this book, the contributors have used the term violence to imply action, rather than thinking or feeling alone, and thus distinct from anger or hostility. The demarcation between violence and aggression is less clear, given that it may not be unreasonable to consider violence as a subset of aggression.

There is then the question of 'pathological violence'. From a victim's perspective, it matters little whether or not violence is pathological. Indeed, the requirements for medical attention for both physical and psychological consequences have much in common even when the 'violence' has followed from a natural disaster with no hint of human causation. The treatment of people who have been violent can also, however, be a legitimate task, and here distinctions between pathology and lack of pathology in the violence become more important. The soldier who kills a designated enemy in a sanctioned war according to the generally accepted rules of combat is unlikely to have committed a pathological act which would merit psychiatric attention or respond to treatment. A young mother who kills her three children and then attempts to kill herself is unlikely to be acting in a healthy way, and almost certainly will require treatment. In common with so many human and other animal characteristics, it seems unlikely that any quality associated with violence is an absolute indicator of pathology. Nevertheless, extremes on a number of dimensions would be suggestive. These would include direction, extent, frequency and direct association with independently recognised psychopathology.

The nearest to a framework for the consideration of some violence as in itself pathological is not dissimilar from that which defines pathology in other areas of human behaviour, for example, a delusion as a pathological form of thinking. Kraupl Taylor defined a psychotic delusion as one based on an absolute conviction of the truth of a proposition which is idiosyncratic, incorrigible, ego-involved and often preoccupying.[4] Few psychiatrists or psychologists working regularly with offenders would fail to recognise a violent equivalent: that is, a violent act, often an extremely destructive act, in itself idiosyncratic and certainly an intensely solitary function, largely unchecked by thoughts of being wrong, or of being caught or punished, and often preoccupying to the extent of being rehearsed in imagination both before and after the event and to the exclusion of other, more conventional kinds of activity. Evidence of psychiatric illness may or may not be present additionally. Professional clinicians have no difficulty in accepting that entirely subjective phenomena such as abnormalities of thought or belief are pathological, and accordingly applying appropriately scientific, medical or psychological approaches to their evaluation, treatment and management, but fully verifiable phenomena such as comparable abnormalities of action are rarely treated with the same scientific rigour. Levin and Fox present a view that is common among clinicians, but wholly incomprehensible to many who, in theory, have less professional expertise.[5]

> The serial killer ... travels around, sometimes from state to state, searching for victims he can rape and sodomise, torture and dismember, stab and strangle. Even these truly sadistic killers are, however, more evil than

crazy. Few of them can be said to be driven by delusions or hallucinations; almost none of them talks to demons or hears strange voices in empty rooms. Though their crimes may be sickening, they are not sick in either a medical or legal sense.

Professional advice from a different source, but to the same effect, was also offered about the same time in England. In the trial of Dennis Nilsen the judge advised the jury:

'There must be no excuses for Nilsen if he has moral defects ... a nasty nature is not arrested or retarded development of mind.' and 'There are evil people who do evil things. Committing murder is one of them.'

The jury manifestly had more difficulty making up its collective mind than did the judge.[6]

The value and appropriateness of medical or psychological skills in assessing and treating the violence of such individuals should rightly be the focus of intense scrutiny. The deflection from this simply by the invocation of evil or wickedness, which the philosopher Midgley regards anyway as 'mostly a vacuum',[7] hardly assists that process, and most certainly does not further understanding and the safe management of antisocial violence.

Other characteristics of violence which may place its management properly in the realm of medical practice are more quantitative than qualitative. It is not uncommon for violence to result in some physical harm to self and others, and for this to be knowingly accepted as a risk, for example, when men engage in fights. When the balance is such that harm to self is the main result, and even the primary goal, the violence is more likely than not to be regarded as pathological, and indeed, in turn, to be associated with pathology. Generally the pathology is a functional neurotic or psychotic illness, but rare physical disorders may be associated with self harm, perhaps the best known being the X-linked recessive chromosomal disorder, Lesch-Nyhan syndrome.

An even more obviously quantitative difference suggesting possible pathology is the extent of damage-inflicting activity. Chance factors often play a greater role in the result of a violent act than is sometimes credited. Few people are anatomically sure in their thrust; a knife that hits a rib is unlikely to be fatal, a knife that slips between ribs much more likely to be so, and yet each of the blows may have been delivered with the same intent, force and approximate direction. Nevertheless, some violence stands out as disproportionate—the delivery of 57 deep stab wounds to one person; the stabbing, strangling, beating and submersion of another, when any one of these activities in itself would have had fatal consequences. On a standard of *'x amount' of violence would probably have killed, but 'x plus 500%'* was delivered, few would dispute the latter degree of violence is grossly abnormal, but who is to say where the cut-off point should be in such a quantitative definition?

Frequency of violence has been the most favoured target of abnormality—and it is easy to see practical reasons why this should be so. If something occurs often, the chances of a skilled professional being able to observe and measure it directly are much greater, and the chances of being able to demonstrate efficacy of treatment much higher. If something—such as homicide—has a low base rate, it is rarely possible to demonstrate that an intervention has been effective. The target feature may never have occurred again anyway. Literature is thus replete with accounts of 'repetitively violent offenders' showing non-specific abnormalities of brain function, and even being regarded as having 'episodic dyscontrol', a sort of epileptic equivalent. The evidence for such a direct, treatable organic abnormality is slight in all but a tiny minority of cases where true epilepsy can be demonstrated, and even more rarely be shown to be directly relevant.[8] On the assumption that there might be something approaching a normal curve for the frequency of violent activity, it is interesting that there is virtually no interest in its low rate or absence.

Finally, it is now recognised that some psychiatric disorders may increase the risk of violence (see Chapters 6–9), and it is for this group of people above all that doctors must play a role in prevention or treatment. The links are increasingly well understood, and it is increasingly apparent that for unacceptable violence—as opposed to other kinds of antisocial activity—the links are often directly to symptoms of the disease and that, insofar as the disease itself is treatable, so is the violence. Successful treatment of such patients will make a tiny contribution to the reduction of violence in society, but be of immense importance to the individual sufferers, their families, and also the health service staff who must from time to time look after them.

Victims and perpetrators of violence alike seek recourse to the law for their problems. In this context, more attention has generally been given to the perpetrators who have a pivotal role in any proceedings, and are entitled to their own lawyers and medical advisers in the due process of the administration of justice. Victims are not so fortunate.[9] Most criminal prosecutions are taken on by the state, and the victim at most has the role of a witness in the case, no rights of representation in court and, in marked contrast to the alleged offender, no absolute rights to protection from, effectively, character assassination by 'the other side'. Regardless of the nature of victimisation—criminal or accidental—medical help and/or compensation for victims has been often dependent on chance, although voluntary agencies now exist to offer information and advice and, as documented later in this volume, the police are increasingly sensitive to the need for information and support by victims of any major trauma.

The victim of adjudicated crime is generally an isolated figure and, not uncommonly feeling more shamed than the perpetrator, rarely presses forward for help. This is perhaps particularly true for children, and for adults who are repeatedly victimised. Wars have proved to be a substantial source of enhanced understanding of the psychological as well as the physical effects of trauma, the USA–Vietnam war being a particular recent landmark. A series of natural, recreational and transport disasters has at last given civilian victims a collective base from which to press their case for survival. Too often still, however, the medical and caring professions have advanced no further than the general public. They can see the physical damage, they can sympathise, even empathise in the short term, but fail to grasp and respond to the longevity of the problems of a substantial proportion of the people who receive violence. The treatment and care both of those who have suffered violence and of those who enact it, which are partly overlapping groups,[10] is demanding in the multiplicity of skills and supports required, and in the length of time that these remain needed. Service planning must be as ready to take individual long-term need into account as the occasional demand for a massive, immediate response to the acute needs of a traumatised crowd or community.

References

1. Maguire M, Bennett T. *Burglary in a dwelling.* London: Heinemann, 1982
2. Novaco RW. A contextual perspective on anger with relevance to blood pressure. In: Johnson E, Gentry D, Julius S, eds. *Personality, elevated blood pressure, and essential hypertension.* Hemisphere Publishing Co, (in press)
3. Gunn J, Gristwood J. Use of the Buss–Durkee hostility inventory among British prisoners. *J Consult Clin Psychol* 1975;**43**:590
4. Kraupl Taylor F. *Psychopathology: its causes and symptoms.* Romney Marsh: Quartermaine House, 1979
5. Levin J, Fox JA. *Mass murder: America's growing menace.* New York: Plenum Press, 1985
6. Masters B. *Killing for company.* London: Jonathan Cape, 1985
7. Midgley M. *Wickedness.* London: Routledge and Kegan Paul, 1984
8. Gunn JC, Fenton G. Epilepsy, automatism and crime. *Lancet* 1971; **i**:1173–6
9. Shapland J, Willmore J, Duff P. *Victims in the criminal justice system.* Cambridge Studies in Criminology No. 53. London: Gower, 1985
10. Hodge JE. Addiction to violence. *Crim Behav Mental Health* 1992;**2**:212–23

Part 1

The origins and causes of violence

Pamela J. Taylor

Head of Medical Services, Special Hospitals Service Authority, London

---

It is easy to make assumptions about violence. A particularly popular myth is that it is currently more pervasive, or serious, or 'nasty' than ever before. Another favourite is that its origins are so clear that policies of tabloid newspaper simplicity will influence its occurrence. Violence is not new, and there is certainly no one simple way of defining, classifying and understanding it.

Epidemiological myths have been addressed both by cross-sectional and by longitudinal approaches. Pearson explored the history of street crime and violence in Britain.[1] Focusing especially on the past 150 years, but taking many earlier examples of violent crime, he searched in vain for 'the golden age' when such deviancy had no place in society. He pointed out that many had placed this age among the 'glories of empire, child labour and workhouse in Queen Victoria's reign', but he showed that the 'traditional lament' about the descent into lawlessness and violence or even the rule of the mob was already established then when, in turn, the impeccable qualities of the 'British way of life' were placed in pre-industrial revolution 'Merrie England'. At least as common as the tendency to invest the more remote past in a rosy glow, Pearson also suggested, is that of locating the decline into chaos and danger within the last 20 years. Falling standards of inner city safety appear to impress people almost as a generational phenomenon, and such perceptions are indeed relatively easily understandable in these terms. For most people, childhood was indeed a time of safety, while the personal responsibilities and anxieties of adulthood may be projected on to the environment, which thus appears so much more dangerous than the parental society. Media reporting of sensational crime tends to reinforce this perception. Although, with changes in societal attitudes to violence, in police and court responses, and in the way that information is collected and interpreted, there will always be some room for doubt over whether regular, apparent rises in crime are real, founded on changing standards of tolerance, or merely artefacts of the systems of recording, Pearson provides a convincing argument that, at the very least, belief in rising violence is disproportionate to the actual change.

The British Crime Survey was the first community survey of crime in Britain and a very important landmark.[2] Disproportionate fear of crime of more explicit numerical proportions was one of the key findings. One person aged 16 years or over was interviewed for each of about 11,000 households in England and Wales and 5,000 households in Scotland. The electoral register was used as the basis of selection. All respondents were asked whether they or any other members of their household had been a victim of crime within the previous 12 months. Those who revealed victimisation were asked for more detailed information and, together with nearly half of those who did not, also completed a follow-up questionnaire about life-style. In common with other comparable national surveys, the victimisation rate was much higher than predicted from official crime figures, but not uniformly so for all crimes. The lowest official reporting rate was shown to be for some relatively trivial offences, including vandalism, while the highest was for car theft. Taken together, incidents involving personal violence became known to police in about four out of ten cases.

Nevertheless, the risks were and almost certainly still are small. The 'statistically average person' aged 16 or over could expect a robbery once every five centuries, an assault resulting in injury, even if slight, once every century, the family car stolen once every 60 years, and a burglary in the home once every 40 years. Thus, the chances of a burglary were slightly less than that of a fire in the home, and the risk of car theft lower than the risk of a family member being injured in a traffic accident. Accepting that the average person is an intangible, relative risks for different groups were calculated. Contrary to popular belief, the characteristics of the group at greatest risk of becoming victims of personal assault include male gender, age under 30, and currently unmarried status. Certain other characteristics perhaps make this cluster more comprehensible: several evenings a week away from the house, heavy use of alcohol, and a history of assault of others. Fear of crime was also elicited. Barely 1% of men under 30 admitted to feeling unsafe, although nearly 8% had been victims of street crime alone. Over one-third of women over the age of 60 felt 'very unsafe', but only 1% had been actual victims.

Although both these studies took a broader view of violence in society than official criminal activity, neither perhaps captured the extent of its influence as a societal phenomenon. The British Crime Survey explicitly excluded children, and both accounts were more or less limited to England, Wales and Scotland and to peacetime activities. John Gunn and Robert Hinde, in this book, probe much more extensively into the complexities of human behaviour regardless of place, creed or time. Hinde (Chapter 2) gives only an introduction to his work, which is published much more extensively elsewhere. He examines how levels of social complexity may make or maintain violence, and risks a note of hope that they may in turn be used or trained to lead to peace. Gunn (Chapter 1), rather more provocatively, suggests that violence, whether widely or sparingly applied, may be one of the key factors in the creation and maintenance of social structures. Indeed, he advances an interesting and plausible definition of pathological violence as that violence which excludes the perpetrator from a place in a successful social group or hierarchy.

The balance and nature of violent approaches in establishing individuals in society, or excluding them, is given weight by Eric Taylor's overview of violence in human development (Chapter 3). The complexity of the interactions between the individual and his society is again inescapable. Deviant violence nearly always has its roots in childhood, and yet both aggression and frank violence are so common among children, and some of the reinforcing factors so strong, that it is more tempting to emphasise the remarkably low levels of violence that emerge in society than to regard them as high. Taylor stresses how often violence produces immediate gratification. Over a disputed toy, the more violent child is more likely to gain the immediate goal. A child who persists in this approach, however, finds himself increasingly marginalised by both adults and other children, and thus in turn in a less advantageous position for observing and learning more adaptive strategies, and is the loser in the long term. Taylor goes on to consider the individual differences that may lead to persistent problems, not only in the child's environment and sociey, but also within the child, and in the child–environment interaction.

Clive Hollin (Chapter 4) similarly explores individual differences, and their relevance both in the environmental context for developmental pathways and also for a particular act of violence. He shifts the focus to the more overtly deviant. In addition, he is more explicit about possible points of intervention—whether for control or prevention—and presents the little available evidence to date of the impact of professional attention. As might be expected from an interactional phenomenon, attention has been directed at influencing the environment as well as the perpetrator.

Almost inevitably, the chapters focus implicitly if not explicitly on male violence. In full physical expression violence is almost certainly more a part of the male than the female world, but Tony Maden (Chapter 5) to some extent redresses the balance of understanding. Examining the challenge that violent women may be regarded as psychiatrically disordered solely because of the excessive statistical deviance of this one area of their behaviour, he shows that there are no simple routes to understanding. There is nevertheless an urgency to address the management of a problem which has often been ignored because of its infrequency. Service provision for small numbers of people is expensive, and it is apparent that the cost in this instance has not so far been readily accepted by society. Crudely, violent women are too often managed either as deviant men—with those designated as the most dangerous residing in a small high security unit within a male prison[3]—or as sick individuals. If categorised as the latter, they may generally expect to be shrugged off to the extremes, either of unsupported struggle in a community that has been or has become hostile towards them, or of maximum security hospital confinement.

The first part of this book sets out the various substrates of violence within and between individuals and at various levels of social grouping. One of the key factors in deviant violence may be a relative incapacity for joining a social group. Thus, as well as an understanding of the individual pathology or deviance, the importance of a real understanding of the possibilities for positive and negative reinforcement from societal structures is crucial to helping an individual who has been the perpetrator of violence, or the recipient, or indeed both.

References

1. Pearson G. *Hooligan: a history of respectable fears*. London, Basingstoke: Macmillan, 1983
2. Hough M, Mayhew P. *The British Crime Survey* (first report). Home Office Research Study No. 76. London: HMSO, 1983
3. Lester A, Taylor PJ. '*H*' *wing, HM Prison Durham*. Unpublished document, 1989. Available from Women in Prison, London

1 | Human violence: a biological perspective*

John Gunn
Department of Forensic Psychiatry, Institute of Psychiatry, Denmark Hill, London

> See that living legend over there?
> With one little squeeze of this trigger
> I can put that person at my feet
> moaning and groaning and pleading with God[1]

We are told we live in a violent age and crime statistics for violence seem to be constantly rising. The fear of violence can be a political factor in Parliament and in elections. We are also engaged in a debate about the deployment of particular kinds of destructive weapons. Throughout all these discussions, the one thing that everybody seems to be agreed upon is that violence is bad. Yet, anything so persistent, so pervasive must have important biosocial functions. Violence is an integral part of any complex social system, and social activity does not exist without it. However, it is also fairly clear that levels of violence vary widely between societies.

Violence and aggression are not just mammalian characteristics, nor are they confined to higher or more successful animals. These phenomena occur throughout the animal kingdom. They are associated with motility, sociability and complexity. For examples of animals that are non-violent, it is necessary to concentrate on relatively immobile, asocial and simple creatures, such as barnacles and earthworms.

Concepts

In this chapter 'violence' is used to mean destructive physical aggression—usually encompassing physical assault. 'Aggression' is broader. Violence is usually included under the umbrella of aggression, but more than physical assault is involved in aggression. Aggression is an attacking *process*, the process by which advantage and dominance are gained. Violence is relatively rare, and is the most obviously destructive component in that process.

* First published in *Criminal Behaviour and Mental Health* 1991; **1**. Reproduced by permission of Whurr Publishers Ltd.

This paper will be concerned with intraspecies violence. Interspecies violence, such as hunting, preying and the like, is a different topic. There is some overlap between the two, but the concepts are best treated separately. All social creatures are violent at times whether or not they are carnivorous.

The first and obvious thought about violence is that it is of survival advantage to an individual animal. The strongest animals can beat off others, and thereby ensure a better food supply and the best mates in which to implant their seed. More importantly, an individual can mark out a piece of territory. Territoriality seems universal among higher animals and is often directly related to feeding, mating and infant rearing. This view is, of course, Darwinian, and has been refined in this century.

Aggression is not always successful, and in some situations there may be optimal levels of aggression that are appropriate for success. Total destruction is rarely necessary for dominance; indeed, it is almost a contradiction in terms. Inappropriately severe aggression can lead to a failure to dominate: a businessman who loses his temper and throws a punch is unlikely to clinch a successful deal! Aggression is an integral part of social living, but violence seems to be only occasionally necessary or even useful for success.

Social functions

A simple social function of aggression may be to spread a densely populated species over a wide area. In other words, the fighting that occurs in many animals is not necessarily to ensure that the strongest animal gets the most food, but rather to see that the group spreads out so that as a whole it has a better chance of obtaining food, and of strengthening the genetic pool by diversification of breeding. In turn, of course, always assuming that the food supply holds up, this will lead to an increase in the numbers in that group, which is clearly of advantage to a gene associated with fighting and spreading.

An important series of observations was made by Zuckerman.[2] Almost 100 baboons were released into an enclosure at Regent's Park Zoo. Zuckerman described a violent community where brute force ruled. Aggressive and dangerous outbursts from high-ranking individuals toward their inferiors were commonplace. Dominant monkeys would grab as much food as possible, more than they needed, and mothers would even take food from their own offspring—all this despite the abundant supply of food provided by the zoo keepers. Fights were frequent, and a number of violent deaths took place. Females, weaklings and youngsters suffered the most. Zuckerman saw one male attacking a baby monkey which died later that evening. Baboons, it seemed, are savage, violent animals.

This supposition was held for some time until observations were made on baboons in the wild in Africa. Hall and De Vore noticed, like Zuckerman, that the baboon group is organised around the dominance hierarchy of adult males.[3] Often there is only one adult male with two to nine females and offspring up to the age of 18 months. No observations were made of one baboon killing another, although low-ranking males were sometimes driven from an established group. Attacks occurred when a dominant animal charged at another, seized his victim, bit him and rubbed him in the dust. Even though these attacks were vicious, they were usually short-lived and no great damage was done. However, in another captive group of baboons, Hall noticed something akin to the Zuckerman observations.[4] At Bloemfontein Zoo, an alien adult male and female were introduced into an established group of 17 baboons. The resulting disturbance completely destroyed the social structure of the colony and many of the animals were killed or died of their injuries.

So, lethal intraspecies violence is not confined to mankind. Differing social circumstances lead to quite different rates of violence. The introduction of strangers and incorrect sex ratios seem especially provocative. Even when the social system is stable and no lethal violence is observed, there is obvious aggression. Threats of violence and minimal violence still persist.

Functions of social living

All primates, including mankind, live in complex social groups. Indeed, so do many successful animals, and this is as true of insects, such as ants and bees, as it is of mammals. Why should social systems arise?

A group can deal more effectively with predators than can a lone individual, but perhaps the supreme importance of a group is that it can undertake many activities which an individual cannot. The massive division of labour which occurs in human societies is perhaps the extreme case, but it has led this one, somewhat puny, animal to conquer all other species and the environment. Every human achievement is dependent upon division of labour.

Intelligence is clearly of great advantage in mastering an environment. Division of labour can be based upon an ability to learn. Skills such as housebuilding, food gathering and environmental control are all skills that require knowledge—more knowledge than can be acquired in the lifetime of one individual. The method of communication between generations can either be genetic, as in the ant, or by teaching, as in mankind—the latter has highly flexible intelligence. Individuals are born with a capacity to learn but without much in-built knowledge or behavioural pattern. Man is thus born with great potential but few skills, and has a long period of immaturity and dependence. The sophisticated group structures which have developed in man enable the immature individual to be nurtured, while he or she is learning complex skills.

Hierarchies and sanctions

A sophisticated group structure and division of labour requires social order, which means hierarchies with some individuals being dominant or managing and others subservient. In some species, this hierarchy may be so all pervasive that the dominant creature is dominant in every respect. In others, particularly man, individuals may be domi-nant in one hierarchy and subservient in another, but the general point remains that a socially successful animal needs to develop complex systems of management and control. To put it simply, it is not much good everybody having their own ideas about how a house should be built. A plan has to be drawn up, someone has to be in charge of it, to ensure that each of the workers does his part according to the plan, and there has to be a complex system of sanctions against aberrant behaviour.

Power operates in all sorts of ways: social status and wealth are two obvious ones. Yet social status and wealth confer power only within a complex set of rules that are agreed by the relevant society. If the rules are broken discreetly, an individual may improve his position in the hierarchy and his power, but if overt breaches of the rules occur the offended group will apply sanctions.

Sanctions are the connection between aggression and group living. Hierarchies depend upon sanctions; sanctions are a form of aggression. Hence aggressive behaviour is at the heart of our most subtle and important characteristic—our social living. It is true that most aggres-sion falls far short of violence, but aggression is only aggression because ultimately it is supported by physical force. No matter how non-violent a social system may appear on the surface, violence is somewhere in the background. In a peaceful, non-violent society an individual who breaks the rules, for example by stealing something, may have various sanctions directed against him. The likeliest is that he will have to pay a financial penalty for his behaviour. If the offender refuses to do this, however, other more physical penalties will be imposed, such as imprisonment. If offenders try to resist imprisonment, they will be forced, if necessary by violence, to go to prison where they will have to be totally subservient and may be manhandled aggressively if they fail to conform. Resistance to the hierarchy is exhibited eventually by some form of violent behaviour and provokes a violent response.

Excess violence

It seems nevertheless that man's violence often goes beyond the level necessary to support social stability. Where does this excess violence come from?

Ordinary competitiveness can lead to violence. Individuals or groups do not necessarily accept the power structure of a social system precisely as it is given; in fact, few do. Attempts to change it constitute part of the spectrum of normal aggression in a society. Most of the time this aggression stops short of violence. Occasionally, however, it takes the form of manifest overt violence, for example, armed uprisings or terrorism. These outbreaks of violence are also related to the under-lying social structure, but will probably occur, to some degree, in every society. Whether or not such violence is called excess depends to some extent on its degree, but also on the subjective views of the observer.

One important source of excess violence may be an individual's personal failure to use his aggressive equipment skilfully. The most successful individuals use their aggression sparingly with appropriate timing, and steadily progress up the social hierarchy. They find a comfortable level of status and almost never resort to physical aggres-sion. *Un*successful individuals find that their aggressive behaviour only leads to greater failure. Given the nature of the aggressive response, this in turn leads to a heightening of the aggression and a sharp counter-aggressive response from other individuals. Sometimes these poor skills seem to be constitutional (for example, in the very unintelli-gent), sometimes related to defective learning, and sometimes attribu-table to illness or mental disorder (for example, schizophrenia). The successful man is seldom violent. The repeatedly violent man is seldom successful. These generalisations fail for exceptional individuals in revolutions when power systems are in turmoil, and also at the bottom of the social ladder where a rung or two may be gained by violence, but they apply for most of the time.

It is not only individuals who can develop or exhibit excess violence; social systems can too, as with monkey hill at London Zoo. The baboons were strangers to one another and to the environment, and the sex ratio was wrong. They had little or no social stability, and the violence seems to have been their mechanism of striving to create that stability. It may well have been successful over an extended period of time.

A vivid illustration of social failure manifesting itself in severe violence, and so causing a high death rate, was the natural experiment of the mutineers from the *Bounty* trying to establish a new heterosexual society among strangers on Pitcairn Island. Thirteen of the 15 settlers died by violence within ten years.[5,6] The analogy suggests that rapid growth and rapid change of either individuals or systems produce ferment and instability and an increase in aggression, perhaps an increase in crime and, in extreme cases, riots and/or uprisings. At an individual level, people who experience rapid social changes often experience alienation, anomie, frustration, relative deprivation, all of which are factors that may be associated with excess violence.

Another source of excess violence is paradoxical. Authoritarian leadership with firm control of social movement or severe oppression can reduce violence. For a time violence is pointless because it will fail. Such regimes may even reduce violence in the long term if there is opportunity within the system for lower levels of aggression to operate, that is, opportunity for individuals to move up and down in the hierarchy and to innovate. However, there are many examples in which such suppression seems to lead to a reaction, and therefore eventually to frank violence, and sometimes to massive social change which, in turn, leads to further violence. The eighteenth century French revolution is an illustration of this process.

Finally, let us remember that what is sometimes regarded as an *excess* of violence is in fact a *magnification* of violence. Man is a physically weak animal who has developed no natural weapons. When two naked people fight, neither is very likely to kill the other. Consequently, man has not developed the sophisticated submission mechanisms that animals with deadly natural weapons have usually developed. Submission gestures in one such animal will switch off the attack in the other. The former becomes the winner and neither gets killed. Man's weapons result from his intelligence, and he has at his disposal highly lethal tools which have evolved in a few thousand years. Behavioural mechanisms dependent upon genes would take hundreds of thousands or even millions of years to develop. Man therefore has not developed by evolution powerful means of appeasing an aggressor, and so an aggressive act magnified by a weapon rapidly becomes lethal. Many domestic murders are due to the availability of weapons.

There is yet a further problem created by weapons. Modern technology, guns, bombs and the like, means that one individual can kill another from a distance. In such circumstances, the victim does not have an opportunity to send *any* submission signal.

Theories of violence

Perhaps the oldest theory of human violence is that it is 'innate', 'instinctive' or 'evil'. These terms all seem to imply an inner force which must be satisfied, perhaps like the drive to feed or drink. However, there is no obvious internal homoeostasis which is upset if we are pacific for a long time, and it certainly is not the case that the likelihood of a person being aggressive is proportional to the time since he or she was last aggressive! However, it has to be acknowledged that most mammals are status seekers, some individuals more so than others according to their personalities. Equally, it is clear that our aggressive behaviour depends upon an apparatus partly located in the brain. Damage the apparatus and abnormalities of aggressive behaviour appear. Just as important, however, are social learning, on the one hand, and social contact or social pressures, on the other. Attributing all aggressive behaviour to internal factors is clearly inadequate. Sociobiology has now largely abandoned instinct theory.[7,8]

Another theory of violence which has also proved inadequate on its own is purely social—the frustration hypothesis. In the 1940s Dollard *et al.* set out a theory explaining aggression in terms of frustrated drives.[9] They went so far as to say that aggression is always a consequence of frustration. Frustration is certainly a useful word in any discussion on violence because, in the broad and colloquial sense, violence is frequently the result of frustration. At a personal level, we all understand the feelings of frustration, anger, rage and ultimately violence that can accompany continued failure to achieve an important aim by non-violent social manipulation, and in that sense the Dollard theory is valid. However, it is not immediately obvious that all wars are started by frustration. A bank robber may or may not be a frustrated individual in the ordinary sense of that term. A sadist may be frustrated only in terms of the number of opportunities for his sadism. A dictator may purge his initial frustration but remain a violent man. Above all, the soldier going into battle is not a frustrated man—he is simply obeying orders. It is clear that to study violence at an individual level, a number of mental mechanisms have to be considered: anger, hate, paranoia, obedience, isolation.[10] Frustration can link several of these, and so is a useful second-order explanation.

Learning theory has given rise to what Bandura calls a social learning theory of aggression.[11] In essence, he sees individuals acquiring behavioural styles through observational learning (modelling), reinforcement of performance (rewards), and structural determinants (physique, brain structure). These styles are then instigated towards aggression by incoming stimuli, such as threats, attacks and frustrations, by internal emotions and by learning. The resultant aggressiveness is regulated by rewards and punishments, both social and self-determined, by mechanisms such as dehumanisation, attribution of blame to victims, moral justification and the like. This theory proposes that, to a large extent, aggression is rational, in that there is a cognitive

or intellectual analysis of a received stimulus and the resultant response is related to the result of that analysis, to the level of emotional
arousal experienced and to the type of behaviour previously learned as
an appropriate response.

Learning theory is thus flexible, heuristic and wide-ranging. Yet,
whilst it acknowledges internal structural determinants, for example,
anatomy and physiology, it ignores external structural determinants,
that is social structure. The theory deals with aggression as if man were
only casually connected with other people. In reality, man lives in a
complex, intense, functional social system. It is therefore postulated in
this chapter that social learning theory can be considerably enhanced
by the addition of a social dominance theory.

The social hierarchies in which man and all other primates live
necessarily establish systems of social competition. Status and power
result from being at the top of the hierarchy, aggression is used as a
means of climbing the hierarchy, successful aggression is backed by
latent or potential violence, and actual violence is used on rare
occasions as the ultimate sanction or bid for power. Frustration is the
sentiment experienced by the loser, and it may provoke a violent
challenge and counter-challenge in a battle for power and dominance.
Clearly violence is not always successful (someone has to lose), but it is
interesting that even when dominance is lost violence may still bring
some rewards such as attention and resources. Riots, for example, may
result in government grants, political change and other benefits; a
defeated country may attract new investment.

It is even possible to explain the delights of violence in terms of social
dominance theory. It may be that the pleasure experienced is not so
much from the violence itself but from the dominating, even if that is
short-lived. For an hour or two the looter can be rich and a hero. The
glory of warfare is in the conquering. A close analysis of sexual sadism
reveals that it is domination and control which is the underlying
currency.[12] Similar mental mechanisms may even apply to groups that
have common ideals, aims and frustations. Individuals within a well-
structured group obey their leader. Thus, a nation seeks more power,
and soldiers carry out the necessary violence under instruction. The
joy of domination is spread among the victorious participants and
citizens. It could be that it is the anticipation of power and its pleasures
that sends men into battle with smiles on their faces.

To understand the full extent of man's battles, the concept of
competitiveness has to be broadened from that which will suffice for
other primates, because man is a creature with ideas. Territory is a
major stimulus to mammalian conflict and man has philosophical and
ideational territory as well as physical territory. Our culture, behaviour and social structure are all determined by our ideas. Battles to

determine which ideas are dominant may be even more important than battles about food supplies. Some of the most fearsome wars in history have been religious or ideological.

Social dominance theory

Put briefly, the social dominance theory being postulated here says that those who are violent are seeking control, power or glory, and have usually failed to achieve sufficient of these by lesser forms of aggression. Put this way, it sounds pretentious and grandiose to talk of a theory—it all seems quite obvious—but common parlance does not yet discuss the conflict of power in relation to individual violence. Politicians' favourite explanations for such violence include 'wickedness', 'criminality' and other individualistic explanations that hark back to instinct theory.

The importance of the social dominance explanation is that it predicts that, whilst violence is ever present in any social system of whatever species, the violence will vary widely in frequency and severity according to the ways in which power is distributed. This provides an opportunity to search for variables which correlate with violence and for means to control and minimise violence and destruction. For experimental study of the theory, measures of control and power would have to be developed. It is relatively easy to think of ways of measuring subjective feelings of powerfulness and powerlessness, but much harder to think of ways of measuring power systems objectively, especially in human social systems and groups. Yet it seems inherently possible that these difficulties could be overcome eventually and that, in the process, a great deal would be learnt about the distribution of power in human society. That very learning process could give ideas about variables to manipulate to reduce power differences to non-dangerous levels both in macro-society and in the domestic environment.

At an individual level, the theory gives immediate possibilities for trials of treatment. Anything that will reduce a violent individual's feelings of weakness and helplessness is worthy of such a trial. As emphasised earlier, the theory does not conflict with social learning theories of violence—it is complementary to them. For example, it is thought that children may learn violence from violent parents by modelling on the adult behaviour. Perhaps they also learn something of the parents' sense of powerlessness. Certainly, a child developing in a family which is deprived of power has to learn that fact realistically. Similarly, it is possible to understand the phenomenon of monkey hill or Pitcairn Island partly in terms of a power struggle. Individuals thrust together in a new environment with little pre-existing social structure need to develop a balance of power, and they may do this initially by means of brute force; sophisticated live and let-live systems come later with continued mutual experience. However, the speed with which stability is obtained, the identity of the eventual dominant individuals and the persistence of the new social order will depend upon individual skills and therefore on previous learning and experience. It will also depend upon the level of mutual understanding between the warring parties' experience of each other's tactics and strategy which leads to subtle and effective mutually beneficial compromises.

Psychiatry and psychology

Within about the last century the problems of excessively violent individuals have started to be studied. Something of the developmental and social factors that lead to their disabilities are now understood,[13] it is being learnt which types of brain and psychological pathways are associated with violence,[14,15] and there are even some attempts to treat these people.[10,16−19] It is also known that children reared violently will, in turn, probably become violent adults,[20] and that there is an association between alcohol consumption and certain types of violence,[21,22] yet so far appropriate social responses are not capitalising on this basic information. More fundamentally, investment research in this area is pitiful.

For those whose neurotic and personality problems or family backgrounds have pushed them to the bottom of the social hierarchy, excessive agressiveness is an attempt to regain some control and status. As suggested above, their plight may be made worse if, as is usually the case, they are deficient in the skills of acceptable and lesser violent forms of aggression, for then they are frequently forced back to the ultimate and ineffective response of physical attack.

Psychotic patients are more complex. Some are reacting to loss of status and to a multitude of frustrations like their neurotic counterparts. Others, however, are responding to psychotic ideas: perhaps they are getting in the first blow to defend themselves against a frightening enemy, perhaps they are responding to the commands of 'God' or some other hallucinatory experience. In these cases, the aggression does not fit easily into any theory constructed by observers because the patient's world and experience are different from those of the observer. To understand why the paranoid man strikes the first blow, it is necessary to know something of his inner world, his terror and the nature of his delusional enemies. However, when there is some understanding of that inner world, the 'irrational' violence usually becomes meaningful and, like other forms of violence, can often be understood in terms of feelings of powerlessness.

Criminal and group violence

The study of criminal violence cannot be approached adequately here. One or two points seem apposite though. If the social dominance theory expounded above is useful, it will of course apply to criminal violence just like all other types of violence. It should be possible to understand why individuals or groups break the rules about the use of aggression in any given society. According to the theory, they will break the rules to achieve status and power which they feel is denied to them by other routes. They may have psychopathology, they may simply be socially inept because of their learning experiences, they may be under severe social pressure, or they may find glory and self-esteem within their peer group.

In a careful 25-year cohort study, West and Farrington[23] and Farrington[24] have shown that there are powerful precursors of crime, such as having criminal parents, poor parental handling of the growing child, low family income, large family size, clumsiness, school failure, low intelligence, parental authoritarianism. Admittedly, the crimes to which West and Farrington allude are mainly property crimes, but their delinquency samples also include violent people, and most forms of theft, especially intrusive ones like burglary, are also aggressive. These data are useful because they fit with the social dominance theory and give clues to the reduction of excess violence. Their work suggests that progress might be made in violence reduction if social policies were introduced that would reduce poverty and provide extra support for vulnerable families, and educational policies to provide special education, especially pre-school education for the underprivileged. Farrington has proposed the methodology of such an experiment.[25]

Some years ago the USA was gripped by a series of urban and racial riots. At relatively low cost, an urgent National Commission was established to ascertain the causes. Within a year the Commission produced a report which suggested that there were five ingredients acting as riot catalysts:

- frustrated hopes;
- a social climate approving of violence;
- intense feelings of powerlessness;
- a new mood of enhanced racial pride among black people; and
- the black man's view of the police as a symbol of white power and white repression.[26]

These are all findings compatible with the social dominance theory. The Commission recommended that neighbourhood action task forces be established and comprehensive grievance response mechanisms set up, that local government be brought closer to the people, ghetto residents be given better police protection, more redress for grievances against the police be provided and more negroes be recruited into the police force. These recommendations were nearly all implemented, and some of the towns concerned have been free from riots for nearly 20 years. A great deal may have been achieved quite cheaply.

Domestic violence

The home is the scene of much serious violence. A questionnaire survey in the USA suggested that perhaps 3% of American families cause deliberate injury to children.[27] A British survey has suggested that one in 1,000 children under the age of four years will be severely injured each year, and one in ten of these will die.[28] In evidence to Parliament, the Metropolitan Police suggested that in London there are between 6,000 and 8,000 reported wife assaults and 15–23 husband/wife murders each year.

Steele and Pollock found that some parents expected and demanded a great deal from their children, much more than an infant could provide—a phenomenon sometimes called role reversal.[20] They quote Kaufman as stating that 'the child is not perceived as a child, but some symbolic or delusional figure'. Carter has suggested that harsh punishment is part of a power game in which an insecure parent reacts to the uncontrollable demands of an apparently powerful baby like an unstable totalitarian ruler faced with a rebellion.[29] Faulk described five types of battering husband:[30]

- a dependent passive husband with a querulous demanding wife;
- a dependent suspicious husband, jealous of his wife;
- a violent bullying man;
- a dominating man, often successful at work, unable to cope with any challenge; and
- a man in a previously stable and affectionate relationship which is destabilised by illness, for example, depression.

In all these descriptions, the importance of the power structure as perceived by the violent individual can be seen.

Warfare

Warfare is undoubtedly the greatest human violence problem of all, nevertheless man is not the only creature that fights in groups. Macaque monkeys in India have undoubted tribal battles,[31,32] battles that lead to savage injuries and sometimes death for individuals engaged in combat. Chimpanzees have been seen to take over another troupe forcefully.[33] Armies of ants go remorselessly into battle and inflict terrible damage on their enemies. Two important differences between human warfare and the warfare of other species are military technology and meaning. As far as we know, other animals do not battle for ideas or ascribe meanings to their battles.

It is important to notice that hitherto for some societies, notably our own, war has produced benefits.[34] Wars produce and accelerate social development, and help to disseminate ideas. European culture and the spread of the English language have probably been accelerated in the twentieth century by two world wars. The obvious advantage of turning aggression outwards from a community that is in dissent is almost too well-known to mention, yet it is important because it increases internal social stability. Almost as obvious is the acquisition of new resources for the victor: energy, food, space to live in and so on. Most important of all, war may greatly facilitate the mixing of genes by producing a mixture of cultures which brings new vigour to both victor and vanquished alike. War, then, may be an evolutionary agent bringing, after a period of turmoil, social stability, prosperity, dissemination of genes, and technological and cultural development.

There is also a further dimension to human warfare. Man is not basically horrified by wars, indeed he both revels in and glorifies them. The outbreak of World War I was greeted with jubilation. More recently the British set about fighting the Argentinians with glee. Our recent concern about warfare is not about war as such but the understanding there now is of what some of the sophisticated weapons can do. Paradoxical though it may seem, warfare elevates the human spirit. It produces art, glory, heroism. Vera Brittain wrote:

> It has often been said by pacifists that war creates more criminals than heroes, that far from developing noble qualities in those who take part in it, it brings out only the worst. If this were altogether true, the pacifist's aim would be, I think, much nearer of attainment than it is. It seems to me that his task, our task, is infinitely complicated by the fact that war, while it lasts, does produce heroism to a far greater extent than it brutalises.[35]

This is not to say that the usual view of the costs of war (for example, the loss of fit young males, brutalisation, spread of harmful drugs) is wrong; rather it emphasises that wars have benefits which may be powerful motivators.

In spite of its crucial importance, warfare is almost unresearched. Research about war is of course difficult, given the nature of the topic and its cross-cultural characteristics. However, one academic discipline which may be of great value is social anthropology. Human warfare is probably so different from other forms of mammalian group violence, because of the technologies and especially the meanings mentioned earlier, that the ethological approach, used so far in this paper, which derives from zoology, is no longer appropriate. As one social anthropologist puts it:

> In the battle between social anthropology and ethology social anthropology's strength may come from the stressing of the *meaning* that is intrinsic to all human social life.[36]

Riches describes how, in spite of being regarded as peaceful because of the absence of warfare, the Eskimo indulges in female infanticide and the pre-emptive killing of strangers. As Eskimos have no corporate social systems, no government, and live in very loose-knit groups which are well spaced from other groups by the low population densities, warfare is almost impossible. However the Yanomama in South America, who have a similar social structure, are among the fiercest people on Earth with up to 25% of them being killed by violence. The crucial difference seems to be that the South Americans are agricultural and live in much closer proximity to one another.[37] As Riches puts it, it is not that population 'pressure' itself causes problems which have to be resolved through violence, rather it is that a high proportion of strangers live together. As for the Eskimos, warfare in a European sense does not occur for there is no government or state structure, but the fierce and lethal tribal battles amount to much the same thing.

Another useful academic discipline could be political history. Given that human warfare has meaning, it is probably by and large a rational activity. It may be that nations go to war only when they believe they can win something or prevent themselves losing something. History could be scrutinised to see if this is true by looking for examples of apparently pointless or purposeless warfare. A careful study of the causes of wars could also be of political significance. At the very least it could be the basis of cross-national collaborative endeavour.[38]

If war is indeed a rational activity, this gives a glimmer of hope for the future of Earth, and it may be the reason that the uneasy nuclear truce has worked for 40 years. A second glimmer of hope comes from the hypothesis that one of the biological functions of warfare is cultural and genetic dissemination. We now live in a highly mobile era. Cheap travel may actually reduce the natural pressure to invade by other means. Perhaps we could consciously capitalise on this kind of process. It might be possible, for example, for enemy countries to agree to educate an equal and considerable number of each other's students, postgraduate at first, undergraduates later. Each side would hope to disseminate its own ideas. Intermarriage would certainly occur. Bombing cities is less palatable if they contain significant numbers of your own citizens.

Evolution of co-operation

Perhaps the most hopeful thought has come recently from a series of studies of the prisoner's dilemma by Axelrod.[39] The prisoner's dilemma is a problem of conflict. Two thieves are caught and questioned separately. They are each offered little or no punishment if they renege on the other (defect). Clearly, each will do well if he defects and the other does not. However, if both defect, they will both do badly. They will each do moderately well if they *both* keep quiet because evidence against both is weak without the other's information. The dilemma is thus clear. Mathematically, it seems that to defect is as good a solution as can be achieved. However, this is true only if the situation is a once-only situation. As soon as there is a chance that the situation could be repeated with the same individual, who of course will remember last time, co-operation becomes increasingly profitable as the dilemma is repeated.

Axelrod invited computer programmers to write a program that would score highly in an iterated prisoner's dilemma game against all other programs. One program turned out to be particularly robust, and to win consistently and score more points than the others, even when others knew what they were up against. This program, called TIT FOR TAT, began by co-operating, and then followed each defect and each co-operation by precisely the same tactic. The program did not beat every other program especially in short series, but overall it acquired more points as time and opponents went by. Further, it became good at acquiring points as soon as it found a co-operative partner. Co-operation with other programs gradually emerged, and proved ineffective only when the future (the series of games) could be predicted to end soon.

The principles which emerge from Axelrod's study are that (1) an eye for an eye, and (2) do unto others as you would that they should do to you, are both useful, and (3) co-operation emerges when (1) and (2) are understood. Axelrod goes further, and says that in any conflict the advice which works is 'don't be envious, don't be first to defect, reciprocate both co-operation and defection, and don't be too clever'.

Perhaps the most interesting feature of the TIT FOR TAT solution to the iterated prisoner's dilemma is that it does not emerge as the overall winner of the series of games by beating other programs but by co-operating with other programs. Moreover, the foundation of co-operation is not really trust, but the durability of the relationship. Whether or not the players trust each other is less important in the long run than whether the conditions are ripe for them to build a stable pattern of co-operation with each other. Friendship is not necessary for co-operation to evolve. To illustrate this point, he points to the remarkable levels of co-operation which occurred between soldiers of opposing sides in the trenches in World War I, much to the fury of commanders who were not faced with the day-to-day contact which the infantry had.[40]

These interesting findings fit with the social dominance theory because it seems that power sharing is, in the long run, more successful than power acquisition. Short-term acquisition works and works well in some circumstances, but those circumstances do not include the longer term in which the contestants remain in contact. Retaliation is important, but only as a means of controlling the level of aggression received from an opponent.

Axelrod ends with a note of caution:

> The core of the problem of how to achieve rewards from co-operation is that trial and error in learning is slow and painful. The conditions may all be favourable for long-run developments, but we may not have the time to wait for blind processes to move us slowly toward mutually rewarding strategies based upon reciprocity. Perhaps if we understand the process better, we can use our foresight to speed up the evolution of co-operation.

Conclusion

Hitherto, violence has variously been explained in terms of an aggressive instinct, frustration or social learning. The instinctive view of violence seems to have waned. However, the remaining theories, whilst being extremely useful, tend to explain violence without sufficient reference to social structure and without sufficiently distinguishing between aggression and violence.

In this chapter the notion of social dominance is advanced as a way of understanding the fundamental purpose of aggressive behaviour, including fighting. Physical assault, fighting and violence are seen as one end of the spectrum of social aggression. It is probable that some violence, or at least the threat of violence, is present in any social system because it has important functions in resolving escalating conflicts, setting limits and maintaining stability. Excess violence over and above the minimum required for social stability and non-violent power redistribution is the major issue to explain. It is hypothesised here that individuals or groups who are violent are seeking control, power or glory, and have usually failed to achieve sufficient of these by lesser forms of aggression. Some violence may be achieving a new social order, but much within an otherwise stable culture is related to powerlessness (real or imagined) and ineptitude. Some is related to anomie—to feeling or being largely outside the stable social system. Within the framework of violence some of the excess destructiveness is a magnification of violent behaviour by intelligence and technology.

The problem of violence in mentally abnormal people can also be understood partly in social dominance terms, as can the violence of outsiders and criminals, and violence in the home. Many violent aggressors feel and indeed are relatively powerless. They are therefore on the receiving and losing end of effective and sophisticated social aggression for most of the time. Their attempts to fight back are often unsophisticated and largely unsuccessful. To understand fully the triggers for violence in a mentally abnormal individual, some attempt to understand his or her inner world has to be made.

Urban and civil disturbance can often also be seen in terms of power struggles between groups in which the balance of power has swung to the point where the less powerful are achieving little by non-violence and where the penalties of non-violence are outweighing the benefits. Warfare, too, fits into this framework but, although it is on the continuum of group aggression, and although it has counterparts in other species, it is best considered as a special human problem. It is a product of dominance behaviour between groups magnified by technology and fuelled by ideas. Many conflicts are at least as much concerned with ideas and philosophies as with physical territory. Man glorifies war, and uses it to disseminate his beliefs and culture, and also to gain resources and power.

The social dominance theory lends itself to pragmatic enquiry and possibly remedy. New approaches to an objective measure of the distribution of power within and between social groups could lead to testing of the theory and also to increased understanding of the nature of human power. Political experimentation could be started by the identification of fairly obvious power imbalances and making attempts to reduce them.

The theory also fits with a remarkable series of observations from computer strategies developed to solve the prisoner's dilemma. These experiments suggest that, given time, in any system of conflict, co-operation between adversaries will evolve provided each contestant can conceive a medium- to long-term future incorporating the other contestant(s). Such co-operation emerges because it has long-term advantages for all participants. It could take a long time to emerge, although an animal with foresight may well speed up the process.

Peaceful resolution of conflict is one of man's most urgent tasks at both the micro and the macro levels. Knowledge is always more powerful than speculation from ignorance, yet the study of human conflict is notable for its dearth of knowledge. Investment in conflict research is miniscule compared with the task in hand and with investment in many lesser problems. No manufacturing business could survive on such a low investment ratio. All our futures would be better safeguarded by serious attention to this deficiency.

Acknowledgements

I am grateful to Pamela Taylor, David Farrington and Donald West for comments on the manuscript, and to Maureen Bartholomew for secretarial assistance.

References

1. Hinckley J. *(Poem) Newsletter Am Acad Psychiatry Law* 1968; **13**: 15
2. Zuckerman SG. *The social life of monkeys and apes.* London: Kegan Paul, 1932
3. Hall KRL, De Vore I. Baboon social behavior. In: De Vore I, ed. *Primate behavior.* New York: Holt, Rinehart & Winston, 1965
4. Hall KRL. Aggression in monkey and ape society. In: Carthy JD, Ebling FJ, eds. *The natural history of aggression.* London: Academic Press, 1964
5. Rutter O. *The court martial of the 'Bounty' mutineers.* Edinburgh: Hodge & Co, 1931
6. Hough R. *Captain Bligh and Mr Christian.* London: Hutchinson, 1972
7. Adams E, Barnett SA, Bechtereva NP *et al.* Statement on violence. *Med War* 1987; **3**: 191–3
8. Ike BW. On 'the biology of war'. *Med War* 1987; **3**: 33–42
9. Dollard J, Miller NE, Doob LW, Mowrer OH, Sears R. *Frustration and aggression.* New Haven, CN: Yale University Press, 1939
10. Gunn J. *Violence in human society.* Newton Abbott: David & Charles, 1973
11. Bandura A. Psychological mechanisms of aggression. In: Green RG, Dounerstein EI, eds. *Aggression, theoretical and empirical reviews (vol 1).* New York: Academic Press, 1983
12. Fromm E. *The anatomy of human destructiveness.* London: Cape, 1974
13. Martin JP. *Violence and the family.* Chichester: Wiley, 1978
14. Boelkins RC, Heiser JF. Biological bases of aggression. In: Daniels DN, Gilula MF, Ochberg LFM, eds. *Violence and the struggle for existence.* Boston, MA: Little, Brown & Co, 1969
15. Mark VH. Sociobiological theories of abnormal aggression. In: Kutash IL, Kutash SB, Schlesinger LB, eds. *Violence.* San Francisco: Jossey-Bass, 1978
16. Lion JR. *Evaluation and management of the violent patient.* Springfield, IL: Charles C. Thomas, 1972
17. Gunn J. Psychiatric aspects of violence and violent offenders. *Forensic Sci* 1975; **5**: 219–27
18. Kutash IL, Kutash SB, Schlesinger LB, eds. *Violence.* San Francisco: Jossey-Bass, 1978
19. Roth L. *Clinical treatment of the violent person.* Rockville: US DHHS, 1985
20. Steele BF, Pollock CB. A psychiatric study of parents who abuse infants and small children. In: Helfer RE, Kempe CH, eds. *The battered child.* Chicago: University of Chicago Press, 1968
21. Bennett RM, Buss AH, Carpenter JA. Alcohol and human physical aggression. *Quart J Stud Alcohol* 1969; **30**: 870–6
22. Goodwin DW. Alcohol in suicide and homicide. *Quart J Stud Alcohol* 1973; **34**: 144–56
23. West DJ, Farrington DP. *The delinquent way of life.* Heinemann: London, 1977
24. Farrington DP. Stepping stones to adult criminal careers. In: Olwens D, Bloch J, Yarrow MR, eds. *Development of antisocial and prosocial behaviour.* New York: Academic Press, 1986
25. Farrington DP. Delinquency prevention in the 1980s. *J. Adolescence* 1985; **8**: 3–16
26. National Advisory Commission on Civil Disorders. *Report.* Washington: US Government Printing Office, 1968
27. Gil DG. Incident of child abuse and demographic characteristics of persons involved. In: Helfer RE, Kempe CH, eds. *The battered child.* Chicago: University of Chicago Press, 1968

28. Royal College of Psychiatrists. Evidence to the Select Committee on violence in the family. In: *First report from the Select Committee on violence in the family, session 1976–77. Vol II, Evidence.* London: House of Commons, HMSO, 1977

29. Carter J. *The maltreated child.* London: Priory Press, 1974

30. Faulk M. Men who assault their wives. *Med Sci Law* 1974; **2**: 180–3

31. Southwick CH, Beg MA, Siddiqi MR. Rhesus monkeys in north India. In: De Vore I, ed. *Primate behavior.* New York: Holt, Rinehart & Winston, 1965

32. Southwick CH. Aggressive behaviour of rhesus monkeys in natural and captive groups. In: Garattini S, Sigg EB, eds. *Aggressive behaviour.* Amsterdam: Excerpta Medica, 1969

33. Goodall J. *The chimpanzees of Gombe.* Cambridge: Belknap Press, 1986

34. Hall JA. War and the rise of the west. In: Creighton C, Shaw M, eds. *The sociology of war and peace.* London: Macmillan, 1987

35. Brittain V. *Testament of youth.* London: Gollancz, 1933

36. Riches D. Violence, peace and war in 'early' human society: the case of the Eskimo. In: Creighton C, Shaw M, eds. *The sociology of war and peace.* London: Macmillan, 1987

37. Chagnon N. *The Yanomama: the fierce people, 2nd edn.* New York: Holt, Rinehart & Winston, 1977

38. Holsti OR. The 1914 case. *Am Political Sci Rev* 1965; **59**: 365–78

39. Axelrod R. *The evolution of co-operation.* New York: Basic Books, 1984

40. Ashworth T. *Trench warfare 1914–18: the live and let live system.* Basingstoke: Macmillan Press, 1980

2 | Aggression at different levels of social complexity

Robert A. Hinde

MRC Group on the Development and Integration of Behaviour, Madingley, Cambridge

Introduction

The same word, aggression, is used to refer to violence intentionally inflicted by one individual on another, and by members of one group or nation on those of another. This chapter summarises evidence that the processes involved are in fact very different.[1]

In general, in considering human social behaviour, it is useful to distinguish a number of levels of social complexity:

- individual behaviour;
- short-term interactions between individuals;
- relationships involving a series of interactions over time between individuals who know each other such that each interaction is affected by preceding ones and often by the expectation of future ones;
- groups; and
- societies involving a number of distinct or overlapping groups.

Each level has properties that are simply not relevant to the level below: for instance, an important property of an interaction is the extent to which the behaviour of each participant fits with that of the other, but this is a property irrelevant to the behaviour of an individual in isolation. However, each level affects, and is affected by, those adjacent to it. Thus, the nature of a relationship is affected by the nature of its constituent interactions, and by the nature of the group in which it is embedded. Furthermore, each of these levels affects, and is affected by, the 'socio-cultural structure' which includes the values, beliefs, norms, and institutions, which are more or less common to the individuals of the group or society concerned (Fig. 1).[2]

With this as background, the nature of aggression at three levels of social complexity may now be considered.

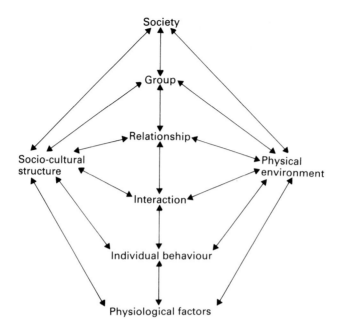

Fig. 1. *Dialectical relations between successive levels of social complexity.*

Individual aggression

An individual aggressor nearly always risks injury to him- or herself. Furthermore, aggression often involves much more than an attempt to hurt another individual. It may, for instance, involve an attempt to gain access to some object or situation, to show off to bystanders, or self-defence. Thus, aggressive acts are not to be ascribed simply to aggressive motivation but to a complex of motivational factors.[2]

Factors giving rise to aggression

In attempting to understand how aggressive motivation arises, it is useful to distinguish between the ontogenetic, the predisposing and the immediately precipitating factors. Among the ontogenetic factors are the genetic constitution of the individual involved,[3] learning experiences in the family of origin,[4] and especially the nature of the individual's relationships with his or her parents.[5,6]

Also important are extra-familial role models, influences from the peer group, the media and so on.[7,8] Among the predisposing factors are personality characteristics, crowding, arousal, uncomfortable or stressful conditions,[9,10] and social norms that value or do not denigrate aggression. Among the more important eliciting factors are frustration,[11] fear and pain,[12] the nature of the victim,[13] and the availability of weapons.[14] A high proportion of aggressive acts occur between individuals known to each other, and even within families[15]—but even within families the factors influencing the incidence of aggression are multiple and complex.[16] Violence within a family may spread from one dyad to another,[17] and may be perpetuated across generations.[18,19]

Aggression between groups

Factors deriving from the dynamics of the group situation enter into aggression between groups. A collection of individuals constitutes a group when those individuals perceive themselves to have some degree of interdependence and evolve rules and norms more or less specific to the group.[20,21] They tend to view themselves as similar to one another, and to exaggerate the difference from members of outgroups, who tend to be denigrated.[22,23] The nature of a group may influence, and be influenced by, the nature of its leader.[24]

When two groups come into conflict, the aggression shown is not the sum of that of the component individuals. If aggression is valued highly by the group, individuals may be more prone to behave aggressively in order to gain admiration from their peers. The group situation may affect the aggressiveness shown because of concomitant arousal, because of the anonymity of the group situation, through the example and exhortation of leaders and so on.

International war

A distinction between group conflict and war is not easy to draw, but international war involves a much greater differentiation of roles than does group conflict. To understand war it is necessary to come to terms both with the dynamics of the many groups and sub-groups involved and with the effects of their leaders. But, more importantly, it must be recognised that war is an institution.[25] Marriage is an institution in which husband and wife have roles: the behaviour of the incumbents of those roles is determined in part by the rights and duties adhering to their roles. Similarly, the behaviour of voters, Members of Parliament, and Ministers is, in part, determined by the rights and duties consequent upon their roles in the institution of Parliament. In war, the behaviour of generals and soldiers, politicians, munition and transport workers, doctors and nurses is in large measure determined by their roles in the institution of war. Even the behaviour of the soldier in combat is influenced at most only to a very limited extent, if at all, by aggressive propensities, and is determined principally by his duty.

Factors maintaining the institution of war

If the incidence of wars is to be reduced or eliminated, therefore, an understanding of the factors that maintain war as an institution must be sought, together with the psychological and other processes through which they operate.[26] Some of these are everyday issues, involving the manner in which war is sanitised in books and films.[27,28] The media only rarely portray war as it really is and, when they do, it often prompts accusations of bad taste. War toys introduce children to the mechanics of war, and tend to make them accept war as normal. The UNESCO (1974) recommendation that peace education should be promoted is disregarded by virtually all countries, Finland being an honourable exception.[29]

Other factors tending to maintain war as an institution are pervasive in the culture. Some countries have a long record of belligerence and others, like Switzerland, of neutrality. Religion often plays a part, with some religions condoning and even praising war. Even in Christian countries church leaders have justified war in the name of religion, and glorified death in war by equating it with Christ's sacrifice.[30] International law no longer condones war, but great power rivalry has made it relatively ineffective in stopping wars. By recognising that some wars are just it has in the past, in fact, supported war as an institution.[31,32]

In war, individuals undergo hardship and expose themselves to danger against their own individual interests, seeing this as their duty. Their actions, and the institution of war itself, are supported by cultural values and propaganda whose effectiveness depends upon basic human propensities—aggressiveness, fear of strangers, the tendency to denigrate outgroups, and the desire to rise in status by acting in conformity with cultural norms. War propaganda creates an image of the enemy as evil and dangerous.[33]

War is not merely an institution, but a nested set of institutions, which Eisenhower referred to as the military–industrial–(scientific) complex. Each of these is maintained by its own inertial forces and by the career ambitions of those involved.[34,35]

Conclusion

The nature of aggression changes as we move from individual aggression through group aggression to war, the increase in complexity being accompanied by the increasing importance of group factors and institutionalisation. To reduce the incidence of war, not only are relatively short-term measures needed, such as the restriction or abolition of the arms trade, but also measures to understand and hence undermine the institution of war. Peace education, involving amongst other things a recognition of the value of cultural differences, can make an important contribution to this.

References

1. Abbreviated from Hinde RA. Aggression and war: individuals, groups and states. In: Tetlock TE, Husbands JoL, Jervis R, Stern PC, Tilly C, eds. *Behaviour, society and violence in war* (in press)
2. Hinde RA. The interdependence of the behavioural sciences. *Philosophical Transactions of the Royal Society of London* 1990; **329**:217–27
3. Manning A. The genetic bases of aggression. In: Groebel J, Hinde RA, eds. *Aggression and war.* Cambridge: Cambridge University Press, 1989
4. Feshbach S. The bases and development of individual aggression. In: Groebel J, Hinde RA, eds. *Aggression and war.* Cambridge: Cambridge University Press, 1989
5. Baumrind D. Current patterns of parental authority. *Developmental Psychol Monographs* 1971; **4**:No. 1
6. Maccoby EE, Martin JA. Socialization in the context of the family: parent–child interaction. In: Hetherington ME, ed. *Mussen handbook of child psychology, vol 4.* New York: Wiley. 1983:1–101
7. Groebel J. International research on television violence: synopsis and critique. In: Huesmann LR, Eron LD, eds. *Television and the aggressive child.* Hillsdale, NJ: Erlbaum, 1986
8. National Institutes of Mental Health, 1982
9. Freedman JL. *Crowding and behavior.* San Francisco: Freeman, 1975
10. Anderson CA, Anderson DC. Ambient temperature and violent crime. *J Personality Social Psychol* 1984; **46**:91–7
11. Dollard J, Doob LW, Millar NE, Mowrer OH, Sears RR. *Frustration and aggression.* New Haven: Yale University Press, 1939
12. Ulrich RE. Pain as a cause of aggression. *Amer Zoologist* 1986; **6**:643–62
13. Olweus D. *Aggression in the schools.* New York: Wiley, 1978
14. Berkowitz L, Frodi A. Stimulus characteristics that can enhance or decrease aggression. *Aggressive Behavior* 1977; **3**:1–15
15. Goldstein JH. *Aggression and crimes of violence.* New York: Oxford University Press, 1986
16. Engfer A. *Kindesmisshandlung: Ursachen, Auswirkungen, Hilfen.* Stuttgart: Enke, 1986
17. Christensen A, Margolin G. Conflict and alliance in distressed and non-distressed families. In: Hinde RA, Stevenson-Hinde J, eds. *Relationships within families: mutual influences.* New York: Oxford University Press, 1988
18. Caspi A, Elder GH Jr. Emergent family patterns: the intergenerational construction of problem behaviour and relationships. In: Hinde RA, Stevenson-Hinde J, eds. *Relationships within families: mutual influences.* New York: Oxford University Press, 1988
19. Hinde RA, Stevenson-Hinde J, eds. *Relationships within families.* Oxford: Clarendon Press, 1988
20. Rabbie J. Determinants of instrumental intra-group cooperation. In: Hinde RA, Groebel J, eds. *Cooperation and prosocial behaviour.* Cambridge: Cambridge University Press, 1991
21. Middleton H. Some psychological bases of the institution of war. In: Hinde RA, ed. *The institution of war.* Basingstoke, Hants: Macmillan, 1991:30–46
22. Tajfel H, Turner JC. The social identity theory of inter-group behavior. In: Worchel S, Austin WG, eds. *Psychology of intergroup relations.* Chicago: Nelson-Hall, 1986
23. Turner JC, Hogg MA, Oakes PJ, Reicher SD, Wetherell MS. *Rediscovering the social group: social categorisation theory.* Oxford: Blackwell, 1987

24. Kenny DA, Zaccaro SJ. An estimate of variance due to traits in leadership. *J Appl Psychol* 1983; **68**:678–85

25. Hinde RA. Aggression and the institution of war. In: Hinde RA, ed. *The institution of war*. Basingstoke, Hants: Macmillan, 1991:1–8

26. Hinde RA, ed. *The institution of war*. Basingstoke, Hants: Macmillan, 1991

27. Fussell P. *The Great War and modern memory*. London: Oxford University Press, 1975

28. Wainter J. Imaginings of war: some cultural supports of the institution of war. In: Hinde RA, ed. *The institution of war*. Basingstoke, Hants: Macmillan, 1991: 155–77

29. Phillips B. The institution of conscription: the case of Finland. In: Hinde RA, ed. *The institution of war*. Basingstoke, Hants: Macmillan, 1991:229–43

30. Sykes S. Sacrifice and the ideology of war. In: Hinde RA, ed. *The institution of war*. Basingstoke, Hants: Macmillan, 1991:87–98

31. Collier JG. Legal basis of the institution of war. In: Hinde RA, ed. *The institution of war*. Basingstoke, Hants: Macmillan, 1991:121–32

32. Greenwood C. In defence of the laws of war. In: Hinde RA, ed. *The institution of war*. Basingstoke, Hants: Macmillan, 1991:133–47

33. Hinde RA. A note on patriotism and nationalism. In: Hinde RA, ed. *The institution of war*. Basingstoke, Hants: Macmillan, 1991:148–54

34. Kaldor M. Do modern economies require war or preparations for war? In: Hinde RA, ed. *The institution of war*. Basingstoke, Hants: Macmillan, 1991: 178–91

35. Elworthy S. Defence decision-making and accountability. In: Hinde RA, ed. *The institution of war*. Basingstoke, Hants: Macmillan, 1991:192–228

3 | The roots and role of violence in development

Eric Taylor

Reader in Developmental Neuropsychiatry, MRC Child Psychiatry Unit, London

Introduction

The roots of violence are nearly always in childhood. Aggression is a normal part of development and brings benefits to the individual as well as risks. Highly aggressive adults can nearly always trace their violence back to an antisocial conduct disorder in their childhood. The antecedents and consequences of violence in early life are therefore the subject of this chapter. I shall describe some normal pathways of development and some of the common factors that determine individual differences. My main theme is the presence of several different pathways into a violent adjustment, and the stability of the aggressive adjustment once it has developed.

There is a large body of developmental and clinical research in childhood that is germane to this theme. To review all the reviews would involve a lengthy account. The reader is therefore referred to Rutter and Garmezy[1] and Earls[2] for much more detailed accounts that can also provide an entry into the extensive literature.

Normal development

Aggression is a part of normal development and it is not all deviant. This is sometimes lost sight of because very high levels of aggression and antisocial behaviour in childhood are such good predictors of excessive adult aggressiveness.[2] This is true, but does not mean that milder degrees of antisocial behaviour carry a risk of later antisocial personality. The predictiveness of aggression comes from a literature about individual differences (especially at the extremes of the range). A distinction must be maintained between this and the normative study of the course of development.

Very young children are quite aggressive in several ways: tantrums, rough-and-tumble play, and instrumental violence to serve their own ends. This everyday observation leads at once to some scientific difficulties. It is not yet clear whether these types of violence should be seen as reflections of an underlying construct of aggressiveness or whether violence should be subdivided and, if so, how. This chapter will deal separately with some possible subdivisions of types of behaviour—not categories of people—all of which are aspects of normal development.

Types of aggression

Tantrums

Children do not need to learn how to have rages. Perhaps the earliest form of aggression is tantrums, which appear in a constant form during early childhood in all societies. Tantrums are well-organised sequences of behaviour provoked by frustration when wishes are not fulfilled and include shouting, kicking, hitting, and vocal as well as physical violence. The effect upon adults is powerful. Tantrums are highly aversive, so adults are strongly motivated to bring them to an end, whether by direct forbidding or by yielding to the wishes that provoked them. The form of adult reaction varies with the age of the child. To begin with, tantrums are often taken as signals of need, and the need is met, but as the children get older their caregivers become less compliant. Tantrums are coercive and bring out control strategies from parents. The developmental course of this varies between cultures, and transcultural research is a promising way forward in understanding parent–child interactions.

The requirement to control tantrum behaviour is therefore one of the major early socialisation demands. This is not necessarily a repressive or distorting aspect of development, but a major opportunity. The important abilities of self-control and self-determination might not emerge in the same way if children were an endless delight to their parents. Autonomy is based upon conflict.

The expectations of parents are partly met. Aggression at home declines gradually from three to ten years old. Tantrums become modified in form; frustrated outbursts still happen but less often involve violence to others. Furthermore, the timing of angry outbursts becomes less closely tied to immediate frustration and more determined by long-term factors and retaliation.

The process of controlling tantrums can break down for several reasons (see section on individual differences):

- inadequate opportunity to learn what is required;
- a pattern of contingencies that maintains them; and
- impairment of the child's ability.

However, it is important that high levels of tantrums are not seen only as a failure of control. Sometimes the apparatus of control is intact, but the levels of frustration are so high that this form of 'protest' aggression is an expected and understandable response.

As children get older, their anger and aggression come under increasingly complex control. Experimental studies have been used to try to disentangle the multiple factors. Social situations can be artificially contrived so as to seem to the child that ordinary events are happening, yet to give the experimenter control over which possible provokers of rage are present. These studies indicate that frustration of wants is indeed a way of eliciting aggressive behaviour to other children, but that for most children other factors are also needed. For instance, after the age of about three years frustration is not sufficient to elicit violence to others under experimental conditions. There must be both a frustration and also some form of permission for aggression to be shown. The existence of a model is one kind of tacit permission: if a child sees another person acting aggressively, he or she is more likely to do likewise.[3]

Developmental research still has to track the course of this kind of reactive aggression into later development. Common sense will see a good deal of similarity between the child's tantrum and the kind of outburst under provocation and frustration that characterises some clinically referred problems of aggression. However, such a similarity of form does not mean that there is also a deep similarity in the processes involved. At the very least, an increasing complexity of determinants must be considered. There will also be an interaction with other lines of development that contribute to aggression.

Why does tantrum aggression decrease or, to put it another way, why do children show increasing degrees of control as they become older? It is partly, but not solely, because of the outside expectations that society imposes, especially the following of rules laid down by adults. This is unlikely, however, to be the whole story. Socialisation has a complex effect. To some extent, children learn not to be nice to other people as they appreciate the rewards of aggression, but they also come increasingly to understand other people as beings with motives and rights of their own, and thus the scope of prosocial behaviour increases.

Rough-and-tumble play

Another form of aggression, not necessarily linked to frustration, is rough-and-tumble play. It appears with contact with other children, and is commoner in males. It is not yet clear whether it constitutes a developmentally separate line of aggression, but I suspect that it does, that individual differences in childhood predict the recreational use of violence by young men, and that the maintaining factors are those deciding how successful a boy will be as a fighter. There are many 'tough kids' who take great pride in their prowess as fighters, for whom it is a useful source of self-esteem, and who are not necessarily psychiatrically disturbed. It seems very similar to the excitement and display functions. In practice, our knowledge of individual differences is based chiefly upon adults' ratings of aggression that put all the different patterns together, so the idea of a distinct line of development here is not well founded. What is clear is that peer relationships between boys tend to become increasingly aggressive during the school years. Indeed, it has been thought for a long time that this is in part a function of the relationships themselves. Thus Patterson *et al.* found that non-aggressive children who interacted a good deal with other children soon came to be aggressive in their interactions.[4] Non-aggressive boys remained non-aggressive only if they interacted little with others.

Instrumental violence

A conceptually different pattern is instrumental violence, by which I mean the use of violence as a means of resolving a conflict between people, such as getting a toy that is in another child's possession. This form of aggression can of course be deeply involved with the other two forms I have stressed. Both tantrums and rough-and-tumble play have operant effects which presumably may affect their frequency, but there are also other ways of using coercive force to overcome resistance by another person to what a child wants. Instrumental violence is common in nursery and playgroup interactions, but tends to become somewhat less common—or at least less overt—as schooling proceeds. It has some obvious benefits, for on the whole the child tends to get what he wants—provided of course that he chooses the right sort of victim.

Aggression in family interactions

These coercive processes are important in families as well as in peer interactions. Patterson stressed, firstly, the extent to which coercion of parents by children is rewarded by the details of the interactions and, secondly, the extent to which this process is maintained by poor communication, lack of clear limits and contingencies, poor tracking of antisocial and prosocial behaviours and maternal irritability.[5]

One type that deserves particular mention is violence in response to threat. This is of course dependent upon perceiving a threat to be present. The importance of this comes from the association between conduct disorder in boys and their attribution of hostile intent to other people in ambiguous situations.

Classification of types of aggression

It is possible to multiply the types of aggression, and many tentative classification schemes exist, all of which have serious weaknesses: the empirical evidence for the existence of valid subtypes is lacking; it is common to see the different types all present in the same person; and longitudinal studies have not indicated that the different forms of aggression have distinct outcomes but, on the contrary, that the consequences of violence tend to maintain it whatever the initial routes towards it (see below).

These weaknesses of existing schemes are not, however, arguments against the enterprise of classification. The absence of empirical validation of the different types is a function chiefly of the relative dearth of studies examining the question. When it is examined, some differences can be found. Gender differences, for example, are not identical for different types of aggression. A meta-analysis by Hyde of published studies reporting gender differences found significant variations according to the type of aggression examined and the method of measurement chosen.[6] Rough-and-tumble play fighting is much more characteristic of boys than instrumental aggression, and prosocial violence—that is, the use of violence to enforce the norms of the group—shows little difference between the sexes. Age differences, too, may help to distinguish the types. Tantrum violence reduces with increasing age in contrast to instrumental aggression. Further investigation of differential correlates with other types of factor such as family circumstances and relationships seems worthwhile. Furthermore, the issue of different types of aggression needs to be distinguished from that of whether there are different types of aggressive people. This second question has sometimes been addressed, but the former rarely.

Developmental consequences of aggression

The consequences of aggression are complex and include both risks and benefits.

Benefits of aggression

The first and most obvious benefit to the aggressor is simply and crudely that it often works. Instrumental violence can get the aggressor what he or she wants in the immediate term. The result may only be a small reward, but it comes at once. The habit can therefore be readily learned on the basis of immediate, though small, reinforcement of an aggressive operant. This formulation of the way that violence is maintained leads directly to a form of management. Parents are often counselled to manipulate the immediate contingencies of their children's behaviour so that reward is withheld if the children are violent or otherwise coercive. There is merit in this approach, but its effects are not usually large, and for many referred children it is not sufficient intervention.

Children have to learn how to resolve conflict. Aggression may well play a part in this for many of them. During the pre-school years, it may be one way through which clashes of interest, especially with other children, are effectively handled. As a result, the child may learn useful lessons about the resolution of such clashes, for example, that they can be resolved, and that it is not necessary always to back off from a dispute. These lessons may be useful in later stages of development after non-violent methods have been acquired.

Indeed, it can be argued that opposition to rules is a universal and valuable aspect of social development. The learning of rules of conduct is not solely one of 'heteronomy', the following of passively acquired instructions, but there is also a 'homonymous' process in which children develop rules for themselves. They do this by reacting to and learning from the reactions of other people, especially other children, and their own assertion of their own needs (including acts of aggression) creates the framework for this learning.

Aggression may also bring benefits in self-esteem and in peer status. The investigation of this possibility is likely to have a focus much more upon the 'enjoyable' sort of rough-and-tumble violence that so far has attracted relatively little developmental research. As already noted, some children in the early and middle school years take considerable pride in their prowess as fighters. It is one source of their self-esteem and one for which other children may admire them. To be sure, such an effect upon peers is a two-edged sword. Sociometric investigations of children rated high in aggression tend to show that aggression is a source of unpopularity rather than peer esteem. Such studies, however, may not fully reflect the full range of aggression in children. They tend to base measures of aggression upon rating scales completed by adults that yield scales not only of physical aggressiveness but of the particular type associated with disobedience and antisocial acts. There is little doubt that this is indeed aversive to other children, who resent experiences of bullying or exploitation, but effective fighting can be admired, and—being a behaviour orientated to other children and not seen by teachers—this is not included in teachers' ratings.

Risks of aggression

The risks for development entailed by aggression are often described and do not need to be laboured. The danger and unpleasantness for other people are all too clear. The consequences come not only for others but also for the individual who is behaving aggressively.

One hazard is that aggressive children are the targets of a good deal of hostile and critical emotion from adults. Ratings of negative expressed emotion can be made reliably, and are more characteristic of the parents of defiant and aggressive children than of the parents of controls.[7] At least some of this relationship is probably secondary to the behaviour, for levels of hostility in parents fall when the child's behaviour is treated successfully with medication.[8] In turn, the critical reaction of parents probably maintains and prolongs the severity of aggressive and otherwise antisocial behaviour, for persistence of disorder is associated with high levels of negative emotion.[7]

Aggression also antagonises other children. Conduct disorder is often associated with poor peer relationships. There are some suggestions in the literature about the processes involved in this association. Aggressive boys are often incompetent at making friends with other children, and this incompetence is associated with poor performance in experimental tests of processing social information about peer relationships.[9] However, aggression is not necessarily associated with a general social incompetence, but aggressive boys are often characterised by a tendency to attribute hostile intention to other children in ambiguous situations. In turn, aggressive behaviour tends to make other children dislike the child who has attacked them. Treatment with medication has also clarified these relationships. When the child's behaviour is improved, so the relationships made with other children tend to become more rewarding.[10]

The reactions of other people may also have long-term effects. To understand this better will involve more information about the emotional adjustment of aggressive children. Recent longitudinal studies have indicated the possible importance of this. Harrington *et al.* followed into adult life a group of children who had been diagnosed as showing a conduct disorder.[11] They found, by comparison with controls, an increase not only in the behaviours characteristic of conduct disorder but also a high rate of depression. The full reasons for this will need to be clarified, but it seems likely that the boys and young men who showed conduct disorder tended to make for themselves a rejecting and adverse environment—and became depressed in reaction to this.

Individual differences

Knowledge of the course of development is sometimes taken to imply an invariant course. For example, it has been argued (admittedly by politicians) that social deprivation is not a cause of criminality because aggression develops in all societies and contexts. In fact, of course, to consider normative development is only to describe the context in which individual differences appear, not to negate their importance.

Individual differences are usually studied by clinically orientated child researchers, so they most commonly choose measures that reflect what is presented to clinicians. Parents or teachers complete rating scales about children that include a wide range of 'symptoms', most of them aggressive or otherwise antisocial behaviours that are unpleasant to involved adults. In short, the measures concentrate essentially on high-frequency aggressive behaviours that are seen by or directed towards adults. Not surprisingly, they are highly correlated with other sorts of high-frequency antisocial behaviours that constitute defiance of adult rules. Indeed, the main factor that emerges from factor analyses of such scales is a combined one of aggression, defiance and disruptive behaviour. It is not clear that it makes much clinical sense to try to distinguish this type of aggression from other kinds of disruptive behaviour disorder.

To focus on one type of aggression is in a sense rather partial, but this kind of overt disruptiveness is quite a good predictor of later adolescent unruliness, and indeed of violent and antisocial traits in adult life.[2]

The stability of high aggression is one of the major issues for a developmental psychopathology. Not only does aggression tend to persist but so does the wider antisocial cluster that includes aggression. To explain this, some students have been led to the idea of an antisocial syndrome and to stress a lack of plasticity once the syndrome has developed. Constitutional and biological causes are therefore emphasised. This does not have to be true, however—it could also be that the stability resides in factors outside the child. If violence results from reaction to adversity in the environment, the reason for the stability may be that the environment remains adverse.

Many processes could be affected to give rise to particularly high levels of aggression. The major processes that are possible candidates can be taken from the consideration of normal development above:

1. That high aggression is determined by a high level of an aggressive drive. To modern ears, this sounds rather tautological, in that there is no evidence for the existence of such a drive apart from the presence of the aggressive behaviour that the notion of a 'drive' is invoked to explain.
2. That particularly high levels of frustration are responsible, especially in combination with models that will make frustration more likely to be expressed in aggression.

Other likely processes include:

- stress;
- an inability to inhibit immediate reaction (impulsiveness);

- the expectations of others for inhibition;
- the extent to which other conflict resolution skills are learnt and empathy developed;
- the extent to which social relationships are dominated by the perception of threat; and
- the nature of the consequences of aggression (eg rewards of attention and successful coercion).

Aetiology of high aggressiveness

Research has now developed to the point where quite a lot is known about many factors associated with high levels of aggression. The problem is to develop from correlations to mechanisms, and to work out how the risk factors do in fact operate. I shall consider the associations of high aggression in the three groups of those that:

- are essentially the coexistence of other forms of psychopathology;
- represent the constitution of the child; and
- involve the impact of the physical and psychosocial environment.

These distinctions are somewhat arbitrary, and there is considerable overlap.

Other psychological problems

Defiance and other antisocial behaviours are so commonly associated with aggression that it is hard to see them as truly different problems.

Impulsiveness, in the sense of immediate reward-seeking and under-control, is associated but not the same. Block and Gjerde, for example, have shown how impulsiveness and antisocial behaviour in teenagers have a different set of family correlates. They tend to be towards permissiveness for the former, and authoritarian discipline for the latter.[12]   Hyperactivity is also distinguishable from aggression. It is a form of inattentiveness and restlessness, often associated with developmental delays. While it is often present in aggressive children, many classification studies have indicated it to be a distinct dimension of psychopathology.[13] A developmental perspective is needed to understand the reason for the frequent coexistence of both problems in the same child. Hyperactivity leads to aggression, not vice versa.[7] The developmental mechanisms involved need more research. It seems possible that the reactions of other people to the hyperactivity may determine whether antisocial problems appear later.

The overlap of these types of disruptive behaviour has led to some fragmentation of the literature. Different volumes of research have been generated by hyperactivity (or attention-deficit disorder with

hyperactivity (ADDH)), delinquency, aggression and conduct disorders, and substance abuse. Yet the people studied by these traditions
are so similar that it is highly artificial to consider them in separate
chapters of a textbook or in unconnected research projects. Most
hyperactive children are aggressive, and most aggressive children
hyperactive.[13] The hyperactive are at high risk for substance abuse
and delinquency later.[14,15] Indeed, in a recent USA/UK diagnostic
study of Diagnostic and Statistical Manual of Mental Disorders
(DSM-III) and International Classification of Diseases (ICD-9)
diagnoses applied to disruptive boys, there was very little agreement
between clinicians on which boys should be categorised as hyperactive,
which as conduct disordered, and which as both.[16] When both types of
problem were present, UK clinicians tended to see the disorder as one
of conduct, and USA clinicians as one of activity control. Accordingly,
recent reviewers have seen an immediate issue of research as one of
attempting a valid subtyping of the heterogeneous disorders that
present with disruptive conduct (for example, references 13, 17 and
18).

Emotional symptoms such as anxiety and depression are quite often
present in aggressive children who have been referred to clinics, but
epidemiological studies make it clear that this association does not hold
in the general population.[7] Emotional and conduct disorders are
essentially independent statistically, but both are common so mixed
cases can often be attributed to chance. It may well be that when both
are present together the problems are intractable and persistent, and
therefore more likely to be referred to clinics.

In short, there are several reasons for the coexistence of aggression
with other types of psychopathology. Comorbidity needs to be taken
into account by all researchers into the way that aggression develops
in childhood.

Constitutional factors

Genetic inheritance
Although genetic inheritance is probably a factor, the size of its
contribution is still unclear. There is no dispute that there is a
clustering of antisocial relatives in the families of disruptive children.
The finding is clear, and is not only because of comorbidity between
aggressive conduct and hyperactivity (for which a genetic contribution
is clear) since even non-hyperactive conduct disorder still shows a high
rate of antisocial relatives.[7] The reasons for the association are not
clear.

Is there a genetic link? The Scandinavian adoptive study, described
by Bohman and Sigvardsson,[19] and re-analysed by Bohman et al.,[20]

suggested that there was indeed a genetic inheritance of something related to antisocial conduct disorder (but separate from alcoholism). On the other hand, an adoptive study of the offspring of psychiatrically disturbed or normal parents suggested that the genetic link between parental illness and childhood disturbance was present for hyperactivity rather than for other types of disturbance.[21] Twin studies in the past found little evidence for genetic inheritance in delinquent young people. However, suggestions that there may indeed be a genetic link in young children with marked aggression and in older adults with antisocial personality call for a new generation of twin studies that can examine the issues of developmental changes in heritability and the problem of what it is that is inherited. The techniques are now in place for genetic studies using family pedigree, twin and adoption designs and the methods of molecular genetics. They have considerable promise for clarifying what is inherited, the subtyping of disorders, and whether the familial association is for a temperamental attribute (e.g. of activity or 'difficulty') or for a psychiatric syndrome. They should be an early priority in research.

It is, however, unlikely that genetic inheritance accounts for the whole of the association with adverse aspects of family life. There is probably a direct effect of family relationships (see below). These are factors operating for the individual child, rather than across the entire family, and may well represent family reactions to behavioural deviation rather than be the initiating cause. Once established, however, they probably form part of the family adversities and maladaptive patterns of parent–child interaction that are known to predict poor outcome for hyperactive as well as antisocial children.[22] Perhaps they represent part of the way that children's constitutions shape their environments.[23] Improved measures of family function should therefore be applied primarily to the longitudinal issue of how qualities of children interact with the way they are treated to determine outcome. For this purpose, it will be desirable to establish and follow up the relatively rare groups of children who have good family function in spite of their disruptiveness, and vice versa, as well as the usual groups of children who show problems in both domains or in neither. Intervention studies (see below) also offer the chance of modifying family factors, and effective interventions would be a helpful way of determining what is causative.

Gender differences
The area of gender differences also deserves a good deal more research. The higher prevalence in males is a highly robust finding, for which comparisons of affected males with affected females could suggest reasons. If the difference stems from the different ways in which boys

and girls are treated, this would be a useful indication of which features in the psychological environment should be targets for modification. It is probable that some of the difference between the sexes comes from biological factors. Hormonal changes probably play a part. First, pre-natal exposure to androgens tends to 'masculinise' later behaviour for female children, which includes a higher level of aggressive behaviour in the exposed girls than in controls. Secondly, naturally occurring levels in circulating hormones are associated with aggressive behaviour. Boys with higher testosterone levels tend to be more violent—though this is not a necessary or a sufficient explanation.[24]

Altered neuropsychological processes

Constitutional alterations in the physiological function of the brain have often been suggested, but this has not yet been established as a cause of violence, except of course in the uncommon cases where a postictal alteration of mental state can lead to episodic aggression, and in the even rarer cases where an outburst of aggression can be directly traced to a complex partial seizure.

The idea of 'minimal brain dysfunction' is often invoked but has little to commend it. The concept is not neurologically coherent and its supposed components (EEG and psychometric test changes, and motor abnormalities) do not in fact tend to correlate one with another.[25]

Investigations of neurotransmitter metabolism have not yet given a consensus. Such studies have of course begun to be reported about all the disorders involving disruptive behaviour, including aggression and ADDH, but they are scanty and contradictory in their findings (see reference 26 for a review).

Aggressive children nevertheless show a higher prevalence of various impairments of neuropsychological function.[27] Poor test performance is linked particularly to the inattentive component of disorder, and especially to the restricted definition of hyperkinetic disorder.[7] There is a need for more research here to obtain closer descriptions of cognitive behaviours such as orientation, search, scanning and preferences, their developmental course, the factors that determine them, and how they relate to difficulties in learning. However, current knowledge suggests that the available measures of neuropsychological deviation are not directly associated with aggression, but rather with the behavioural problems such as hyperactivity that tend to be comorbid with it. The line of pathogenesis is probably complex, and it would be wrong to think of aggression as the direct consequence of a defined brain dysfunction.

Social processing

Other research at the level of individual pathology may usefully focus upon the information processing that underlies social competence and incompetence with other children. An example comes from the work of Dodge *et al.*[9] who have conceived of social behaviour as a function of children's processing social environmental cues through encoding, mental representation, accessing potential responses, selecting a good response and enacting it. They set competent and incompetent children to watch videotapes of children interacting and, separately, to enact a similar situation. Processing skill predicted actual performance, and better performance was associated with natural popularity. Processing about a peer group entry situation did not predict aggression, but processing about a situation involving provocation was indeed associated with more aggression.

The enhancement of social processing may come to join the armamentarium of therapeutic interventions. This is difficult research, and the determinants of performance will need to be specified. The situation specificity of much disruptive behaviour should be a caution against over-rapid acceptance of any general explanation based on individual pathology. One of the goals of research is to clarify the situational as well as the personal determinants of behaviour.

Environmental factors

Differences between neighbourhoods in the prevalence of behaviour problems are known and strong. Urban–rural differences are known for many types of psychiatric pathology,[28] but they seem to be especially strong for disorders involving aggressive and hyperactive behaviour.[29] They are presumably generated by co-existing disadvantage rather than by urban environment *per se*. For example, a disadvantaged rural population in mainland China was found to have higher rates of antisocial and hyperactive behaviours than an urban population.[30] One set of major factors operating is probably those causing the family problems already mentioned,[28] but they may also work through variations in the effectiveness of schools.

Family relationships

One of the most solidly established findings of medical epidemiology is that family relationships are very often discordant in conduct disorder. It is probably through the family that many of the other types of social disadvantage have their impact (e.g. poverty, unemployment, living in an inner city), but the directions of effect are not always clear—for example, an aggressive boy will tend to create discordant and coercive family relationships around himself, so these will be present even when a brain disorder such as autism or temporal lobe epilepsy is the initiating cause of aggression.

The major research questions now are therefore to clarify how the various types of problematic relationships come about. To do this, it will be necessary to have a fuller description of the types of relationship disturbance that are encountered and how they interact with other causes of aggression. Are they a necessary step in pathogenesis, or are there alternative routes into high aggression?

Maudsley Hospital family study

There are several difficulties in this research. It requires the subtyping of cases, so large numbers of serious problems have to be examined. Clinically gathered data may therefore be useful in a preliminary examination of the factors involved. I shall therefore describe some findings from clinically referred children at the Maudsley Hospital in London. The clinicians assessing the children complete a standard questionnaire about findings in each case. This set of clinical information is a useful basis for descriptive clinical surveys.

The first need is to describe the psychosocial problems of children clinically diagnosed as showing an aggressive (or otherwise antisocial) conduct disorder. Between 1973 and 1983, 1,010 children were diagnosed at the Maudsley Hospital as showing 'conduct disorder of childhood' (ICD-9, classification 312), 87% of whom were also diagnosed as having at least one of the psychosocial diagnoses from axis 5 of the multiaxial version of the World Health Organisation's 9th revision of the ICD. Most of the individual diagnoses are not more common than in the other children seen at the same hospital: over-involvement is present in 12% of conduct disorder cases and 15% of controls, poor family communications in 13% *vs* 10%, acute stresses on the family in 12% *vs* 13%, and mental disorder in other family members in 22% *vs* 20%. However, discord is significantly commoner in conduct disorder cases (40% *vs* 29%) and lack of warmth (in 13% *vs* 8%). This is in keeping with a picture of cold and rejecting relationships as a specific aspect of the pathology of conduct disorder, and one that probably helps to shape its development.

The next issue relates to those children in whom no psychosocial disorder is present. What characterises the 13% of conduct disorder cases whose backgrounds seem to be normal? They might show a more subtle operation of the same factors, but clinical ratings of abnormal personal relationships suggest they do not characterise those without an axis 5 diagnosis. In comparison to those with a conduct disorder who have a 'psychosocial' diagnosis, disturbance of the child–mother relationship is significantly less common (present in 46% *vs* 74%; $\chi^2 =$

27; df $= 1$; $p < 0.0001$). The same is true for child–father relationships (disturbed in 29% vs 60%; $\chi^2 = 29$; df $= 1$; $p < 0.0001$), while child–sibling relationships are similar in both groups (problematic in 43% vs 49%). (Children with subnormal intelligence are excluded from these analyses.)

The scores on two scales of 'disruptive behaviour' and 'emotional disorder' also differentiate the groups. Children from non-deviant social backgrounds are less disruptive (mean, 6.8; SD, 4.5) than those from deviant backgrounds (10.1 (4.9); $F = 22.4$; df $= 2,880$; $p < 0.0001$) and less emotionally disordered (mean, 2.3; (SD, 3.0) for those from non-deviant backgrounds; 3.1 (3.1) for the remainder; $F = 4.7$; df $= 2,920$; $p < 0.01$).

Children from 'normal' family and social backgrounds are more impaired in cognitive development, and 35% of them are intellectually retarded compared to only 12% of the conduct-disordered with abnormal families. A further 17% show disorder of comprehension of language (vs 7% of those with psychosocial diagnoses), and 30% have an expressive language problem (vs 9% of those with psychosocial diagnoses).

The suggestion is therefore that there is some heterogeneity in this group of referred children with antisocial conduct disorders, and that neurodevelopmental problems and adverse family relationships constitute alternative pathways into the development of disorder.

Environmental toxins

Environmental toxins have often been blamed for the high rates of behavioural deviance in inner cities. Of these, lead has received by far the largest amount of research attention. There has been general agreement that high tissue lead levels are weakly correlated with disruptive behaviour and psychological test impairment. It has also been generally recognised that high lead levels are a marker to social disadvantage as well as being potentially harmful in themselves. The causative pathway is therefore obscure.

This is a common situation for the factors known to be associated with conduct problems. The unusual aspect of the lead work is that its political (rather than medical) importance has attracted enough funding to allow for the types of study that will be important. Several groups of investigators have reported multiple regression analyses, in which the association between lead and behaviour is examined after allowing for the effects of adverse social circumstances (see reference 31 as an example). Most of these investigations find that the association is attenuated but still statistically significant after the statistical controls have been made.[32] The research issues are worth highlighting because progress will have to be made before any clear conclusions are possible.

Some of the disagreement arises from technical differences. First, the more factors that are controlled for, the greater becomes the risk of over-correction in the multiple regression. Obviously, too, the choice of factors to be controlled for may, on the one hand, miss the key environmental circumstances or, on the other, remove the influence of lead itself. Finally, the effect size is small, and often on the very boundary of statistical significance with the sample sizes taken.

However, even when technical considerations are solved, there are still problems of interpretation. Children's behaviour may itself increase their exposure to lead (as may be implied by the higher levels of blood lead in boys than in girls). The causal relationship may therefore run from behaviour to the supposed risk factor. It will be desirable therefore to seek groups of children in whom exposure to lead is determined by factors that are obviously not the consequence of their behaviour (e.g. their geographical proximity to a newly started industrial source of pollution), and (again) to use a longitudinal strategy.

It is, in short, an arduous and expensive business to determine the details of pathogenesis even of a single well-defined factor, yet the details of pathogenesis are crucial for decisions about prevention and treatment.

Conclusions

What can be concluded from the developmental research so far? Clearly, much remains to be learned, but what needs to be known has become somewhat clearer. There are several routes into high aggression in childhood: hyperactivity, language delay, and possibly emotional disturbance. Rare causes include autism, some forms of epilepsy and many kinds of brain damage. The largest single factor is violence in other close family members. Whatever the route into aggression, it tends to propagate itself. The reaction of others maintains an environment that confirms the child's belief of being under threat and isolated, and so tends to make a vicious cycle of increased aggression.

References

1. Rutter M, Garmezy N. Developmental psychopathology. In: Mussen H, ed. *Handbook of child psychology. Vol IV. Socialization, personality and social development.* New York: Wiley, 1983
2. Earls F. Oppositional-defiant and conduct disorders. In: Rutter M, Taylor E, Hersov L, eds. *Child and adolescent psychiatry, 3rd edn.* Oxford: Blackwell Scientific Publications (in press)
3. Bandura A. Social-learning theory of identification processes. In: Goslin D, ed. *Handbook of socialization theory and research.* Chicago: Rand-McNally, 1969

4. Patterson GR, DeBarysh BD, Ramsey E. A developmental perspective on anti-social behaviour. *Am Psychologist* 1989; **44**:329–35

5. Patterson GR. *Coercive family processes.* Eugene, OR, USA: Castilia Press, 1982

6. Hyde JS. How large are gender differences in aggression? A developmental meta-analysis. *Dev Psychol* 1984; **20**:722–36

7. Taylor E, Sandberg S, Thorley G, Giles S. *The epidemiology of childhood hyperactivity.* Maudsley Monographs 33. Oxford: Oxford University Press, 1991

8. Schachar R, Taylor E, Wieselberg M, Thorley G, Rutter M. Changes in family function and relationships in children who respond to methylphenidate. *J Am Acad Child Adolesc Psychiatry* 1987; **26**:728–32

9. Dodge KA, Pettit GS, Braun MM. Social competence in children. *Monograph Soc Res Child Dev* 1987; **51**:no. 2

10. Cunningham CE, Siegel LS, Offord DR. A developmental dose–response analysis of the effects of methylphenidate on the peer interaction of attention deficit disordered boys. *J Child Psychol Psychiatry* 1985; **26**:955–72

11. Harrington R, Fudge H, Rutter M, Pickles A, Hill J. Adult outcomes of childhood and adolescent depression. II. Links with antisocial disorders. *J Am Acad Child Adolesc Psychiatry* 1991; **30**:434–9

12. Block J, Gjerde PF. Distinguishing between antisocial behavior and undercontrol. In: Olweus D, Block J, Radke-Yarrow M, eds. *Development of antisocial and prosocial behavior.* Orlando, FL, USA: Academic Press Inc, 1986

13. Taylor EA. Attention deficit and conduct disorder syndromes. In: Rutter M, Tuma AH, Lann IS, eds. *Assessment and diagnosis in child psychopathology.* New York: Guilford Press, 1988

14. Gittelman R, Mannuzza S, Sheriker R, Bonagura N. Hyperactive boys almost grown up. I. Psychiatric status. *Arch Gen Psychiatry* 1985; **42**:937–47

15. Satterfield J, Hoppe CM, Schell AM. A prospective study of delinquency in 110 adolescent boys with attention deficit disorder and 88 normal adolescent boys. *Am J Psychiatry* 1982; **139**:795–8

16. Prendergast M, Taylor EA, Rapoport JL *et al.* The diagnosis of childhood hyperactivity: a US-UK cross-national study of DSM-III and ICD-9. *J Child Psychol Psychiatry* 1988; **29**:289–300

17. Rutter M. Attention deficit disorder/hyperkinetic syndrome: conceptual and research issues regarding diagnosis and classification. In: Sagvolden T, Archer T, eds. *Attention deficit disorders and hyperkinetic syndrome.* Hillsdale, NJ, USA: Erlbaum, 1988

18. Werry JS, Reeves JC, Elkind GS. Attention deficit, conduct, oppositional and anxiety disorders in children. I. A review of research on differentiating characteristics. II. Clinical characteristics. *J Am Acad Child Adolesc Psychiatry* 1987; **26**:133–55

19. Bohman M, Sigvardsson S. A prospective longitudinal study of children registered for adoption. *Acta Psychiatr Scand* 1980; **61**:339–55

20. Bohman M, Cloninger CR, Sigvardsson S, von Knorring A-L. Predisposition to petty criminality in Swedish adoptees. I. Genetic and environmental heterogeneity. *Arch Gen Psychiatry* 1982; **29**:1233–41

21. Cunningham L, Cadoret R, Loftus R, Edwards JE. Studies of adoptees from psychiatrically disturbed biological parents. *Br J Psychiatry* 1975; **126**:534–9

22. Weiss G, Hechtman LT. *Hyperactive children grown up.* New York: Guilford Press, 1986

23. Scarr S, McCartney K. How people make their own environments: a theory of genotype-environment effects. *Child Dev* 1985; **54**:424–35

24. Olweus D. Aggression and hormones: behavioral relationship with testosterone and adrenaline. In: Olweus D, Block J, Radke-Yarrow M, eds. *Development of antisocial and prosocial behavior.* Orlando, FL, USA: Academic Press Inc, 1986

25. Schmidt MH, Esser G, Allehoff W, Geisel B, Laucht M, Woerner W. Evaluating the significance of minimal brain dysfunction—results of an epidemiological study. *J Child Psychol Psychiatry* 1987; **26**:803–22

26. Oades RD. Attention deficit disorder with hyperactivity (ADDH): the contribution of catecholaminergic activity. *Prog Neurobiol* 1987; **29**:365–91
27. Douglas V. Attentional and cognitive problems. In: Rutter M, ed. *Development neuropsychiatry*. New York: Guilford Press, 1983
28. Quinton D. Annotation: urbanism and child mental health. *J Child Psychol Psychiatry* 1988; **29**:11–20
29. Boyle MH, Offord DR. Ontario Child Health Study. I. Methodology. II. Six-month prevalence of disorder and rates of service utilisation. *Arch Gen Psychiatry* 1987; **44**:826–36
30. Shen Y-C, Wong YF, Yang XL. An epidemiological investigation of minimal brain dysfunction in six elementary schools in Beijing. *J Child Psychol Psychiatry* 1985; **26**:777–88
31. Silva PA, Hughes P, Williams S, Faed VM. Blood lead, intelligence, reading attainment, and behaviour in 11-year-old children in Dunedin, New Zealand. *J Child Psychol Psychiatry* 1988; **29**:43–52
32. Taylor E. Toxins and allergens. In: Rutter M, Casaer P, eds. *Biological risk factors for psychosocial disorders*. Cambridge: Cambridge University Press, 1991

4 | Contemporary psychological research into violence: an overview

Clive R. Hollin
*School of Psychology, University of Birmingham; and Glenthorne
Youth Treatment Centre, Birmingham*

Introduction

Contemporary psychological research into violence, like that from other disciplines such as biology and sociology, is concerned with the individual person and with the environmental influences on individual behaviour. Thus, in discussing individual factors these should be understood with reference to the environmental context in which the behaviour takes place. Conversely, environmental factors need to be understood with reference to individual differences. As is becoming increasingly clear from the research on developmental pathways from childhood troublesomeness to adolescent delinquency and ultimately to adult criminal behaviour, highly complex models are needed to account for the interplay between environmental factors and individual behaviour.[1] In order to give a flavour of what such a model of violence should encompass (without claiming to offer anything like a model), I have drawn together in an ordered manner some of the research findings on the topic of violent behaviour. This illustrates a logical way of seeking to advance our understanding of violence.

Conceptual bases of violent behaviour

The basis for understanding violent behaviour in terms of an environment–person interaction may be shown simply as in Fig. 1. In this scheme, there are three stages:

- the *situation* in which the violence takes place;
- the *person* part of the scheme, the individual's thoughts, feelings and actions; and
- the *impact* of the violent behaviour on the environment.

This sequence of three stages provides a helpful way to consider the research findings on violent behaviour. It is important to emphasise that this is not the only way to understand violent behaviour. There are many different ways to explain the phenomenon of violence, including attempts from several disciplines: for example, biology, anthropology, neurology and sociology have all made valuable contributions to our understanding of violence. From psychology alone there have been a variety of explanations of violence, based on psychodynamic, instinct and drive, behavioural and personality theories, and theories from social psychology. (For reviews of the psychological theories see references 2, 3 and 4.)

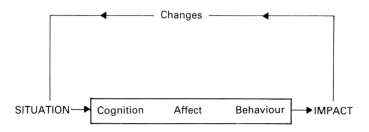

Fig. 1. *Stages in the cognitive–behavioural model.*

It is important at the outset to be clear with respect to terminology. There are two particular terms in common use, sometimes used interchangeably in the literature: *aggression* and *violence*. Megargee[5] and Siann[6] both suggest the following use of these terms:

- *aggression*, which refers to the intention to hurt or gain physical advantage over other people, without necessarily involving physical injury;
- *violence*, which involves the use of strong physical force against another person, sometimes but not always impelled by aggressive motivation, that results in the physical injury of the other person.

In this chapter, the terms aggression and violence are used in the sense suggested by Megargee and Siann.

Situational analysis

Henderson conducted an analysis from self-reports of adult male violent offenders about the types of situation in which they behaved in a violent manner.[7] This study is of interest because it gives an indication of the settings in which violent incidents are most likely to occur, at least those involving adult males.

Henderson's analysis revealed four broad categories of violent situation:

- violence in conjunction with another crime—sometimes intentionally as with robbery and sometimes in panic as when discovered committing another crime such as burglary;
- in a family context, directed towards both women and children;
- violence in public places such as clubs and bars; and
- violence in institutions (police stations and prisons in Henderson's study) directed towards fellow inmates, police officers and prison staff.

While not part of Henderson's analysis, violence in institutions can be extended to other institutions such as hospitals, and to other professional staff such as nurses and doctors, social workers and probation officers.

Henderson's study illustrates the distinction between premeditated or instrumental violence, as for example in a robbery, and *angry* or *hostile* violence which is impulsive and unplanned.[8] Situational analysis has pointed to a number of factors that increase the likelihood of this latter type of violent outburst. These factors fall into two broad groups.

Physical factors

The first group covers the aspects of the situation that do not involve social interaction with other people. These physical factors include high temperature, air pollution and overcrowding. There is strong evidence to suggest that they are all related to rises in the number of violent acts over a given period.[9,10] A study by Jarrell and Howsen investigated the effects of *transient* crowding on rates of criminal behaviour.[11] Transient crowding refers to increases in the population density caused by an influx into a given area of 'strangers' such as tourists, students or shoppers. Jarrell and Howsen report that this has the effect of increasing the rates of burglary, larceny and robbery, but a negligible effect on rates of assault, murder and rape.

An explanation for this pattern of results might be that the crimes that increase in frequency are crimes of acquisition, which can involve *instrumental violence*: the more people there are in an area, the greater the number of opportunities for taking another person's property, sometimes by force. However, crowding has little or no impact on crimes often associated with angry violence, that is murder, assault and sex offences. These types of violent act are often closely bound in with close personal relationships, so the number of strangers passing through an area would therefore be less likely to have an effect on this form of violence.

Social factors

The second group of factors are social in nature, and refer to the words
and actions of other people. This is perhaps associated more strongly
with angry violence. In this context, the violent act might be precipitated by verbal provocation, such as an insult, physical intimidation,
as with jostling or pushing, or the other person's behaviour breaking
some social rule. However, these social factors are in the eye of the
beholder: one person's social rule is not necessarily another's, so what
one person finds provoking and insulting may not have the same effect
on another. When seen in this way, it becomes less easy to separate
social and personal factors. In order to understand the impact of social
factors, it is necessary to turn to the person part of the sequence.

The person

Background

The longitudinal studies, such as the Cambridge Study of Delinquent
Development, have paid some attention to the issue of background
predictors of violent behaviour. Farrington and West suggest a significant continuity between childhood forms of violent conduct and
violent adult behaviour.[12] However, the early predictors of violence
were essentially the same as for non-violent offences: eg economic
disadvantage, family criminality, troublesome behaviour at school.
Farrington and West conclude therefore:

> Aggression was merely one element of a more general antisocial tendency,
> which arose in childhood and continued through the teenage and adult
> years ... Violent offenders were very similar to non-violent frequent
> offenders in childhood, adolescent, and adult features ... the causes of
> aggression and violence were essentially the same as the causes of persistent
> and extreme antisocial, delinquent and criminal behaviour (Ref. 12,
> p. 131).

Stattin and Magnusson reported a prospective longitudinal study of
the relation between aggressiveness at early school age and criminal
behaviour in later life with a sample of 1,027 young people followed
from the age of 10 years through to the age of 26 years.[13] It was found
that for both males and females, high ratings of aggressiveness by
teachers were strongly associated with later criminal behaviour, in
terms both of the seriousness and of the frequency of these acts. This
relation between early aggressiveness and later criminal behaviour was
independent both of intelligence and of the education level of the
parents.

Denno[14] carried out a study of background, psychological and biological factors in the development of violent behaviour and concluded, rather like Farrington and West, that a complex admixture of the influences was needed to account for criminal behaviour generally, with the boundaries between violent and non-violent crime somewhat blurred.

Widom[15] reported a thorough examination of the literature concerned with the hypothesis that 'violence breeds violence'; in other words, that abused and neglected children will become the next generation of abusers, that the victims of violence will become the violent perpetrators when their turn comes. Despite the intuitive appeal of this notion of intergenerational transmission of violent behaviour, as Widom notes in concluding her review of the evidence:

> Not all children who grow up in violent homes become violent adults. . . . Certainly a wide variety of environmental stresses, potential triggering mechanisms, and many other factors are involved in the learning process. Nevertheless, because many children appear not to succumb to the adverse effects of abuse or neglect, it is important to determine why this is so and what it is that protects them from those negative consequences (Ref. 15, p. 24).

While DiLalla and Gottesman[16] followed Widom's paper with the argument for a strong genetic component to the transmission of violence, in a later paper Widom[17] suggests that the evidence may not be so compelling after all. If there is little difference in the backgrounds of violent and non-violent criminals, perhaps more can be learnt from the violent person's immediate response to situational cues. This response to situational cues can be divided into three components: cognition, emotion, and action.

Response: cognition

Dodge[18] defined a sequence of steps in the effective processing of social information:

- encoding social cues;
- the cognitive representation and interpretation of these social cues;
- searching for appropriate ways to respond;
- deciding the best way to respond.

After completing this sequence, the person then acts according to his decision. The first part of this cognitive sequence involves the person in perceiving and interpreting situation cues, particularly the words and actions of other people. There is a body of research evidence to suggest that aggressive and violent people, perhaps especially aggressive and violent children and adolescents, search for and perceive *fewer* social cues than non-violent people (e.g. ref. 19). Further, it is also clear that violent people are much more likely to interpret cues in a hostile fashion.[20] This hostile, aggressive interpretation of social cues may well be a fundamental component of violent behaviour. Indeed a study by Stefanek *et al.* demonstrated that this tendency is evident even in aggressive young children.[21] Stefanek *et al.* recorded the self-statements of groups of young children when they were faced with social contact with other children, and found that aggressive children were much more likely to describe to themselves social encounters in an aggressive fashion: 'that child doesn't like me', or 'they want to take my toys'. If this line of argument is followed, the violent person must see the other people's actions in a hostile manner so that the world must seem to be a perpetually threatening place.

The next part of the sequence demands the ability to generate suitable responses to an understanding of the situation, sometimes referred to as social problem solving. Effective social problem solving demands the ability both to generate solutions—that is, effective courses of action—and to select the most expedient alternative. Some studies have pointed to limited social problem solving skills, in terms of generating solutions and considering the consequences of their actions, for interpersonal conflicts in aggressive and violent populations (eg reference 20). However, as other research has shown, this finding extends to delinquent groups generally and so may not be peculiar to violent individuals.

The limited problem solving ability for violent populations can be accounted for in one of two ways. First, violent people experience difficulty with social problem solving: that is, they have not mastered the requisite skills to generate effective, socially acceptable solutions to interpersonal problems. Alternatively, it may be that *defining* an interaction as aggressive, due to a limited perception of the situation and a hostile interpretation of what has been seen, cuts down the number of options generated by violent people. Thus, the argument could be advanced that rather than limited problem solving ability leading to the generation of fewer solutions, it is in the nature of violent situations that they offer fewer alternatives for action. Following this line of thought, the eventual decision to act in a violent manner is entirely understandable: if an individual is being threatened, to retaliate in kind is a perfectly reasonable and rational response. It is not surprising, in this view, that aggressive people often select a violent response, viewing their violent behaviour as an acceptable, legitimate course of action.[20]

Response: emotion

This cognitive sequence of perception, interpretation, and problem solving may be influenced significantly by the individual's level of emotional arousal. The widely cited work of the American social psychologist Raymond Novaco has suggested that there can be reciprocal relationships between environmental events, both physical and social, cognitive processes and angry emotional arousal.[22,23]

Specifically, Novaco's original analysis of anger suggested four stages:

- external triggering events;
- angry thoughts;
- heightened angry emotional arousal, including both physiological and psychological elements; and
- action

Novaco suggested that complex reciprocal relationships might function between these components; for example, another person's remark (triggering event) might be appraised in a hostile manner, leading to angry thoughts. This heightens emotional arousal, in turn intensifying the angry thoughts. The interplay between cognition and arousal thereby increases the likelihood of the individual acting in a violent manner.

Response: action

In the final part of the response sequence the individual carries out a violent act. Violent behaviour can, of course, take many different forms. Most typically, it involves an unarmed physical assault, such as kicking, punching, slapping and strangling. Less typically, a weapon is used, most often a broken bottle or a knife, sometimes a gun.[7] Most violent incidents are not planned in advance, and often the use of a weapon is the result of one of the people involved in the incident grabbing whatever comes to hand. Thus, it is not surprising that the countries with the highest level of firearm availability have a higher firearm homicide rate.[24] The premeditated use of weapons, particularly firearms, can be seen in crimes such as armed robbery. In this type of crime, the weapon is used to increase the chances of success through intimidation and fear, which is not to say that the weapons would not be fired if opposition was encountered.

The sequence of cognition, emotion and action should not be thought of as static. There may be a number of dynamic interactions, involving changes in thought and deed prior to the violent act; in other words, there may be an escalation of behaviour as an interpersonal exchange becomes more heated and out of control. This possibility is discussed below in considering the impact of the person's behaviour on the other people in the situation.

Impact of violent behaviour

The individual's actions have the effect of changing the situation. Violent behaviour may often be a highly rewarding strategy. A display of violence may produce some financial or social reward that would otherwise not be forthcoming; for example, a successful robbery can produce both hard cash and peer group status. Violent behaviour is an excellent way to avoid social situations or escape from unwanted tasks; for example, an assault on a teacher is a remarkably effective strategy to avoid lessons and escape from the constraints of the classroom. For some people, the victim's fear and pain are the rewards. The history of criminology is littered with criminals who perform sadistic acts of torture on their victims, sometimes recording or photographing the results of their actions, to enjoy repeatedly the power and control afforded by their victim's suffering.

Role of the victim

Violent behaviour has an impact on other people, often producing a response to the offender's actions. It follows that to understand violence it is necessary to look at the role of the victim in the violent event. A violent act involving offender and victim can be portrayed as an interaction, with those involved continually shifting and moving in response to each other's actions. Such a dynamic interchange is described in a classic paper by Luckenbill which examines violent acts that culminate in murder.[25] Based on analysis of case material, Luckenbill documents the typical pattern of events culminating in murder as a series of transactions between offender and victim (often when one or both have been drinking). Luckenbill notes that in many instances of murder the opening move comes from the victim. This may take the form of a verbal comment, flirtation with another person or a refusal to comply with a request. In some cases, the provocation is clearly intended, in others the offender interprets the victim's actions as provocative.

   The next transaction involves the offender in checking his or her perception of insult or refusal. This may be by directly asking the victim or onlookers, or by the victim's refusal to obey a command to stop. Thus, the offender sees his or her own perception of refusal as accurate when, for example, a screaming child does not comply with an instruction to be quiet.

   In the next stage, the offender opts not to retreat but to engage with the other person to sort things out, in the main through verbal retaliation and the issue of threats, although in a minority of cases the first level of retaliation is physical, resulting in murder. More usually, however, the victim responds in some way to the offender's actions, making a verbal or even physical counter-attack. Luckenbill suggests that such a move by the victim appears to confirm to the perpetrator that violence is appropriate. The offender attacks and in many cases, as Luckenbill notes, 'dropped the victim in a single shot, stab or rally of blows' (Ref. 25, p. 185).

Violence towards women and children

While Luckenbill's analysis exemplifies the social, interactive nature of violent acts, it would be unwise to assume that all violence is 'victim-precipitated'. This can be seen, for example, in situations in which men are violent towards women or children. (For extended reviews by psychologists, see references 26 and 27.) Thus, Dobash and Dobash argue strongly against universal application of the notion of victim precipitation of violence.[28] They are of the view that violent episodes against women should be understood as intentional acts by the man. Indeed, rather than contributing to violence, many women victims try to avoid or avert the onset of violence, and negotiate a safe outcome for themselves and sometimes their children. An understanding of this type of violence, Dobash and Dobash suggest, requires an analysis that involves the male's gender identity and its associated roles and meanings within a social and cultural context.

A recent study by Goldsmith looked at abuser characteristics as perceived by the abused spouse.[29] The most frequently nominated characteristics were that the man was violent when angered—and was easily angered—domineering, accepted violence as a problem solving technique, a heavy drinker and displayed macho type behaviour. Within this list elements of the type of male gender identity referred to by Dobash and Dobash are perhaps seen: a constellation of attitudes, beliefs and emotions that for the offender legitimise and even excuse his violent behaviour.

It is clear that different types of violent act will demand different levels of explanation, a task that is far from simple. The last words here belong to Widom:

> The study of social problems such as child abuse and violence places a heavy burden on the researcher to cross disciplinary boundaries in developing theories and designing research to address these important questions.[17]

Reducing violence

If the use of a cognitive-behavioural model helps to start to understand violence, what does it suggest as strategies for reducing violence? It indicates three directions which may be taken:

- *prevention* of the situation in which the violence occurs;
- *treatment* of the violent person; and
- *sentencing*, or the consequences that follow violence.

Prevention

There are a number of crime prevention strategies that might be expected to reduce the level of violent crime:

- environmental design, such as better lighting in public places;
- neighbourhood watch schemes;
- more police patrols; and
- transport schemes to remove victims from potentially dangerous situations.

All these are examples of ways in which to lessen the chances of violent attacks by muggers, armed robbers, and rapists.

'Situational crime prevention' has become enormously popular over the last decade. However, on a note of caution, there is considerable debate about its value both in terms of whether such initiatives as neighbourhood watch really do lower the crime rate, and about the possibility of 'displacement' of crimes to other more vulnerable targets.

Moving away from these broad social measures to more personal areas, the last few years have seen increasing attention being paid to the prevention of face-to-face violence. Many professional people, such as nurses, police, probation officers and social workers, are regularly exposed to situations in which violence may erupt with them as victims. A number of researchers have examined such potentially dangerous face-to-face situations, and have formulated various strategies to minimise the risks of becoming a victim of a violent assault (eg references 30 and 31). These strategies include, for example, developing *personal skills* to heighten awareness of the risk of violence. They can be as basic as familiarisation with case material prior to an initial family visit, or learning the specific non-verbal cues associated with anger so as to recognise the early warning signs of likely violence.

Strategies for managing violent incidents are also important: tactics such as effective *time management* to avoid keeping potentially aggressive clients waiting and growing more angry, or provoking anger by cutting short appointments. There are obvious points to be made:

- guarding private addresses and telephone numbers;
- letting colleagues know where you are going and what time to expect to hear from you;

- paying attention to office design so that there are no heavy objects to hand or easily barricaded doors;
- paying attention to aspects of clothing might also save injury, such as plastic lenses for spectacles, tying back long hair, and not wearing hanging earrings.

Perhaps most importantly, there should be clear articulated policies within a group or staff team as to the procedures to be followed should a violent incident occur. It should go without saying that those responsible for the implementation of policy should ensure that *all* staff are aware of and understand the policy. Indeed, given the mood of some sections of the legal profession at the moment, not to have a policy and staff trained in accordance with it could leave both individuals and their employers in a vulnerable position.

Treatment

The assumption underpinning a treatment approach is that violent behaviour can be stopped by changing the violent person. In this light, a number of treatment techniques based on cognitive-behavioural theory have proved popular in recent years.[32] These treatment approaches can be broadly divided into those that aim to change cognition and those that aim to change behaviour.

Of those that seek to change cognition (together with the associated angry arousal), *anger management* has proved enormously popular.[33] Of the techniques aimed at changing behaviour, *social skills training* has been widely used with violent people.[34,35] Both these approaches have, within limits, proved to be moderately successful. However, the next generation of treatment programmes looks even more promising. A number of North American researchers and practitioners, principally Robert Ross in Canada and Arnie Goldstein in the States, are developing *multimodal programmes*. The Reasoning and Rehabilitation programme developed by Ross and Fabiano[36] has begun to show beneficial effects with a range of types of offender.[37] However, for present purposes, the Aggression Replacement Training (ART) programme developed by Goldstein and his colleagues is of interest.[38,39] ART utilises three main approaches:

- structured learning training, including social problem solving and social skills training;
- anger control training; and
- moral education

The outcome studies strongly indicate that ART does lead to improved skills, greater self-control and lower rates of violent behaviour.

Context

It is recognised by most practitioners that context is an important determinant of the success of a treatment approach to working with offenders. In looking specifically at the management and treatment of violent behaviour, Gentry and Ostapiuk have raised some important issues concerning the relative effectiveness of treatment in institutions and community settings.[40]

The characteristics of institutions and communities are quite different in a number of important respects. For many reasons, including legal requirements, protection of staff, other residents and the public, institutions are characterised by security and the predictability of routines. These factors, of course, produce a highly artificial environment compared to the community, which very often lacks such rigid and controlling security, structure and definition of rules and boundaries.

Overlaying this dichotomy of institutions and community, *management* needs and *client* needs may be distinguished. The former, reflected in the characteristics of institutions, involves an effective means by which to ensure compliance, containment and adherence to routines in order to impose control over the client's behaviour. In contrast, in order to survive in the community the client needs to develop self-control to ensure continued freedom and independence.

It follows that if the aim is to treat violent people in institutions, there are a number of problems to be solved. The secure artificiality of the institution may control the violent behaviour, but this does not mean that the violent person has been changed. The problem has not been solved; it has simply been put to one side for a period of time. Further, the artificiality of the institution may lead to a low rate of generalisation of treatment gains back into the community after release.

In the community, the position is reversed: the professional may have such little control over the violent person's environment—friends, family, drinking, etc—that intervention has little chance against such odds. The control offered by the institution is simply not to be found in the community. However, in the community, the generalisation problem is solved at a stroke. As the intervention takes place in the environment where the behaviour occurs, so generalisation is 'built-in'.

Two issues remain:

- how to construct institutional regimes to move from management imposed external control to person-centred internal control prior to release; and
- how to begin in the community to gain some degree of control over the violent person to engage him in changing his violent behaviour.

These issues seem to be increasingly raised in the literature, and it may well not be too long before more solid suggestions are made.

Closing remark

I hope I have shown how a cogent theoretical position can be applied both to the understanding of violence, and how that understanding can be used to begin to generate means by which to develop professional practice.

References

1. Robins L, Rutter M. *Straight and devious pathways from childhood to adulthood.* Cambridge: Cambridge University Press, 1990
2. Archer J, Brown K, eds. *Human aggression: naturalistic approaches.* London: Routledge, 1989
3. Hollin CR. *Psychology and crime: an introduction to criminological psychology.* London: Routledge, 1989
4. Howells K, Hollin CR, eds. *Clinical approaches to violence.* Chichester: Wiley, 1989
5. Megargee EI. Psychological determinants and correlates of criminal violence. In: Wolfgang ME, Weiner NA, eds. *Criminal violence.* Beverly Hills, CA: Sage Publications, 1988
6. Siann G. *Accounting for aggression: perspectives on aggression and violence.* London: Allen & Unwin, 1985
7. Henderson M. An empirical typology of violent incidents reported by prison inmates with convictions for violence. *Aggressive Behavior* 1986; **12**:21–32
8. Buss AH. *The psychology of aggression.* New York: Wiley, 1961
9. Anderson CA. Temperature and aggression: ubiquitous effects of heat on occurrence of human violence. *Psychol Bull* 1989; **106**:74–96
10. Rotton J, Frey J. Air pollution, weather, and violent crimes: concomitant time-series analysis of archival data. *J Personality Social Psychol* 1985; **49**:207–20
11. Jarrell S, Howsen RM. Transient crowding and crime: the more 'strangers' in an area, the more crime except for murder, assault and rape. *Am J Econ Sociol* 1990; **49**:483–94
12. Farrington DP, West DJ. The Cambridge Study of Delinquent Development: a long-term follow-up of 411 London males. In: Kerner H-J, Kaiser G, eds. *Criminality: personality, behaviour and life history.* Berlin: Springer-Verlag, 1990
13. Stattin H, Magnusson D. The role of early aggressive behavior in the frequency, seriousness, and later types of crime. *J Consulting Clin Psychol* 1989; **57**:710–8
14. Denno DW. *Biology and violence: from birth to adulthood.* Cambridge: Cambridge University Press, 1990
15. Widom CS. Does violence beget violence? A critical examination of the literature. *Psychol Bull* 1989; **106**:3–28
16. DiLalla LF, Gottesman II. Biological and genetic contributors to violence— Widom's untold tale. *Psychol Bull* 1991; **109**:125–9
17. Widom CS. A tail on an untold tale: response to 'Biological and genetic contributors to violence—Widom's untold tale'. *Psychol Bull* 1991: **109**:130–2
18. Dodge KA. A social-information-processing model of social competence in children. In: Permutter M, ed. *Minnesota Symposium on Child Psychology* (vol 18). Hillsdale, NJ: Erlbaum, 1986
19. Dodge KA, Newman JP. Biased decision-making processes in aggressive boys. *J Abnormal Psychol* 1981: **90**:375–9

20. Slaby RG, Guerra NG. Cognitive mediators of aggression in adolescent offenders:
    1. Assessment. *Developmental Psychol* 1988; **24**:580–8
21. Stefanek ME, Ollendick TH, Baldock WP, Francis G, Yaeger NJ. Self-statements
    in aggressive, withdrawn, and popular children. *Cognitive Res Therapy* 1987; **11**:
    229–39
22. Novaco RW. The functions and regulation of the arousal of anger. *Am J Psychiatry*
    1976; **133**:124–8
23. Novaco RW, Welsh WN. Anger disturbances: cognitive mediation and clinical
    prescriptions. In: Howells K, Hollin CR, eds. *Clinical approaches to violence*. Chiches-
    ter: Wiley, 1989
24. Lester D. Crime as opportunity: test of the hypothesis with European suicide rates.
    Br J Criminol 1991; **31**:186–8
25. Luckenbill DF. Criminal homicide as a situated transaction. *Social Problems* 1977;
    25:176–86
26. Browne KD. Family violence: spouse and elder abuse. In: Howells K, Hollin CR,
    eds. *Clinical approaches to violence*. Chichester: Wiley, 1989
27. Frude N. The physical abuse of children. In: Howells K, Hollin CR, eds. *Clinical
    approaches to violence*. Chichester: Wiley, 1989
28. Dobash RE, Dobash RP. The nature and antecedents of violent events. *Br J
    Criminol* 1984; **24**:269–88
29. Goldsmith HR. Men who abuse their spouses: an approach to assessing future risk.
    In: Pallone NJ, Chaneles S, eds. *The clinical treatment of the criminal offender in
    outpatient mental health settings*. New York: Haworth Press, 1990
30. Breakwell G. *Facing physical violence*. Leicester/London: BPS Books/Routledge,
    1989
31. Davies W. The prevention of assault on professional helpers. In: Howells K,
    Hollin CR, eds. *Clinical approaches to violence*. Chichester: Wiley, 1989
32. Hollin CR. *Cognitive-behavioral interventions with young offenders*. Elmsford, NY:
    Pergamon Press, 1990
33. Feindler EL, Ecton RB. *Adolescent anger control: cognitive-behavioral techniques*. Elms-
    ford, NY: Pergamon Press, 1986
34. Henderson M. Behavioural approaches to violent crime. In: Howells K, Hollin
    CR, eds. *Clinical approaches to violence*. Chichester: Wiley, 1989
35. Howells K. Social skills training and criminal and antisocial behaviour in adults.
    In: Hollin CR, Trower P, eds. *Handbook of social skills training, vol. 1: applications
    across the life span*. Oxford: Pergamon Press, 1986
36. Ross RR, Fabiano EA. *Time to think: a cognitive model of delinquency prevention and
    offender rehabilitation*. Johnson City, TN: Institute of Social Science and Arts, 1985
37. Ross RR, Fabiano EA, Ewles CD. Reasoning and rehabilitation. *Int J Offender
    Therapy Comp Criminol* 1988; **20**:29–35
38. Goldstein AG, Keller H. *Aggressive behavior: assessment and intervention*. Elmsford,
    NY: Pergamon Press, 1987
39. Glick B, Goldstein AP. Aggression replacement training. *J Counseling Development*
    1987; **65**:356–67
40. Gentry MR, Ostapiuk EB. Violence in institutions for young offenders and
    disturbed adolescents. In: Howells K, Hollin CR, eds. *Clinical approaches to violence*.
    Chichester: Wiley, 1989

5 | Women as violent offenders and violent patients

Tony Maden
Senior Lecturer, Department of Forensic Psychiatry, Institute of Psychiatry, London

Gender differences in offending

Women commit less offences than men, a difference so marked that some authors have described it as the most significant feature of recorded crime.[1,2] In England and Wales in 1989, a total of 396,500 convictions or cautions for indictable offences was recorded against men compared to 76,200 for women, a ratio of 5:1.[3] Within these figures, violence against the person is even less common in women, accounting for 10% of their indictable crime compared to 16% in men. Property offences account for most crime in both sexes, and male to female ratios for different types of crime are given in Table 1.

Table 1. Male to female ratios for different types of crime.

Type of crime	Male to female ratio
Theft	3:1
Violence against the person	8:1
Drug offences	9:1
Criminal damage	11:1
Sexual offences	106:1

These figures are limited to recorded crime. In 1950, Pollak, without producing any hard evidence, argued that gender differences in crime were artefactual and resulted from a combination of female crime being more difficult to detect and a chivalrous legal system, which was reluctant to prosecute and convict women who were detected.[4] D'Orban found little evidence to support this view, concluding that gender has an influence on the treatment of offenders at all stages of the criminal justice system,[5] but the effects are complex and cannot be explained in terms of unitary concepts such as chivalry.[6,7]

Subsequent work on 'hidden' offending also fails to support Pollak's ideas. Increasing recognition of domestic violence may have exposed the non-accidental injury of children as an offence often committed by women, but has also revealed far more hidden offending by men within the home against their partners or their children. The British Crime Surveys confirmed the importance of under-reporting in crimes by men and women, and provided no evidence to suggest that the inclusion of unreported offences would alter the broad pattern of gender differences.[8] Under-reporting applies mainly to less serious offences, and it can be assumed that official figures are a valid if incomplete measure of gender differences in violent offending.[9]

A more serious limitation of these figures is that they reveal little about qualitative differences in the violence of men and women. For example, the victims of women who commit murder are more likely to be family members or intimate friends than is the case for men.[10,11] These differences are reflected in the prison statistics. The sentenced female prison population in June 1989 contained 218 women sentenced for violence against the person, 17% of all sentenced women.[12] The male sentenced population of 36,734 included 8,449 men sentenced for violent offences,[13] amounting to 23% of all sentenced men, and a male to female ratio of 39 to 1. For every woman serving a sentence for homicide or attempted homicide there were 27 men, whilst the ratio among those sentenced for other violent offences was 53 to 1. Women are sent to prison for violent offences much less often than men, and tend to be sentenced for a different type of violence.

Causes of gender differences

The causes of gender differences in violent offending have been the subject of much debate, often amounting to little more than a repetition of the nature–nurture discussion. A detailed account is beyond the scope of this review, but D'Orban reviews some well-known theories,[5] Morris[14,15] gives a more recent account, including an overview of feminist critiques, and Mandaraka-Sheppard describes the different theoretical frameworks that have been used to explain gender differences.[16]

Whatever the causes, it has been suggested that there has recently been an increase in female offending in general, and violent offending in particular, partly as a consequence of the women's movement leading to greater participation of women in areas of society from which they were once excluded.[17] Box and Hale attempt a critical examination of this question, and point to the considerable methodological problems involved—problems which have not been surmounted by most studies in the area.[18] Their own study found no relationship between four measures of female liberation and female crime rates during the years 1951–79. Jones argues that fears of a rising tide of female lawlessness based on little evidence have surfaced at various points in history, but reflect male insecurity about changing gender roles rather than a deterioration in female standards of conduct.[19]

Growth of feminism

The growth of feminism has given a new impetus to the study of gender and violence, with attempts to relate violence by women to their role in society. Hartmann describes 12 middle-class Victorian women found guilty of murder, and suggests that their acts of violence were extreme solutions to problems faced by many of their contemporaries.[20] Jones adopts a similar approach, in an ambitious attempt to relate changes in the nature of female homicide to the history of women in America.[19] The value of these approaches is that they abandon simple deterministic accounts, and demonstrate the futility of explaining gender differences in violent offending without reference to the wider context of women's role in society. Their weakness is that by emphasising the common ground between women who kill and the majority who do not—suggesting that female murderers are 'just like other women'—it is easy to lose sight of those factors that do distinguish this tiny minority. Jones makes the point, overlooked by many other authors, that gender differences in homicide are not absolute. Some men also murder those they love, just as some women kill for money, in the heat of an argument or, occasionally, for pleasure.

Provocation in domestic killings

Concern that the law, administered mainly by men, gives insufficient recognition to the nature of women's violence has focused recently on the plight of victims of domestic violence who respond by killing their partner. A defence to the charge of murder on the grounds of provocation may fail, as Lord Goddard in R v. Duffy (1949) referred to the necessity to demonstrate 'a sudden and temporary loss of control', and argued that the longer the delay between the provoking events and the killing the less likely that the defence would apply. Defence counsel in R v. Thornton (1991) argued without success that a long history of violence by her husband amounted to provocation, even when the defendant delayed her attack until the man was asleep and defenceless, for reasons of self-preservation.

This controversy has revolved around alleged miscarriages of justice in individual cases, but evidence that they reflect a general principle is

less convincing. Wasik found that juries and courts often interpret the
concept of provocation more generously than Lord Goddard's statement suggests.[21] In response to the controversy over the Thornton
case, the Home Office produced figures to show that provocation was
used as a successful defence in a higher proportion of 'domestic'
homicides where the accused was female.

Female violence and psychiatric disorder

Psychiatric studies of violent women are often limited by their concentration on highly selected groups. D'Orban describes the 89 women
remanded to Holloway over a six-year period charged with attempted
or actual filicide.[22] Psychiatric disorder was found in 75 (84%),
including 14 (16%) who were suffering from psychosis. Rates of
psychiatric disorder are high, but the selective nature of the sample
precludes generalisation to other violent women in prison, let alone
violent women in other settings. In a more comprehensive study, West
compared 148 cases of murder followed by suicide and a control group
of 148 other murder cases.[23] Women accounted for 60 (41%) of the
murder-suicide group, compared to only 11.5% of the murder group,
and a high proportion of the murder-suicide offenders were suffering
from mental disorder.

Psychiatric disposal

Court samples give an overall picture of the processing of mentally
disordered offenders, and show that women appearing before the
courts are roughly twice as likely as men to be dealt with by psychiatric
means.[24] This is a consistent finding: psychiatric disposals accounted
for 0.8% of all women convicted in 1961, compared to 0.5% of men.[25]
Despite the gender difference, a psychiatric disposal accounts for a tiny
proportion of all cases appearing before the courts.

Edwards, using interviews with female defendants and criminal
justice professionals, finds evidence to suggest that women's criminality
is more likely to be seen as an indicator of mental disorder deserving of
treatment, although comparative information on male offenders is not
provided.[26] A study of magistrates' courts found that 9.3% of men and
7.1% of women were remanded for medical reports in Inner London,
whilst the comparable figures in Wessex were 4.3% and 5.5%,
respectively.[27] Medical remands were imposed on 31% of all women
charged with violent offences against property, compared to 15% of
men facing a similar charge.[28] For indictable offences, hospital orders
accounted for a greater proportion of male disposals, and psychiatric

probation orders for a greater proportion of female disposals, although there was great variation with type of offence. The figures indicate complex qualitative and numerical differences between the treatment of men and women.

Reasons for different sentencing practices

In order to elucidate these differences, Allen examined the decision-making processes surrounding the trials of female and male defendants, selecting cases in which psychiatric evidence was likely to be important.[24] Her qualitative study was based on a sample of 24 female and 25 male homicides (selected at random), 11 male 'domestic' homicides, and 36 female and 33 male cases referred for psychiatric reports. The diversity of psychiatric disposals available to the court, and the flexibility of the rationales for their use, was found to allow ample scope for discretion and the operation of bias, including a sexual bias.[29] Most psychiatric disposals are made at the point of sentencing, and this is where gender bias is most apparent, favouring a psychiatric disposal for the female offender.

Allen warns against any simple explanation in terms of a systematic tendency '. . . to psychiatrise female offenders *per se*'.[30] She argues that existing medico-legal structures are 'a hotch-potch of provisions', so it is hardly surprising that they produce anomalous and contradictory outcomes. For example, she found that sentencers tended to regard disorderly female offenders as less deranged than many disorderly males, which should mitigate against their psychiatric disposal, but the actual outcome was the opposite. A psychiatric probation order can be imposed irrespective of whether a diagnosis is made, and the less disturbed offender fits more readily into community-based treatment facilities. The male offender who is regarded as more disturbed faces two barriers to a psychiatric disposal. Greater weight is attached to moral and retributive factors in male cases, favouring punishment rather than treatment, and there is a grave shortage of facilities for the chronically and dangerously disordered offender.

Allen's work is based on a selected and non-representative sample but is quoted at some length because it is one of the few studies to examine how decisions on psychiatric disposal are reached. It stresses the complexity of the forces which impinge on these decisions, and provides an alternative to simplistic accounts of the 'psychiatrisation' of female offenders, violent or otherwise. Finally, Allen makes the point that the discrepancy between the treatment of female and male offenders can be seen in large part as a reluctance to recognise and treat equivalent mental disorder in male offenders.

Surveys of violent offenders

All surveys of offenders are likely to exaggerate the importance of psychiatric disorder in women. If mental disorder causes some violence in both men and women, this 'abnormal' violence may be more conspicuous in the female population where the baseline level of 'normal' violence is lower. As a result, percentage figures are likely to be misleading. Maden showed the prevalence of psychosis to be similar (about 1–2%) in men and women serving a prison sentence in England and Wales, whilst the estimated numbers of prisoners with this diagnosis were 680 men and 16 women.[31]

Community surveys overcome the problems associated with selective samples, but have difficulties of their own. They are expensive and there is no comprehensive survey of violence and psychiatric disorder in England and Wales. In the former German Federal Republic, Hafner and Boker described all mentally disordered offenders who committed a crime of homicidal violence against the person in the period from January 1955 to December 1964.[32] Among the 533 offenders 23% were women, and there were important qualitative differences between men and women in the sample. Women accounted for a majority of depressed offenders, the victims usually being their own child in a carefully planned offence that took the form of an extended suicide. The typical male subject suffered from schizophrenia, and the index offence was often preceded by other attacks or threats, the victim often being a partner in a relationship characterised by long-standing tension and discord. This emphasises the complexity of the gender differences in mentally disordered offenders, and will have relevance when considering the treatment needs of women in secure hospitals.

Violence by women within prisons

Women in prison have been notorious for a high level of disturbed behaviour since 1862,[33] and a report in 1910 comments on the need for higher staffing levels to manage the women's section of Millbank prison.[34] Dobash *et al.* review the historical development of prison regimes for women, drawing attention to the 'conventional wisdom' that women, whilst less violent outside prison, behave more violently than men once locked up.[35]

In England and Wales, women within prison are punished for disciplinary offences more often than men, and the rate of offences per 100 prison population for all female establishments in 1985 was 335 whereas for men it was 160.[36] However, most offences are disobedience or disrespect rather than violence. In a comparison of the disciplinary record of the men and women in the survey by Gunn *et al.* of sentenced prisoners,[37] Maden found that more women had a record of offences against prison discipline but were much less likely to have been punished by loss of remission.[31] They were also less likely than men to have been transferred between prisons for disciplinary reasons. It appears that more male prisoners commit serious disciplinary offences, but a greater proportion of women are punished for trivial offences. This point has been made by Carlen, who suggests that regimes in female prisons are more oppressive, as they require a higher standard of behaviour.[38]

Mandaraka-Sheppard studied women in three open and three closed prisons and concluded that institutional rather than individual characteristics were more important in accounting for violent incidents.[39] She criticised the trivial nature of many recorded offences, the vague nature of some rules, and the consequent inconsistency in their application. It has also been suggested that the nature of female prison officers is partly responsible for the high number of trivial offences recorded in women's prisons.[40]

All these factors may be important. Any comparison with male prisoners is complicated by the difference in regimes. Among sentenced prisoners, the long lock-up periods that characterise male prisons, even those for long-term inmates, are less common in female prisons which often allow considerable freedom of movement within a secure perimeter.[41] This allows more interaction with prison officers, and increases the potential for transgressing minor prison rules. Overall, there is little evidence to suggest that women in prison are more likely than men to be violent toward staff or other inmates.

Self-injury

One of the main criticisms of Holloway prison has been the high rate of self-injury by inmates, which is often regarded as a reflection of the conditions in which they are held.[42] While not disputing the importance of the environment as a cause of self-injury, empirical studies have looked for associations between self-injury and other characteristics of the women concerned. Cookson described self-injury by women in Holloway, and found that women who injured themselves tended to be younger than average with longer sentences and more violent offences—that is, there is an association between violence towards the self and violence towards others.[43] She concluded that the rate of self-injury is high, but did not compare it to the rate in male prisons.

A more recent study by Wilkins and Coid found that 7.5% of all remands to Holloway had a history of previous self-injury by cutting.[44] Compared to remanded women with no history of self-mutilation, they were more likely to have had a disturbed and deprived childhood, and showed high rates of behavioural disturbance, substance abuse and personality disorder. There was also an association with violence and arson. The authors concluded that self-cutting was an indicator of severe psychopathology. Maden found an association between self-cutting, past experience of being in care, violent offending and problem drinking.[31] The same pattern of associations was found in male sentenced prisoners, who reported a similar lifetime prevalence of self-cutting. Dooley found that only 1.7% of all prison suicides were female in the period 1972–87, although women accounted for 3% of the prison population.[45] It is interesting that self-injury in male prisoners has received less attention in the literature than its prevalence would warrant. The emphasis on self-injury in female prisoners may be related to a general expectation that women in prison are more likely to be psychologically disturbed.

Violent women in hospital

As women commit less violence than men, they would be expected to form only a minority of patients detained in secure hospitals. About 20% of all patients within the maximum security special hospitals are women. Although this is a minority, it is a substantial one, and the pressure group, Women In Special Hospitals (WISH), has argued that too many women are detained in maximum security as a consequence of the inappropriate labelling of violent female offenders as psychiatrically disturbed.[46]

It has already been shown that a greater proportion of women than men who appear before the courts receive a psychiatric disposal. Nevertheless, men outnumber women among the cases detained for treatment on court orders. During 1961–85, women accounted for 16.4% of unrestricted and 11.5% of restricted hospital orders made by the courts, whilst the average proportion of women among those found guilty of an indictable offence during this period was 14%.[47] Walker and McCabe point out that this ratio is:

> quite different from the sex ratio for other compulsory admissions to mental hospitals, in which women slightly outnumber men.[48]

Women who receive compulsory psychiatric treatment in England and Wales are most likely to do so under 'civil' sections of the Mental Health Act 1983 rather than coming through the courts as offender-patients.

A survey of prisoners transferred to Broadmoor hospital between 1960 and 1983 found that the ratio of men to women was 14 to 1, whereas the corresponding ratio in the adult sentenced prison population was 31 to 1.[49] The debate about women in special hospitals tends to concentrate on comparisons with the prison population, but the choice of prison as a reference point for a *hospital* population is questionable. Severely mentally disordered offenders form an important, but small, minority of around 3% of the sentenced prison population and would not be expected to be typical of prisoners as a whole.[37]

Women outnumber men among the approximately 20% of special hospital patients detained under 'civil' orders rather than coming through the courts. Figures for utilisation of other psychiatric provision reveal that first hospital admission rates in 1989 were 110.7 per 100,000 in women and 102.6 per 100,000 in men (1.1:1). The alternative view of the special hospitals is as a psychiatric facility with a statistical over-representation of men, rather than a prison holding too many women.[50] Neither prisons nor ordinary hospitals provide the ideal comparison group for the special hospitals. A community survey of severely mentally disordered offenders offers an alternative, and Hafner and Boker's finding that 23% of such offenders are female accords very well with the proportion of women being treated in maximum security.[32] This figure may be convenient in explaining the number of women in special hospitals, but it must be qualified by reference to the differences between the men and women in Hafner and Boker's sample. Being a mentally disordered violent offender does not imply the need for long-term treatment in maximum security. None of these figures provides a definitive statement of how many women should be in special hospitals, but they show that the question is more complex than suggested by a simple comparison of prisoners and patients.

The behaviour of women within special hospitals is also relevant to the question of whether they could safely be managed elsewhere. Data are limited, but a survey of violent incidents in Rampton hospital found that women, who account for only 25% of the patient population, were involved in 75% of the incidents.[51] The suggestion is that women form a small but difficult group of patients, although the authors note that a few highly disturbed patients accounted for most incidents, with one woman responsible for 12% of all violent incidents. This uneven distribution emphasises the pitfalls inherent in making generalisations about the nature of women as patients. Outside the special hospitals, Noble and Rodgers' study of violence on a locked acute ward found that women accounted for just over half of all admissions and a similar proportion of violent incidents.[52]

Apart from the question of whether they need to be in maximum secure conditions, another major concern about violent women is the adequacy of the facilities provided for them. Rowett and Vaughan describe women in Broadmoor, drawing attention to their qualitative differences from male patients who have a more extensive offending record.[53] They suggest that women may be disadvantaged by being held in an institution where they are greatly outnumbered by men, and where their specific needs as women may receive low priority. It is also suggested that the regime for women may attach too much importance to 'the cultivation of stereotypically feminine attributes'. Rowett and Vaughan give an uncritical account of the situation of women in Broadmoor, but make the important point that the female mentally disordered offender is always likely to find herself in facilities designed for men, and her specific needs can easily be overlooked.

Conclusions

Women account for a very small proportion of violent offenders, and the differences between violent men and women are more complex than simple figures suggest. The reasons for these gender differences are not fully understood, but an important consequence is that women find themselves in a minority in any population of violent offenders. This has contributed to their neglect by researchers, although the growth of feminism means that this imbalance is now being redressed. Services for the mentally disordered violent offender deal mainly with men and will need to take specific action to address the particular needs of women.

References

1. Wootton B. *Social science and social pathology*. London: Allen & Unwin, 1959
2. Heidensohn F. *Women and crime*. London: Macmillan, 1985
3. *Criminal statistics, England and Wales*. London: HMSO, 1989: 113
4. Pollak O. *The criminality of women*. New York: University of Pennsylvania Press, 1950
5. D'Orban PT. Social and psychiatric aspects of female crime. *Med Sci Law* 1971; **11**:104–16
6. Heidensohn, F. Women and justice. In: *Women and crime*. London: Macmillan, 1985: 31–58
7. Morris A. Women in the criminal justice system. In: *Women, crime and criminal justice*. Oxford: Blackwell, 1987: 79–102
8. Morris A. *op cit*: 21–4
9. Hough M, Mayhew P. *Taking account of crime: key findings from the 1984 British Crime Survey*. Home Office Research Study no. 85. London: HMSO, 1985
10. Gibson E, Klein S. *Murder*. Home Office Research Unit Report no. 4. London: HMSO, 1961
11. Gibson E, Klein S. *Murder 1957 to 1968*. London: HMSO, 1969
12. Home Office. *Prison statistics, England and Wales 1989*. London: HMSO, 1990: 25
13. Home Office. *op cit*: 24–5

14. Morris A. Gender differences in crime. In: *Women, crime and criminal justice*. Oxford: Blackwell, 1987: 19–40
15. Morris A. Theories of women's crime. In: *Women, crime and criminal justice*. Oxford: Blackwell, 1987: 41–78
16. Mandaraka-Sheppard A. *The dynamics of aggression in women's prisons in England*. Aldershot: Gower, 1986: 6–9
17. Adler F. *Sisters in crime*. New York: McGraw-Hill, 1975
18. Box S, Hale C. Liberation and female criminality in England and Wales. *Br J Criminol* 1983; **23**:35–49
19. Jones A. *Women who kill*. London: Gollancz, 1991: xx–xxi
20. Hartmann MS. *Victorian murderesses*. London: Robson, 1977
21. Wasik M. Cumulative provocation and domestic killings. *Crim Law Rev* 1982; 29–38
22. D'Orban PT. Women who kill their children. *Br J Psychiatry* 1979; **134**:560–71
23. West DJ. *Murder followed by suicide*. London: Heinemann, 1965
24. Allen H. Justice unbalanced. Gender, psychiatry and judicial decisions. *Official statistics on psychiatric disposals*. Milton Keynes: Open University Press, 1987: 123–6
25. Walker N. *Crime and punishment in Britain*. Edinburgh: Edinburgh University Press, 1965
26. Edwards SSM. *Women on trial*. Manchester: Manchester University Press, 1984
27. Gibbens TCN, Soothill KL, Pope PJ. *Medical remands in the criminal court*. Oxford: Oxford University Press, 1977
28. Gibbens TCN, Soothill KL, Pope PJ. *op cit*:18
29. Allen H. *op cit*:66
30. Allen H. *op cit*:113
31. Maden T. *Psychiatric disorder in women serving a prison sentence*. London: University of London MD Thesis
32. Hafner H, Boker W. *Crimes of violence by mentally abnormal offenders. The psychiatric epidemiological study in the Federal Republic of Germany*. Cambridge: Cambridge University Press, 1982
33. Mayhew H, Binny J. *The criminal prisons of London and scenes of prison life*. London: Griffin, Bihn & Co, 1862: 180–2
34. Quinton R. *Crime and criminals*. London: Longmans, Green & Co, 1910
35. Dobash RP, Dobash RE, Gutteridge S. Penal regimes. In: *The imprisonment of women*. Oxford: Blackwell, 1986: 62–88
36. *Offences against discipline in women's prisons*. London: NACRO, 1986
37. Gunn J, Maden T, Swinton M. *Mentally disordered prisoners*. London: Home Office, 1991
38. Carlen P, ed. *Criminal women*. Cambridge: Polity Press, 1985: 134
39. Mandaraka-Sheppard A. *The dynamics of aggression in women's prisons in England*. Aldershot: Gower, 1986
40. Kozuba-Kozubska J, Turrel D. Problems of dealing with girls. *Prison Service J* 1978; **29**:4
41. King RD, McDermott K. British prisons 1970–1987. The ever-deepening crisis. *Br J Criminol* 1989; **29**:107–28
42. Moorehead C. The strange events at Holloway. *New Society* 1985; **11**:40
43. Cookson HM. A survey of self-injury in a closed prison for women. *Br J Criminol* 1977; **17**:332–46
44. Wilkins J, Coid J. Self-mutilation in female remanded prisoners: I. An indicator of severe psychopathology. *Crim Behav Mental Health* 1991; **1**:247–67
45. Dooley E. Prison suicide in England and Wales, 1972–87. *Br J Psychiatry* 1990; **156**:40–5
46. Stevenson P. *Perspectives on female violence*. Address to conference, St George's Hospital, London, 8 March 1991
47. Robertson G. The restricted hospital order. *Psychiatr Bull* 1989; **13**:4–11
48. Walker N, McCabe S. *Crime and insanity in England, vol. 2: new solutions and new problems*. Edinburgh: Edinburgh University Press, 1973: 146

49. Grounds A. The transfer of sentenced prisoners to hospital 1960–1983. *Br J Criminol* 1991; **31**:54–71
50. Department of Health. *On the state of the public health for the year 1989—the annual report of the chief medical officer.* London: HMSO, 1990: 54–61
51. Larkin E, Murtagh S, Jones S. A preliminary study of violent incidents in a special hospital. *Br J Psychiatry* 1988; **153**:226–31
52. Noble P, Rodgers S. Violence by psychiatric inpatients. *Br J Psychiatry* 1989; **155**: 384–90
53. Rowett C, Vaughan PJ. Women and Broadmoor: treatment and control in a special hospital. In: Hutter B, Williams G, eds. *Controlling women: the normal and the deviant.* London: Croom Helm, 1981

Part 2
Mental disorder and violence

Pamela J. Taylor
Head of Medical Services, Special Hospitals Service Authority, London

---

The title of this section is problematic. As if violence were not difficult enough to define, 'mental disorder' raises even more difficulties. More often than not, its use in practice is casual, to denote non-specific deviations from mental health. Perhaps a more medically appropriate term would be 'disease'. The entire collection of recognised deviations from mental health is still brought together by the World Health Organisation in the International Classification of Diseases. However, both the World Health Organisation[1] and the American Psychiatric Association,[2] which has produced the overlapping but not entirely co-terminus classification in its *Diagnostic and Statistical Manual*, insist on describing this subgroup of diseases as 'mental disorders'. In Britain, this is slightly confusing, because mental health legislation also adopts the term 'mental disorder', but this legal classification is markedly different and more restrictive. For England and Wales only, the Mental Health Act 1983 uses the widest explicit range of legal classification within the term 'mental disorder'. The categories are:

- Mental illness, which is not defined

- Severe mental impairment, which means a state of arrested or incomplete development of mind which includes severe impairment of intelligence and social functioning *and* is associated with abnormally aggressive or seriously irresponsible conduct (my italics)

- Mental impairment, which means almost the same thing, but the incomplete development is not regarded as severe

- Psychopathic disorder, which means a persistent disorder or disability of mind (whether or not including significant impairment of intelligence) which results in abnormally aggressive or seriously irresponsible conduct on the part of the person concerned.

- Promiscuity, immoral conduct, sexual deviancy, or dependence on alcohol or drugs, as pure disorders are each explicitly excluded from the legal construct of mental disorder.

Definitions in part depend on the purposes for which they are designed. The legal definitions of disorder are provided as the starting point for determining whether or not it would be appropriate to admit or detain persons in hospital for purposes of assessment or treatment, without their free, informed or necessarily comprehending consent. A statute for the legal enforcement of medical assessment or treatment is unique in medicine to the management of people with mental disorders. The British government decided that not all such disorders would warrant loss of free choice in this regard.

The dissonance between the medical and legal classifications of mental disorder both reflects and compounds confusion over what states are reasonably considered to be in the provenance of medical and psychiatric practice. It is not unknown for the legal concepts of disorder to be used as a means of keeping patients out of services when they are likely to be demanding and resource hungry (e.g. ref. 3). For health service staff, the primary issues should remain how much they can offer a patient to relieve distress and treat symptoms, and how far they can engage the patient in co-operating with the services and treatments available. Considerations of compulsory detention are secondary, even if they are occasionally necessary or permitted.

This section takes the broader, clinical view of disorder, without being exhaustive. In the only community survey of the epidemiology of mental disorder and violence, Swanson *et al.* found the impact of substance abuse overshadowed that of all other disorders.[4] Associations between alcohol and violence are covered in Chapter 9 by John Hodge, and other drug use in Chapter 8 by David Forshaw and John Strang. Swanson and colleagues were unable to tackle the difficult question of the epidemiology of personality disorder and violence links. Their criteria for violence ratings were embedded in the personality disorder section of the Diagnostic Interview Schedule which they used for the survey.[5] Few clinicians are satisfied with predominantly medical attempts to find meaningful diagnostic entities within the broad class of personality disorders. Although the Diagnostic and Statistical Manual in the third revised edition provides a tempting face validity,[2] in reality, for each personality diagnosis there is poor agreement on the diagnoses between clinicians, a tendency to multiple classifications and little stability of the diagnoses over time.[6] Nevertheless, the extent of distress and disturbed behaviour within such groups is evident.[7] In Chapter 7 Blackburn offers a way through the morass which seems clinically useful.

Personality disorders are the only disorders of development covered in this volume. The absence of discussion of sexual disorders better reflects the continuing difficulties both in their definition and in the demonstrable effectiveness of treatment rather than any denial that some may be associated with violence. Although there is little doubt about the principle that sexual disorders and sexual offending are different entities, distinctions in practice can be harder to make. Sexual offending is simply a breach of societal code and, as such, sex offenders are wholly dependent on the mores of society at any given time for their definition. Sexual disorders, as recognised in the International Classification of Diseases, fall into three main groups:

1. The paraphilias, defined by arousal in response to sexual objects or situations that are not part of normative arousal or activity patterns, which in varying degrees interfere with the capacity for reciprocal, affectionate activity.
2. The dysfunctions include inhibitions of sexual desire or characteristic psychophysiological changes.
3. Other disorders include disorders mainly centred on distress about body image or sexual orientation.

Of these groups, the paraphilias are most likely to overlap with offending, but by no means all the paraphilias constitute offences, for example, fetishism. Some offences as isolated pieces of behaviour could not possibly be construed as disorder in these terms. Nevertheless, societal attitudes undoubtedly influence some of these decisions. 'Sexual deviancy' is a term which can be advanced as having some legal meaning within the Mental Health Act 1983. As such, there perhaps should be more caution in using the term interchangeably with the concept of sexual disorder. Following from the difficulty in clinical definition, it is almost impossible to say how often sexual disorders may be associated with violence. It is, further, almost impossible to describe with any confidence effective treatments. Aside from one or two studies of the use of libido suppressants, almost all reported work with people with sexual disorders is single-case study based. The topic of sexual disorder and violence awaits future generations of researchers.

The absence of a chapter on mental retardation or learning disabilities perhaps also deserves a word of explanation. It cannot be denied that people with mental retardation, and even those with severe learning disabilities or handicaps, may be violent, but a very low, almost inverse relationship with serious violence has been described until recently (e.g. ref. 8). The draining, but hardly dangerous, violence of frustration among the few in this disorder group that have mis-learned its effectiveness or have an otherwise poor repertoire of social skills is sufficient a problem to have brought about the development of a few specialist units (e.g. ref. 9). Robertson, in his review of the patterns of crime among mentally handicapped offenders,[10] has also shown how little either civil or court provisions, even within the later years of operation of the Mental Health Act 1959, were used to enforce hospital treatment for this group.[11] The Mental Health Act 1983 requires abnormally aggressive or irresponsible conduct as part of the criteria for detention, and the provisions remain little used.

Hodgins' important report of a birth cohort (i.e. unselected for any particular characteristic) of men and women in Sweden suggests, however, that offending of all kinds may be a great deal more common among people with an intellectual handicap than previously recognised.[12]

References

1. World Health Organisation. *Mental disorders: glossary and guide to their classification in accordance with the ninth revision of the International Classification of Diseases.* Geneva: WHO, 1978
2. American Psychiatric Association. *Diagnostic and statistical manual of mental disorders.* 3rd edn, revised. Washington, DC: APA, 1987
3. Coid J. Mentally abnormal prisoners on remand. *Br Med J* 1988;**296**:1779–84
4. Swanson JW, Holzer CE, Ganju VK, Jono RT. Violence and psychiatric disorder in the community: evidence from the Epidemiologic Catchment Area Surveys. *Hosp Comm Psychiatry* 1990;**41**:761–70
5. Robins LN, Helzer JE, Croughan J, *et al.* National Institute of Mental Health Diagnostic Interview Schedule: its history, characteristics and validity. *Arch Gen Psychiatry* 1981;**38**:381–98
6. Tyrer P. Flamboyant, erratic, dramatic, borderline, antisocial, sadistic, narcissistic, histrionic and impulsive personality disorders: who cares which? *Crim Behav Mental Health* 1992;**2**:95–104
7. Coid JW. DSM-III diagnosis in criminal psychopaths: a way forward. *Crim Behav Mental Health* 1992;**2**:78–94
8. Hafner H, Boker W. Crimes of violence by mentally abnormal offenders. Cambridge: Cambridge University Press, 1982. (English translation, Marshall H. Grewaltten geistesgestörter. Berlin: Springer-Verlag, 1973)
9. Day K. A hospital-based treatment programme for male mentally handicapped offenders. *Br J Psychiatry* 1989;**153**:635–44
10. Robertson G. The extent and pattern of crime amongst mentally handicapped offenders. *Apex (J Br Inst Mental Handicap)* 1981;**9**:100–3
11. Robertson G. The 1959 Mental Health Act of England and Wales: changes in the use of its criminal provisions. In: Gunn J, Farrington DP, eds. *Abnormal offenders, delinquency, and the criminal justice system.* Chichester: John Wiley and Sons, 1982
12. Hodgins S. Mental disorder, intellectual deficiency and crime. *Arch Gen Psychiatry* 1992;**49**:476–83

6 | Mental illness and violence

Pamela J. Taylor

Head of Medical Services, Special Hospitals Service Authority, London

'... but why *will* you say that I am mad? The disease had sharpened my senses—not destroyed—not dulled them...

It is impossible to say how first the idea entered my brain; but once conceived, it haunted me day and night. Object there was none. Passion there was none. I loved the old man. He had never wronged me... I think it was his eye!... —a pale blue eye, with a film over it. Whenever it fell upon me, my blood ran cold; and so by degrees... I made up my mind to take the life of the old man, and thus rid myself of the eye for ever.'[1]

Poe's account of dangerous madness captures the clinical essence of the interplay between serious violence and mental illness when they occur together. There is the toying with insight and its rejection, the autochthonous delusion, its gnawing persistence, the detachment of emotion, the limited focus of perception, but the continued capacity for logical thought and action—these last rendered crazy and dangerous only by the false premise. As the story unfolds, so the other relevant behaviours emerge. The delusion creates terror—the only real surviving emotion—but still the decision to kill is slow to follow. Even after the decision the sufferer checks, and seeks evidence that the 'evil eye' remains. Finally, he satisfies himself with evidence not only for the evil eye, but also by the fortuitous meeting of his lantern beam with that eye for the rightness of his solution. The old man is killed and dismembered but, also as is most usual in such cases, the police have to do no detection.[2] The sick killer, initially confident, invites them into his home and the scene of the crime, and then feels driven to reveal his deed, before giving an eloquent account of it.

The assumption of a link between madness and violence is very old. In ancient Greek and Roman civilisations, a habit of wandering and a proneness to violence were considered to be the two characteristic features of the mentally disordered.[3] Monahan, briefly reviewing such attitudes, illustrates their universality and persistence.[4] It is difficult to know whether the media encourage or merely reflect such views, but in prime time American television drama the mentally ill are portrayed as violent nearly twice as often as their mentally healthy counterparts,[5] while the choice of newspaper reporters is such that 86% of all stories printed about former mental patients centre on a

violent crime committed.[6] The general public does, however, seem to
have a growing sense of proportion. In a nationwide survey in the
USA, nearly half those interviewed agreed that 'the mentally ill are far
less of a danger than most people believe'.[7]

Frequency of coincidence of violence and mental illness

The popular fear is not wholly without foundation. Evidence is
mounting that people with some mental illnesses are slightly but
significantly more likely to be violent than those who are mentally
healthy. Many studies which have attempted to quantify the association between violence and psychosis apparently conflict in their
findings, but this is almost entirely due to methodological problems.[8,9,10] Some samples are of prisoners and others of psychiatric
patients, while the latter include some pre-admission groups, hospital
inpatients and post-discharge cases. Case definition is often poor, and
researchers almost never allow for sampling biases, such as the effect of
mental illness on the ease of detection of violence or the time for which
people are at risk.[10] Two sorts of study stand out as more reliable than
most in this field: studies of samples of people who have killed, and the
random community survey.

As most people are aware, while uninvestigated reports of violence
may be greatly exaggerated, true rates of offending behaviour generally exceed crime rates as recorded in the official criminal statistics.
This last discrepancy, however, often known as the dark figure, is not
random. The more serious the reported behaviour, the more likely it is
that a crime will be cleared up. The majority of reported murders are
solved (for example, 97% in West Germany[11]). Studies of complete
samples of homicides for a given geographical area have generally
shown that the proportion of people with schizophrenia in the homicide sample exceeds that which would be expected in the general
population (about 1%). People with other mental illnesses contribute
little. The figures for Scotland[12] and West Germany[11] were relatively
low (about 3%) (Hafner and Boker, however, included attempted
murder[11]). Our study from the Institute of Psychiatry covering London and the home counties found that 11% of men who had killed had
evidence of schizophrenia at the time,[13] as Wilcox showed for a county
in California.[14] Petersson and Gudjonsson found for Iceland in the first
eight decades of this century (when there was a peculiarly stable and
complete population) that no less than 25% of those who had killed
had a psychosis, usually schizophrenia.[15] Nevertheless, absolute
numbers of people with psychosis in all these studies were fairly small.
This is a crucial point in estimating the real risk posed by the mentally
ill. People with schizophrenia constitute only 1% of the general

population, and Hafner and Boker estimated that the risk of serious violence to others by a person with schizophrenia was only about 0.05%.[11]

Swanson *et al.* have presented the only data from a community survey, the Epidemiologic Catchment Area project, in which structured diagnostic interviews were conducted with 3,000–5,000 household residents at each of five sites in the USA between 1980 and 1983.[16] Of the respondents, 368 (3.7%) said that they had been violent (on criteria from the Diagnostic Interview Schedule: for example, 'Have you spanked or hit a child hard enough so that he or she had bruises ... or had to see a doctor?', 'Since the age of 18 have you been in more than one fight that came to swapping blows?', 'Have you ever used a weapon?'). Multiple psychiatric diagnoses according to DSM-III criteria were more dangerous than a single diagnosis, and subjects with alcohol or other drug use disorders a particular risk.[17] The self-reported rate of violence to others was about 2% among those without a psychiatric diagnosis, and not significantly higher for those with either an anxiety state or a depressive state alone. People with mania or bipolar disorder showed a higher rate of violence, but entirely confined to the family, and nobody within this group reported using a weapon. Over 8% of those with schizophrenia alone reported at least one episode of violence, and nearly 13% who had more than one diagnosis but including schizophrenia.

The demonstration of a numerical association between any given disorder and a form of action is of considerable use to service planners. Sound medical treatment in appropriate settings must be available for all people who are ill regardless of their other problems. Such an association does not, however, necessarily imply that mental illness causes or influences violence. Lanzkron, for example, showed that in a substantial minority of cases serious mental illness appeared to have emerged only after an afflicted individual had killed.[18]

Psychosis as a factor in causing violence

Symptomatic triggers of violence

Psychosis may indeed be an important factor in provoking violence, but again techniques in sampling and other aspects of investigation have hampered definitive comment. An almost exclusive reliance on case records for data may have minimised the chances of finding a direct association. Nevertheless, between 25%[19,20] and 76%[11] of serious offenders with a psychosis have been reported as having acted directly on their delusions or in the context of a delusional relationship, with the most frequently reported estimate about 40%.[15,18,21] Only in one study were data from records supplemented with an offender interview conducted by a researcher close in time to the offence, when recall is likely to be at its most reliable.[21] In the two studies of male prisoners in which the issue was addressed no man who was free of psychosis claimed a delusion or other psychotic symptom as a motive for his actions.[19,21]

Contrary to popular belief, although hallucinations, particularly auditory hallucinations of commanding voices, do sometimes trigger action, they have very rarely been implicated in serious violence.[11,21] Hallucinations of smell or taste may be more worrying, but probably only in the context of a delusion that the patient is being poisoned.[22,23]

Disorders of passion are often considered as part of the delusional catalogue. As with other disorders of belief, this element shades from more or less healthy concern through abnormally overvalued ideas to false, unshakeable beliefs which all observers would regard as pathological. De Clerambault argued that delusions of passion were to be distinguished from other delusions, since a striving for fulfilment is at their core, in contrast to, say, delusions of persecution, which leave people fearful but less likely to be committed to any particular course of action.[24] Evasion, for example, may serve as well as aggression. This last was in part borne out in a study of general psychiatric hospital patients with delusions in which 60% of 83 consecutively hospitalised patients acted on their delusions, but only 10% at all violently, with the rest showing a wider repertoire of protective, evasive or complaining activities.[25,26] The other factor which may mitigate in favour of pathological love, jealousy or feelings and beliefs of entitlement being particularly dangerous is that the pathological attention is usually highly focused. Delusional lovers may come in series, but rarely in parallel. Vexatious litigants tend to focus their claims and accusations on one individual. The object of delusional jealousy is almost invariably the spouse,[22,27,28] although one study rates the rival as being at equal risk.[29] Although the hypothesis is plausible that, among people with psychosis, disorders of passion may be exceptionally dangerous, the definitive study has still to be done comparing the proportion of people with, say, delusional jealousy who engage in serious violence with the proportion of people with, say, persecutory delusions or delusions of catastrophe. The most that can be said at present is that delusions of persecution, which are probably the most frequently occurring delusions, and perhaps delusions of passivity or control by other forces, appear to be the most numerically important in triggering violence in clinical practice.

Disorders of passion in quite another sense seem to be important in 'permitting violence' for the person with schizophrenia. In a series of men awaiting trial for having been violent towards others, attitudes and actions towards their victims suggesting an absence of passion were among the features that best distinguished the psychotic men from the non-psychotic comparison group.[30] The men with psychosis were only slightly more likely to have attacked strangers than the non-psychotic, but they were significantly less likely to have reported any feelings about their victim at the time of the attack. Evidence both from the men and from other sources confirms the likelihood of this being a valid representation of affairs. The non-psychotic men were significantly more likely to have inflicted the violence in the course of a quarrel than the psychotic men, who had rarely engaged in any social interaction at the time.

Depression is the only other primary symptom worthy of mention as potentially provocative of violence. This is not to say that other symptoms or states are wholly unimportant, but that in isolation they rarely lead to violence and, when they are implicated in combination with other symptoms or states, the nature, direction or degree of importance of the relationship is unclear. Anxiety is an example in point. Rarely associated *per se* directly with violent action, it may be associated with violence through its links with almost any other disorder.[16] Further, among general psychiatric inpatients, feeling frightened of a particular delusion appeared likely to be one of the factors that most influenced the chances of acting on a particular delusion, although rarely violently.[25]

Depression has been a focus of theoretical interest in relation to violence because of the view that depression and aggression are inversely related.[31,32] Kendell reviewed the evidence for such a hypothesis and found it broadly supportive.[33] In relation to criminal activity, most reports suggest that violence directed against others and depression are rarely associated, but that the seriousness of the violence in some circumstances is undoubted. Depressive homicide, often associated with attempted or completed suicide, is rare, but is the only sphere in non-gender-specific criminal activity (for example, infanticide) in which women outnumber men.[11]

At the other extreme of emotional disorder, mania is extremely rarely associated with serious violence, despite an often threatening demeanour on the part of a patient.[34] Perhaps this is because accompanying grandiose delusions sustain the individual without having to act, or perhaps because the individual is too chaotic and has too short an attention span to see through a calculated act.

Violence and illness careers

There have been many observations that serious violence generally emerges relatively late in the course of a psychotic illness,[11,35] and that mentally abnormal offenders tend, on average, to be older than the mentally healthy.[22,36,37] Even where life-threatening violence emerges in the context of a first episode of schizophrenia, the illness appears to have been well established in most cases. Humphreys *et al.* showed that more than half of one series of such patients had been ill for more than a year, some for many years.[38] In my study of remanded prisoners, it was possible to document criminal, violence and illness careers from a variety of sources, including criminal records, hospital records and each prisoner's own account.[21] For all those with a psychotic illness, whether schizophrenia or a primary affective illness, a general criminal history was as likely to precede as to follow the onset of the illness. By contrast, behaviour which resulted in injury to another person, whether or not criminal, followed the onset of illness in nearly 90% of cases. In other words, psychosis seemed to occur in a few previously violent men—hardly a surprising finding, since it would be unlikely that psychosis would be completely protective—but for the vast majority who had been violent and at some stage come to the attention of the courts, the psychosis seemed a material factor in that violence. Wessely has subsequently confirmed, in a community sample, that the frequency of personal violence and criminal damage for men and women rises after the onset of illness for people with schizophrenia.[39] In this series also, other criminal activities were not affected in this way. The differences in criminal careers between people with schizophrenia and the controls were striking.

Impact of psychosis on general life-style

Although there seems little doubt that symptoms of psychosis are directly relevant to the violence for a substantial proportion of those who have a psychosis and are violent, there remains an equal or slightly larger group for whom this does not appear to be so clearly the case—even though illness and violence career patterns would suggest that the illness is nevertheless relevant. Conversely, only a minority of people with even the most strongly implicated symptoms (delusions) become violent. Other factors must be important. It is not possible here to detail all the possibilities, but clearly both past and current personal and social experiences influence the detail of content of some of the symptomatology and the quality of responses.

The fact of the illness itself has a powerful impact on the sufferer and his life-style. Some would now argue that it commonly (in nearly half the cases) induces a post-traumatic stress disorder (PTSD),[40] and that the negative symptoms, perhaps including the kind of indifference to others referred to earlier, are equivalent to the avoidance and estrangement of PTSD.[41] More conventional wisdom emphasises the impact of psychosis on social circumstances. A tendency towards a substantial decline in socio-economic status is well documented for people with schizophrenia,[42] and is not uncommon among people with other serious chronic mental disease. This, it is argued, may be associated with frustration responses which may include violence. In fact, while this almost certainly has some relevance to non-violent, generally petty offending, such as minor theft or deception (for example, taking food or meals without paying for them, or trespass), the social decline probably has little impact on serious violence. The chronically disabled, socially disadvantaged person with psychosis may sometimes lash out in frustration, but planned and seriously damaging assaults tend to be the province of individuals who are socially, and even mentally relatively intact except for well developed delusional systems.[43]

Psychosis and violence as a product of other primary pathology

An understanding of the impact of the brain on behaviour—whether thinking, feeling or action—is still relatively crude. It is, therefore, perhaps hardly surprising that hypotheses of brain abnormalities or dysfunctions associated with mental illness overlap with those associating brain disorder with pathological violence. For these purposes, pathological violence almost invariably means violence of increased frequency rather than any other kind of abnormality. The attempts to link this with EEG abnormalities or frank epilepsy, or even to refer to the violence as a form of epileptic equivalent have abounded. Most have foundered on a failure to evaluate blind any postulated link between rather non-specific cerebral changes and fairly subjectively related aggressive activities.[44] No study has shown that specific cerebral abnormalities are a necessary associate of repeated violence, but merely suggest that some abnormalities may be more likely in the violent than the non-violent individual. Comparable research has been much more wide-ranging and thorough only among people with psychotic illnesses. Nevertheless, even here, research can best be summed up, perhaps reassuringly, by noting that it tends to confirm the complexity of brain function and dysfunction rather than provide definitive evidence of pathognomonic cerebral damage. It is just possible that for those patients who manifest schizophrenia and show pathological violence the two disorders are linked by a common cerebral aetiology, but data are slight and contradictory. The 'career model' could with value be applied here. Rarely considered, even in schizophrenia research, it is almost wholly absent from violence research when studying cerebral events. Milstein, who followed a group of repeatedly violent psychiatrically ill patients using brain electrical activity mapping techniques, failed to show either a consistent baseline map or a consistent pattern of change in the map with change in clinical state.[45]

If the more objectively measurable possibilities of common causation lead to no definite conclusions, how much more true this is for potentially relevant social factors. Literature is replete with histories of trauma in childhood exceeding chance expectations in a range of people who are mentally ill, among personality disordered groups, and also in criminal and violent samples. The more awareness of the possibility seems to spread, the more reports of such histories emerge. Most researchers, however, have limited themselves to retrospective enquiry within groups defined by their later pathology. In this context, early loss of a parent by death or separation has been shown to be a relatively common occurrence (about 40% of cases) among people both with schizophrenia,[46] and with violence, whether self-directed or toward others.[20,47] In our Institute of Psychiatry studies among violent and psychotic pre-trial prisoners, there was a strong suggestion that parental loss early in childhood, which was of a similar order to that found in these other studies, was less the problem in itself than the nature and quality of the remaining relationship (Taylor unpublished data).

Mentally ill and violent patients within the health service

Health service staff have an interest in violence by patients which must extend beyond the purely objective and altruistic, because their own risk of becoming victims is not insignificant. An important survey by the Health Services Advisory Committee found that in Great Britain NHS staff were three times more likely to be injured at work than industrial workers, principally because of such attacks.[48] Nurses and ambulance staff were most at risk, and psychiatric and geriatric hospitals the focus of the highest rates of violence. Within a general hospital, accident and emergency departments took second place to general medical wards for minor injury, while exceeding them in the other categories of major injury, use of weapons or threat. Important guidance for managers for maximising the safety of the environment follows.

The risks are certainly not confined to British patients, and in the psychiatric sphere it is clear that no type of facility is immune. Lion and Reid, mainly for the USA, collected reports variously from the state and public mental hospital systems, a university hospital, a private psychiatric facility, general hospitals and specialist forensic hospital facilities.[49] All faced important problems in this regard. Most researchers have noted that staff are more at risk than other patients.[50] It is perhaps important to emphasise, however, that, although it is acknowledged that there is widespread underreporting of violent incidents in hospitals,[51,52] this is particularly of less serious assaults.[53] At least within psychiatric settings, when adjusted for length of exposure the risk of *serious* harm to staff or other patients is extremely low.[54]

Violent behaviour in the context of psychiatric illness is almost certainly an important factor in the decision to admit a patient to hospital. Several studies put the occurrence of actual violence to others just preceding admission to hospital at between one in ten and one in three cases.[55–57] Although such rates might seem to suggest that a measure of inpatient violence would be inevitable, there is quite good, if only indirect, evidence to suggest that a rather different group of patients tends to be most responsible for violence once admitted. Tardiff's comparison between inpatients and those at admission suggests they differ as groups by gender, age, diagnosis and, to a rather lesser extent, by simultaneous tendency to self harm.[58] The gender shift, from a male propensity for violence outside hospital to an equivalent or even higher female propensity in hospital, is widely reported, the other consistent finding between studies being that a relatively small number of patients tend to account for a dispro-portionate amount of the violence.[59] In Noble and Rodger's later series, in which the patient population was much less numerically stable, about half the assaulters had attacked only once, while 72 subjects were responsible for 405 assaults.[50]

Health service staff, particularly those working with people with a psychiatric illness, need systems for the accurate evaluation of risk. At all stages, the risk to the patients themselves is high, and must never be forgotten or underestimated in the context of concern about others. Violent patients may be at exceptional risk for suicide.[60] At the time of admission to hospital and after discharge, the psychiatrist's concern is otherwise principally for the patient's family and friends or the general public, while in hospital it is most likely to be for professional staff. The hospital environment may reduce violence risks when its physical qualities are well designed and constructed (see ref. 48), with avoid-ance of the use of temporary, often not specifically skilled staff,[61] and the establishment under strong leadership of a stable, structured, skilled staffing.[62] There are nevertheless some aspects of hospital treatment which may be unavoidable that may actually increase risk, and thus require special planning. Lion *et al.* showed that over half the inpatient assaults on staff had occurred while they were restraining patients.[51] Perhaps with less serious consequences, Nilsson *et al.* found in a small series of psychogeriatric inpatients that over 75% of the aggressive incidents recorded against staff (234 in six weeks) were provoked as the staff helped the patients with the activities of daily living.[63] Frank staff–patient conflict may occur,[64] and staff expectations, fear or overdefensiveness about violence may themselves be provocative factors, while counter-transference may even lead to acts of staff violence or brutality against patients.

The prediction of violence by psychiatrists and psychologists (not always, it must be said, confining themselves to prediction within psychiatric populations) has itself suffered extremes of fortune. Its history is admirably charted by Monahan.[65] Instead of making absolute predictions for all time about dangerousness, physicians who are well skilled and practised in the field will now make cautious predictions about the likelihood of violence—or other dangerous behaviour, such as fire setting—occurring in specified circumstances, and the likelihood of treatment interventions or social management minimising the risks. The chances of violence are always a product of factors in the potentially violent person, the potential victim(s) and the environment. As part of a complete evaluation, the doctor and clinical team must establish, for example, whether there are identifiable potential victims and, if so, whether the potential victims understand the risks and are able to take appropriate measures, which may include avoiding the patient altogether, or learning ways of diffusing mounting tension or anger. With respect to the environment, the availability of weapons or of disinhibiting substances like alcohol, and the pressures of unemployment, financial hardship or threatened loss may all be important.

In relation to each individual patient, a history of violence may be helpful. The literature, indeed, repeats almost monotonously that the best predictor of future violence is past violence, even for psychiatric patients. Statistically, this may be true in a number of studies, but the *importance* of such a statement has been put in perspective by Harry and Steadman, who showed that a history of previous arrests would effectively predict only about 5% of future offending.[66] In fact, as newer generations of researchers turn to the measurement of more illness-specific factors than their predecessors, qualities of the illness emerge as much better predictors of violence, at least within the hospital setting.[67,68] General psychiatric rating scales, in particular the Brief Psychiatric Rating Scale,[69] or more specific scales for focusing on target risk symptoms, such as the Maudsley Assessment of Delusions Schedule,[70] may be of particular help.

Admission to hospital for a patient may be necessary for all sorts of reasons. Symptoms, such as delusions, which in that patient have led to violence or may do so, and which are not responding to treatment may be an important reason for admission, compulsorily if co-operation is in doubt and the risk judged high. Continued failure to respond to specific treatment, or poor compliance with treatment even when it is clearly effective, are factors that may mitigate strongly against the discharge of a patient once admitted. The vast majority of mentally ill patients who commit serious violence have been well-known to psychiatric services at some time, although they are often not in treatment at the time of the violence *and*, where not, have generally been discharged by the psychiatrists previously treating them (for example, ref. 11 and Taylor unpublished data).

As psychiatric inpatient beds become fewer, and civil libertarians both more vociferous and, in relation to the expressed wishes of many patients, more effective in ensuring they do not remain in hospital, a crisis has been recognised in caring for mentally abnormal offenders and those with violent or challenging behaviour that has not been criminalised. For England and Wales, the government has set up a special interdepartmental Committee (Department of Health and the Home Office), chaired by Dr John Reed, to review provision. While the majority of the offending behaviour of the mentally ill is not serious, the principles of service provision apply as well to the violent as the non-violent. These include that:

— mentally disordered offenders should receive care and treatment from health and personal social services rather than in custodial care;
— such services should be provided with attention to the needs of individuals, under conditions of no greater security than is justified by the degree of danger they present to themselves or others, and as near as possible to their own home or community to maximise rehabilitation potential and the chances of sustaining or regaining an independent life.[71]

The rest of the Committee's Report documents the details of the immense challenge these principles pose to the health services, and the extent of the development of services that will be required to honour them. Awareness of the problems has been raised. Appropriate action must follow.

References

1. Poe EA. *The tell-tale heart*. 1845
2. Robertson G. Arrest patterns among mentally disordered offenders. *Br Med J* 1988; **295**:632–4
3. Rosen G. *Madness in society*. Chicago: University of Chicago Press, 1968
4. Monahan J. Mental disorder and violent behaviour. *Am Psychologist* 1992; **47**:511–21
5. Gerbner G, Gross L, Morgan M, Signorielli N. Health and medicine on television. *N Engl J Med* 1981; **305**:901–4

6. Shain R, Phillips J. The stigma of mental illness: labeling and stereotyping in the news. In: Wilkins L, Patterson P, eds. *Risky business: communicating issues of science, risk and public policy.* Westport CN: Greenwood Press, 1991: 61–74

7. DYG Corporation. *Public attitudes toward people with chronic mental illness.* Elmsford, NY: DYG Inc, 1990

8. Taylor PJ. Schizophrenia and violence. In: Gunn J, Farrington DP, eds. *Abnormal offenders, delinquency and the criminal justice system.* Chichester: John Wiley & Sons Ltd, 1982: 269–84

9. Monahan J, Steadman HJ. Crime and mental disorder: an epidemiological approach. In: Tonry M, Morris N, eds. *Crime and justice: an annual review of research (vol 4).* Chicago: University of Chicago Press, 1983: 145–89

10. Wessely S, Taylor PJ. Madness and crime: criminology versus psychiatry. *Crim Behav Mental Health* 1991; **1**:193–228

11. Hafner H, Boker W. *Crimes of violence by mentally abnormal offenders.* Cambridge: Cambridge University Press, 1982. (English translation, Marshall H, 1982. Gewalttaten geistesgestörter. Berlin: Springer-Verlag, 1973)

12. Gillies H. Homicide in the west of Scotland. *Br J Psychiatry* 1976; **128**:105–27

13. Taylor PJ, Gunn JC. Violence and psychosis: I. Risk of violence among psychotic men. *Br Med J* 1984; **288**:1945–9

14. Wilcox DE. The relationship of mental illness to homicide. *Am J Forensic Psychiatry* 1985; **6**:3–15

15. Petersson H, Gudjonsson GH. Psychiatric aspects of homicide. *Acta Psychiatr Scand* 1981; **64**:363–72

16. Swanson JW, Holzer CE, Ganju VK, Jono RT. Violence and psychiatric disorder in the community: evidence from the epidemiologic catchment area surveys. *Hosp Comm Psychiatry* 1990; **41**:761–70

17. American Psychiatric Association. *Diagnostic and statistical manual of mental disorders.* Washington, DC: American Psychiatric Association, 1980

18. Lanzkron J. Murder and insanity. A survey. *Am J Psychiatry* 1963; **119**:754–8

19. Gibbens TCN. Sane and insane homicide. *J Crim Law Criminol Police Sci* 1958; **49**: 110–45

20. McKnight CK, Mohr JW, Quinsey RE, Erochko J. Mental illness and homicide. *Can Psychiatr Assoc J* 1966; **11**:91–8

21. Taylor PJ. Motives for offending among violent and psychotic men. *Br J Psychiatry* 1985; **147**:491–8

22. Mowat RR. *Morbid jealousy and murder.* London: Tavistock Publications, 1966

23. Mawson D. Delusions of poisoning. *Med Sci Law* 1985; **25**:279–97

24. De Clerambault CG. Les psychoses passionelles. In: *Oeuvres psychiatriques.* Paris: Presses Universitaires, 1942: 311–455

25. Buchanan A, Reed A, Wessely S *et al.* The phenomenological correlates of acting on delusions. *Br J Psychiatry* (in press)

26. Wessely S, Buchanan A, Reed A *et al.* Acting on delusions. *Br J Psychiatry* (in press)

27. Psarska AD. Jealousy factors in homicide in forensic material. *Polish Med J* 1970; **9**:1504–10

28. Mullen PE, Maack LH. Jealousy, pathological jealousy and aggression. In: Farrington DP, Gunn J, eds. *Aggression and dangerousness.* London: Wiley, 1985: 103–26

29. Daly M, Wilson M, Weyhurst SJ. Male sexual jealousy. *Ethol Sociobiol* 1982; **3**:11–27

30. Taylor PJ. Schizophrenia and crime: distinctive patterns in association. In: Hodgins S, ed. *Crime and mental disorder.* Newbury Park, CA: Sage Publications Inc, 1993, 63–85

31. Dollard J, Miller N, Doon L, Mowrer O, Sears R. *Frustration and aggression.* New Haven, CN: Yale University Press, 1939

32. Berkowitz L. *Aggression: a psychological analysis.* New York: McGraw-Hill Book Co Inc, 1962

33. Kendell RE. Relationship between aggression and depression. *Arch Gen Psychiatry* 1970; **22**:308–18
34. Schipkowensky M. Affective disorders: cyclophrenia and murder. In: de Reuck AVS, Porter R, eds. *The mentally abnormal offender*. London: Churchill, CIBA, 1968
35. Walker N, McCabe S. *Crime and insanity in England, vol 2. New solutions and new problems*. Edinburgh: Edinburgh University Press, 1973
36. East N. *Medical aspects of crime*. London: Churchill, 1936
37. Taylor PJ. Social implications of psychosis. *Br Med Bull* 1987; **43**:718–40
38. Humphreys MS, Johnstone EC, MacMillan JF, Taylor PJ. Dangerous behaviour preceding first admissions for schizophrenia. *Br J Psychiatry* 1992; **161**:501–5
39. Wessely S. *The criminal careers of people in one London borough with and without schizophrenia*. Presentation to the winter workshop on schizophrenia, Badgastein, Austria, 1992
40. McGorry P, Chanen A, McCarthy E, van Riel R, McKenzie D, Singh B. Post-traumatic stress disorder following recent-onset psychosis. *J Nerv Mental Dis* 1991; **179**:253–8
41. Stampfer H. 'Negative symptoms': a cumulative trauma stress disorder. *Aust NZ J Psychiatry* 1990; **54**:516–28
42. Goldberg EM, Morrison SL. Schizophrenia and social class. *Br J Psychiatry* 1963; **109**:785–802
43. Taylor PJ, Mullen P, Wessely S. Psychosis, violence and crime. In: Gunn J, Taylor PJ, eds. *Forensic psychiatry: clinical, legal and ethical issues*. Oxford: Butterworth-Heinemann (in press)
44. Kligman D, Goldberg DA. Temporal lobe epilepsy and aggression. *J Nerv Mental Dis* 1975; **160**:324–40
45. Milstein V. EEG topography in patients with aggressive violent behavior. In: Moffitt TE, Mednick SA, eds. *Biological contributions to crime causation*. Dordrecht, Boston, Lancaster: Martinus Nijhoff Publishers, 1988
46. Wahl CW. Some antecedent factors in the family histories of 568 male schizophrenics of the United States Navy. *Am J Psychiatry* 1955; **113**:201–10
47. Humphrey JA. Social loss: a comparison of suicide victims, homicide offenders and non-violent individuals. *Dis Nerv System* 1977; **38**:157–60
48. Health Service Advisory Committee. *Violence to staff in the health service*. London: HMSO, Health and Safety Committees, 1987
49. Lion JR, Reid WH, eds. *Assaults within psychiatric facilities*. New York: Grune and Stratton, 1983
50. Noble P, Rodger S. Violence by psychiatric inpatients. *Br J Psychiatry* 1989; **155**: 384–90
51. Lion JR, Snyder W, Merrill GL. Under-reporting of assaults on staff in a state hospital. *Hosp Commun Psychiatry* 1981; **32**:497–8
52. Convit A, Isay D, Gadroma R, Volavka J. Under-reporting of physical assaults in schizophrenic inpatients. *J Nerv Mental Dis* 1988; **176**:507–9
53. Infantino J, Musingo S. Assaults and injuries among staff with and without training in aggression control techniques. *Hosp Commun Psychiatry* 1985; **36**:1313–4
54. Ekblom B. *Acts of violence by patients in mental hospitals*. Uppsala: Almquist & Wiksolls Boktryseni AB, Scandinavian University Books, 1970
55. Johnstone EC, Crow TJ, Johnson AL, MacMillan JF. The Northwick Park study of first episodes of schizophrenia. 1. Presentation of the illness and procedure relating to admission. *Br J Psychiatry* 1986; **148**:115–20
56. Lagos JM, Perlmutter K, Saexinger H. Fear of the mentally ill: empirical support for the common man's response. *Am J Psychiatry* 1977; **134**:1134–7
57. Tardiff K, Sweillam A. Assault, suicide and mental illness. *Arch Gen Psychiatry* 1980; **37**:164–9
58. Tardiff K. A survey of assault by chronic patients in a state hospital system. In: Lion JR, Reid WH, eds. *Assaults within psychiatric facilities*. New York: Grune and Stratton, 1983

59. Fottrell E. A study of violence behaviour among patients in psychiatric hospitals. *Br J Psychiatry* 1980; **136**:216–21
60. Robertson G. Mentally abnormal offenders: manner of death. *Br Med J* 1987; **295**: 632–4
61. James DV, Fineberg NA, Shah AK, Priest R. An increase in violence on an acute psychiatric ward: a study of associated factors. *Br J Psychiatry* 1990; **156**:846–52
62. Katz P, Kirkland F. Violence and social structure on mental hospital wards. *Psychiatry* 1990; **53**:262–71
63. Nilsson K, Palmstierna T, Wistedt B. Aggressive behaviour in hospitalised psychogeriatric patients. *Acta Psychiatr Scand* 1988; **78**:172–5
64. Sheridan M, Henrion R, Robinson L, Baxter V. Precipitants of violence in a psychiatric inpatient setting. *Hosp Commun Psychiatry* 1990; **41**:776–80
65. Monahan J. The prediction of violent behaviour toward a second generation of theory and policy. *Am J Psychiatry* 1984; **141**:10–5
66. Harry B, Steadman H. Arrest rates of patients treated at a community mental health center. *Hosp Commun Psychiatry* 1988; **39**:862–6
67. Werner PD, Rose TL, Yesavage JA, Seeman K. Psychiatrists' judgements of dangerous inpatients on an acute care unit. *Am J Psychiatry* 1984; **141**:263–6
68. Palmstierna T, Lasserius R, Wistedt B. Evaluation of the Brief Psychiatric Rating Scale in relation to aggressive behaviour by acute involuntarily admitted patients. *Acta Psychiatr Scand* 1989; **79**:313–6
69. Overall J, Gorham DR. The Brief Psychiatric Rating Scale. *Psychol Rep* 1962; **10**: 799–812
70. Taylor PJ, Garety P, Buchanan A *et al*. Delusions and violence. In: Monahan J, Steadman H, eds. *Violence and mental disorder: developments in risk assessment*. Chicago: Chicago University Press, 1992 (in press)
71. Department of Health, Home Office. *Review of health and social services for mentally disordered offenders and others requiring similar services. (The Reed Report)*. London: Department of Health, 1992

7 | Personality and violence

Ronald Blackburn
*Director of Research and Honorary Consultant Clinical Psychologist,
Ashworth Hospital, Liverpool*

Introduction

This chapter examines the contributions of the person to violence. It
considers some recent psychological research on aggression, and
presents some of the author's own work with mentally disordered
offenders. While the intention is not to elaborate a theory of aggression, the approach makes certain basic assumptions:

- violent acts are typically attempts to resolve problems, and human
  aggression can be conceptualised as a form of problem solving
  behaviour;
- human aggression is learned, and is not a biological given;
- the emotion of anger has a biological basis and may be on a
  continuum with defensive aggression in other animals.

However, the experience of anger depends on cognitive appraisals
and attribution, and has more to do with ontogeny than with phylo-
geny.

People clearly vary in the extent to which they experience and
express anger or behave aggressively. I argue that it is quite appropriate to talk of traits or dispositions in this respect, but the notion that
people have stable traits which they carry around with them has had a
bad press in psychology. Social learning theorists argue that people are
not in fact very consistent in their behaviour, and that behaviour is
determined more by the situation than by generalised traits or tendencies. The so-called person-situation debate, however, is about conceptual as much as empirical issues.

Aggression and personality

Acts and dispositions

One issue which is particularly important in considering violence is
the distinction between *acts* and personal *dispositions*. An act is an

intentional, goal-directed behaviour performed by a person in a specific situational context. A violent act, for example, can be construed as the forceful infliction of physical injury by one person on another. A disposition is a tendency or capacity to perform particular kinds of act. The concern here is with aggressiveness as a disposition to inflict harm, which people possess in varying degrees. A disposition is known from *average* behaviour over time and setting. It is a property possessed by the person, whether or not a relevant act is performed on a particular occasion. Traits therefore describe what people *can* do, not what they necessarily *will* do.

Dispositions and acts call for different explanations. An attempt to explain an aggressive disposition may be made in terms of distal factors such as genetic endowment, early family environment or experiences with peers. These, however, do not explain the occurrence of an act of aggression, which depends on more proximal factors such as the situational context, the meanings attached to it by the participants, their emotional state and their interpretations of the behaviour of the other. In the open world, these may often be fortuitous. Studies of homicides, for example, suggest that they are often unpredicted altercations which go further than intended, the outcome depending on the victim–offender interaction and the availability of a weapon.[1]

Violent acts, then, require more than violent actors. One implication is that the relationship between aggressive dispositions and the performance of violent acts is not simple. There are people with marked aggressive tendencies which will not necessarily eventuate in a violent crime. This has been overlooked in much of the research on predicting dangerousness, in which the identification of an aggressive disposition has not been clearly separated from the forecasting of violent acts.[2] Conversely, violent crimes may often be committed by people who are not habitually aggressive. Studies still appear which attempt to establish the attributes of violent people by taking a sample of prisoners or offender-patients defined solely by reference to a single conviction for violence. Many of these, however, will have committed their offence because of situational factors or temporary state rather than a propensity for violence. On the other hand, some will have contributed directly to a violent outcome by characteristics which create the conditions for an act of violence.

Populations of violent offenders are therefore likely to be heterogeneous in personality. This has been clearly established in research with mentally disordered offenders committed to special hospitals because of violent acts. My earliest studies with this population were initially concerned with testing Megargee's hypothesis that those who have committed an act of extreme violence can be divided into over-controlled and under-controlled personality types.[3] Megargee proposed that under-controlled offenders are those with weak inhibitions, who respond aggressively with some regularity, and are likely to be identified as psychopathic personalities. Over-controlled offenders, in contrast, have strong inhibitions, and aggress only when instigation (anger arousal) is sufficiently intense to overcome inhibitions. They are therefore expected to attack others rarely, but with extreme intensity if they do so, and should hence be found more commonly among those who have been extremely assaultive or homicidal. Supporting this hypothesis, extreme assaultives were found to be significantly more controlled, inhibited and defensive on personality tests than moderate assaultives. They were also less likely to have a prior criminal record or to be diagnosed as psychopathic personality.[4]

The over-control hypothesis sheds some light on why typically timid and *unaggressive* individuals are found among violent offenders, but rests on a questionable energy model in which anger arousal accumulates with repeated provocation. Current theorising would predict that anger is most likely to be maintained by the cognitive rehearsal of grievances, resulting in a bias to respond more readily to further provocation.[5] Nevertheless, subsequent research supports the usefulness of the over-controlled–under-controlled distinction.

Consistency of aggression

Some of the strongest evidence favouring the view of aggression as a stable trait comes from longitudinal studies. Olweus reviewed evidence on the stability of aggression in males as measured by observer ratings, peer nominations and direct observation, and identified 12 investigations in which assessments had been made on at least two occasions, which ranged from 6 months to 21 years apart.[6] The average corrected correlation between the two assessments was 0.79. He therefore concluded that there is substantial stability in aggression which cannot be attributed to situational constancy.

Subsequent studies extend Olweus' findings. For example, in research in New York, Huesmann *et al.* found that peer nominations of aggression made at age 8 correlated significantly with self- and spouse-reported aggression and also criminal records 22 years later.[7] In another American study, Caspi *et al.* found that children who exhibited explosive tempers in childhood were judged more under-controlled and irritable 20 years later, and had shown a life-course pattern of educational, occupational and marital failure consistent with a recurring maladaptive coercive style.[8] Similarly, in West and Farrington's study of delinquent development in London boys, ratings of aggression at age 8 to 10 correlated significantly with self-reported aggression in adolescence and adulthood.[9]

Criminal violence appears to be a function of such a disposition. Farrington found that 22% of those rated as highly aggressive by teachers at age 12 to 14 subsequently had a conviction for violence, compared with 7% of less aggressive boys, and that the former accounted for 60% of the violent offenders.[9] Similar data were reported from Sweden by Stattin and Magnusson.[10] Robins also found that fighting in childhood consistently predicts violent behaviour in adults.[11] In all these studies, early aggression was associated with later social deviance in general. This justifies the notion of a 'syndrome' of antisocial behaviour, of which aggression is a prominent feature. However, as will be argued later, this does not necessarily mean that there is a single type of aggressive or antisocial personality.[12]

The notion of aggressiveness as a trait or tendency therefore has some substance. All these studies, however, have a high false positive rate. Although a majority of those who exhibit violence in adulthood have been identified as aggressive in childhood, only a minority of aggressive children go on to be seriously aggressive. Many of the remainder may continue to be aggressive in less obvious ways, but it must be emphasised that stability is only relative in this context.

Individual differences and aggression

The consistency of aggression depends both on personal attributes which determine what the individual perceives as aversive or anger arousing and on what other coping skills are available to the person in conflict situations. Critics of trait concepts point out that adaptive behaviour requires discrimination and flexibility. A high degree of consistency may reflect failures to discriminate between past and present events, and may be associated with maladjustment. This is consistent with the DSM-III definition of personality disorders as traits which are 'inflexible and maladaptive' and result in social dysfunction or subjective distress.[13] It is therefore not unreasonable to suppose that those who are aggressive with some consistency will exhibit characteristics which are dysfunctional.

The traditional assumption is that violent individuals lack internalised controls, although this notion rests on the questionable idea that there is an aggressive instinct or drive which needs to be controlled. Thus, psychodynamic and early learning theorists see individual differences as residing in the acquisition of emotional inhibitions restraining harmful behaviour, such as anxiety, guilt, empathic concern, and tolerance for frustration. However, where traditional approaches focus on affective aspects, recent research emphasises factors which facilitate aggression such as anger arousal, and the cognitive processes which mediate facilitation or inhibition.

Several studies have demonstrated deficits in both cognitive processing and the content of cognition in aggressive children and violent delinquents. Neuropsychological research, for example, suggests that reduced left hemispheric lateralisation may be particularly characteristic of delinquents showing psychopathic traits and a history of violence, and that this may reflect a relative inability to modulate control of behaviour by means of inner speech.[14] Several studies also point to a significant association of aggression with low intelligence. Huesmann *et al.* found a consistent negative correlation of aggression with IQ and attainment over 22 years, although they suggest that intelligence exerts an effect on aggression primarily in childhood.[15]

Research on social cognition in aggressive boys by Dodge suggests that they have a bias to perceive hostile intent in ambiguous interpersonal situations having a negative outcome.[16] He also finds that they are deficient in social problem solving skills. For example, they pay less attention to available information and generate fewer constructive solutions when faced with interpersonal problems. Slaby and Guerra replicated these findings with violent delinquents, and also demonstrated deviant expectations about aggression.[17] Compared with unaggressive adolescents, the delinquents endorsed more positive and neutralising beliefs about the consequences of aggression, such as that it gains tangible rewards, enhances self-esteem and results in minimal suffering to the victim.

Violent delinquents also appear to have deviant beliefs about the self. Threats to masculine self image and self-image promotion or defending were significantly associated with violence in Toch's observations of encounters between police and delinquents.[18] Low self esteem makes a person vulnerable to threat, but people with low self esteem may also adopt coercive means of influence because they lack non-coercive skills with which to achieve power and status.[19]

These studies, then, demonstrate a number of factors which support an aggressive disposition. However, skill deficits or low self esteem are by no means characteristic of all violent offenders. My work with adult mentally disordered offenders in special hospitals suggests that it is an oversimplification to treat aggressive individuals as an homogeneous group.

One study, a cluster analysis of Minnesota Multiphasic Personality Inventory (MMPI) profiles of patients who had committed homicide, supported Megargee's over-control hypothesis, but in fact indicated two over-controlled and two under-controlled types.[20] In subsequent work, a questionnaire has been used which focuses on traits particularly relevant to personality disorder, the Special Hospitals Assessment of Personality and Socialisation (SHAPS).[21] The ten SHAPS scales reduce to two broad dimensions, defined by:

- impulsivity, aggression, and hostility, labelled *aggression* or *psycho-pathy*;
- shyness, social anxiety, and lack of self esteem, labelled *withdrawal versus sociability*.

Cluster analyses of SHAPS profiles have consistently reproduced the earlier fourfold typology. This emerged from a study of those in the legal category of psychopathic disorder,[22] but it also accounts for the main patterns of personality deviation in the special hospital popu-lation as a whole.[23] Four classes may be described as:

1. *Primary psychopaths* (P): impulsive, aggressive, hostile, extroverted, self-confident, low to average anxiety.
2. *Secondary psychopaths* (S): hostile, impulsive, aggressive, socially anxious, withdrawn, moody, low in self esteem.
3. *Controlled* (C): defensive, controlled, sociable, very low anxiety.
4. *Inhibited* (I): shy, withdrawn, controlled, moderately anxious, low self esteem.

The four groups represent combinations of extremes on the two factor dimensions:

- the P and S groups score towards the aggressive extreme of the first factor of aggression, but occupy opposite positions on the with-drawal factor;
- the C and I groups score at a low level on the aggression factor, but again are opposite on the withdrawal-sociability dimension.

This typology seems robust, having been replicated in research in English prisons on 'normal' murderers,[24] and violent offenders more generally.[25]

Studies in the special hospitals have established differences between the four groups on psychophysiological, emotional and behavioural variables, S generally being the most deviant.[26] P and S are more likely to have an early criminal history, but there are differences between the groups in the pattern of offences. P is most likely to have a previous history of violent crimes, I the least. S and I, on the other hand, are more likely to have been admitted following a sexual crime.

Some data obtained from a representative sample of 136 patients resident at one special hospital are currently being examined. Cluster analysis of the SHAPS yields the four groups identified previously (Table 1). Confirming previous findings,[23] the typology shows some relation to the Mental Health Act 1983 classification. P and S make up a higher proportion of the psychopathic disorder category, but the same four types are also found among those classified as mentally ill. The relation of the typology to the DSM-III categories of personality

Table 1. SHAPS groups

Mental Health Act category	Primary psychopath	Secondary psychopath	Controlled	Inhibited
Mental illness	15	17	36	22
Psychopathic disorder	16	12	6	6
MI/PD	0	3	1	2
MCMI high scores	Narcissistic Antisocial Histrionic	Passive–Aggressive Avoidant Schizoid Paranoid Antisocial	Compulsive Dependent	Avoidant Schizoid Dependent Schizotypal Passive–Aggressive

SHAPS = special hospitals assessment of personality and socialisation
MCMI = Millon clinical multiaxial inventory
MI = mental illness
PD = psychopathic disorder

disorder, as assessed by the Millon Clinical Multiaxial Inventory (MCMI),[27] shows marked differences between the groups on most MCMI scales. Of particular interest is the difference between the two under-controlled groups, P and S. Both groups meet Millon's criteria for antisocial or aggressive personality, which he defines in terms of hostile affectivity, social rebelliousness, vindictiveness and disregard for danger. However, where P patients are also narcissistic, S are passive–aggressive, avoidant, and paranoid. This provides further support for the view that aggressive personalities are not a unitary category.

A cognitive-interpersonal model of personality

Aggression and the interpersonal circle

Our current work is concerned with investigating a cognitive-interpersonal model which promises to integrate some of the findings on aggression and personality. The model originates from Leary's interpersonal theory of personality, basic to which is a descriptive scheme known as the *interpersonal circle*,[28] a version of which is shown in Fig. 1.

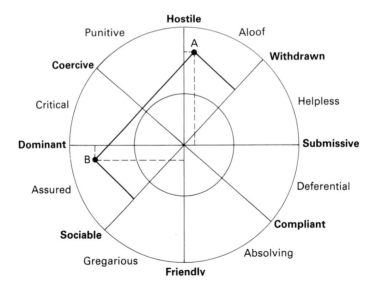

Fig. 1. *The interpersonal circle. A and B represent individuals with different styles but similar degrees of aggressiveness.*

When interpersonal behaviours occurring across a sample of interactions are examined, their intercorrelations typically produce a circular array around a two-dimensional space, known mathematically as a circumplex. The two dimensions relate first to the degree of power or control in an interaction(dominance versus submission), and secondly, to the degree of affiliation (hostile versus friendly). Most kinds of interaction reflect different blends of these two, which accounts for the circular relationships. Thus, an aggressive or coercive interaction entails a combination of dominance and hostility. My current research is focused on the eight points as indicated on the perimeter of the circumplex.

This system now has a firmly established empirical basis.[29] The elements may be individual acts, but Leary developed the notion of *interpersonal style*. He suggests that adaptive functioning requires the ability to produce behaviour represented at all parts of the circle according to situational demands, and hence to have an adequate range of interpersonal skills. However, as a result of early experiences, people tend to acquire a distinctive style which emphasises a particular area of the circle. The inner circle of Fig. 1 represents the normal range. The more a style exceeds this, the narrower the range of interactions on which the person relies. This follows from the circumplex structure, in which segments of the circle are positively associated with adjacent segments and negatively associated with opposite segments. A person with an extreme dominant style, for example, has interactions marked by frequent dominant exchanges. Such a person will also show coercive and sociable characteristics quite often, but submissive, withdrawn or compliant behaviour infrequently. The individual's behaviour will hence be rigid and inflexible. This is consistent with the DSM-III concept of personality disorders as inflexible traits, and the classes of personality disorder can be represented by interpersonal styles at different parts of the circle. The styles of narcissistic and histrionic personalities, for example, fall in the dominant–sociable area, while schizoid and avoidant personalities are characterised by withdrawn–submissive styles.[30]

However, the location of an individual in the circle requires reference to two axes. The positions of A and B in Fig. 1 show how two individuals may have quite different styles but be similar in aggressiveness. A has a dominant–sociable style, while B tends to be hostile and withdrawn. Both, nevertheless, show a similar degree of coerciveness. The nature of their aggressive interactions seems likely to be different.

To look at interpersonal styles in special hospital patients as assessed by nurse ratings, a set of items was developed which sample the interpersonal circle, the Chart of Interpersonal Reactions in Closed Living Environments (CIRCLE). These items are grouped into eight scales to mark the octants around the circle. The results also suggest that psychopathy as a personality dimension may be broadly equated with the coercive–compliant axis of the circle.

The rating scale profiles of the four SHAPS groups provide significant support for the assumption that these groups represent distinguishable interpersonal styles. P patients are characterised by a
dominant–sociable style, and score highest on coercion. This pattern
coincides with their self-reported extroversion, narcissism, and aggressive traits. S, who describe themselves as aggressive but also as avoidant
and passive–aggressive, are also coercive but differ from P in being
more submissive and withdrawn. The interpersonal characteristics of
the C and I groups are also consistent with their self-report patterns, C
tending to be friendly and compliant, I submissive and withdrawn.

Interpersonal style, cognition and the persistence of interpersonal style

A central question is the implication of these differences in explaining
the violent acts of patients and in suggesting strategies of clinical
intervention. The assumption is that these four patterns represent
typical or pre-potent forms of coping with interpersonal problem
situations, of which violence is sometimes, though not invariably, a
consequence. In the case of P and S, the probability of a violent
outcome seems likely to be increased as a result of their typically
coercive approach. For C and I individuals, on the other hand,
violence may represent a last resort when attempts to resolve conflict
through compliance or submission break down. The question is why
some individuals have a persistently coercive style.

Current views attribute persisting aggression primarily to family
modelling and reinforcement. This has been supported by both cross-
sectional and longitudinal studies, and violent adults frequently report
a history of witnessing violence and experiencing physical abuse in
childhood. However, exposure to such conditions is not sufficient to
account for the perpetuation of an aggressive style of interaction across
the life course. Caspi *et al.* identify two forms of person–environment
interaction which promote continuity:[8]

1. *Cumulative continuity* arises when a person's disposition leads to the
   selection of environments which sustain the disposition; for
   example, dropping out of school because of poorly controlled
   temper may restrict career options to frustrating occupational roles
   which evoke further patterns of ill-tempered behaviour.
2. In *interactional continuity* the immediate and recurring consequences
   of coercive exchanges short circuit the learning of more controlled
   forms of interaction.

Carson presents a similar theory in terms of expectancy confirmation processes.[31] In essence, the theory proposes a causal relationship
between what an individual expects, how he behaves and how others

react. People avoid cognitive dissonance by eliciting behaviour from the other in accord with their self concept and perceived role in the interaction. A particular overture involves verbal and non-verbal behaviour which sends a message about the relationship, not necessarily at a conscious level. It invites a complementary response from the other which, if forthcoming, provides feedback confirming the relationship. In this way, people engage in negotiated self-confirmation in their interactions. In the case of rigid interpersonal styles, early experiences create distorted expectations of how others are likely to react, which become *self-fulfilling prophecies*. Thus, a hostile person has expectations of hostile reactions from others and behaves in a way which gets them. People with strong expectations are thus likely to create interactions which minimise the chance of disconfirming experiences.

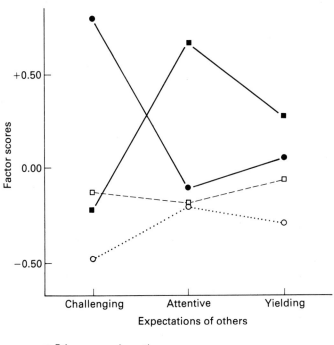

Fig. 2. *Interpersonal expectations of four patient groups.*

A simple measure of social expectations has been used to test this hypothesis. Patients are asked to indicate how often they expect other people to avoid them, criticise them, behave in a hostile way, be sympathetic and so on, the selection of the 32 items being guided by the interpersonal circle. There are three factors in the data which reflect expectations that others are likely to be:

- challenging (argue, wind you up, be sarcastic);
- attentive (friendly, sincere, confiding); and
- yielding (do things your way, be fearful, admit you are right).

There are significant differences between the four SHAPS groups on these factors (Fig. 2). Secondary psychopaths expect others to challenge them and not be friendly or attentive. Primary psychopaths, in contrast, do not expect others to be challenging, but expect attentive interactions, and also expect others to be more yielding. Controlled and withdrawn patients do not expect challenge or attention. The data appear to encourage the theory.

Conclusion

The interpersonal model has clear implications for treatment. To the extent that aggressive offenders create the conditions for violent acts by an interpersonal style which is supported by distorted expectations, the target for change is the individual's dysfunctional belief system. This is the goal of cognitive therapies developed by Beck and Ellis, but several North American therapists, notably Kiesler[32] and Safran,[33] are currently exploring procedures guided explicitly by interpersonal theory. Differentiating interpersonal styles within aggressive offenders may help to structure the therapeutic conditions necessary to change their maladaptive interactions.

References

1. Block R. *Violent crime*. Lexington, MA: Lexington Books, 1977
2. Gordon RA. A critique of the evaluation of Patuxent Institution, with particular attention to the issue of dangerousness and recidivism. *Bull Am Academy Psychiatry Law* 1977; **5**:210–55
3. Megargee EI. Undercontrolled and overcontrolled personality types in extreme antisocial aggression. *Psychol Monographs* 1966; **80**(no. 611)
4. Blackburn R. Personality in relation to extreme aggression in psychiatric offenders. *Br J Psychiatry* 1968; **114**:821–8
5. Zillmann D. *Hostility and aggression*. Hillsdale, NJ: Erlbaum, 1979
6. Olweus D. Stability of aggressive reaction patterns in males: a review. *Psychol Bull* 1979; **86**:852–75
7. Huesmann LR, Eron LD, Lefkowitz MM, Walder LO. Stability of aggression over time and generations. *Develop Psychol* 1984; **20**:1120–34
8. Caspi A, Bem DJ, Elder GH. Continuities and consequences of interactional styles across the life course. *J Personality* 1989; **57**:375–406
9 Farrington DP. Early predictors of adolescent aggression and adult violence. *Violence and victims* 1989; **4**:79–100

10. Stattin H, Magnusson D. The role of early aggressive behavior in the frequency, seriousness, and types of later crimes. *J Consult Clin Psychol* 1989; **57**:710–8

11. Robins L. Sturdy predictors of adult antisocial behaviour: replications from longitudinal studies. *Psychol Med* 1978; **8**:611–22

12. Blackburn R. On moral judgements and personality disorders: the myth of the psychopathic personality revisited. *Br J Psychiatry* 1988; **153**:505–12

13. American Psychiatric Association. *Diagnostic and statistical manual of mental disorders, 3rd edn (revised)*. Washington, DC: American Psychiatric Association, 1987

14. Miller L. Neuropsychological perspectives on delinquency. *Behavior Sci Law* 1988; **6**:409–28

15. Huesmann LR, Eron LD, Yarmel PW. Intellectual functioning and aggression. *J Personality Social Psychol* 1987; **52**:232–40

16. Dodge KA. A social-information processing model of social competence in children. In: Perlmutter M, ed. *Minnesota symposium on child psychology*. Hillsdale, NJ: Erlbaum, 1986

17. Slaby RG, Guerra NG. Cognitive mediators of aggression in adolescent offenders: 1. Assessment. *Develop Psychol* 1988; **24**:580–8

18. Toch H. *Violent men*. Harmondsworth: Penguin Books, 1969

19. Tedeschi JT. Social influence theory and aggression. In: Geen RG, Donnerstein EI, eds. *Aggression: theoretical and empirical reviews (vol 1)*. New York: Academic Press, 1983

20. Blackburn, R. Personality types among abnormal homicides. *Br J Criminol* 1971; **11**:14–31

21. Blackburn R. *The special hospitals assessment of personality and socialisation*. Liverpool: Park Lane Hospital, 1982 (unpublished)

22. Blackburn R. An empirical classification of psychopathic personality. *Br J Psychiatry* 1975; **127**:456–60

23. Blackburn R. Patterns of personality deviation among violent offenders: replication and extension of an empirical taxonomy. *Br J Criminol* 1986; **26**:254–69

24. McGurk BJ. Personality types among normal homicides. *Br J Criminol* 1978; **18**:146–61

25. Henderson M. An empirical classification of convicted violent offenders. *Br J Criminol* 1982; **22**:1–20

26. Blackburn R. On the relevance of the concept of the psychopath. In: Black DA, ed. *Issues in criminological and legal psychology, no. 2*. Leicester: British Psychological Society, 1982

27. Millon T. *Millon clinical multiaxial inventory, 3rd edn*. Minneapolis: Interpretive Scoring Systems, 1983

28. Leary T. *Interpersonal diagnosis of personality*. New York: Ronald Press, 1957

29. Wiggins JS. Circumplex models of interpersonal behaviour in clinical psychology. In: Kendall PC, Butcher JN, eds. *Handbook of research methods in clinical psychology*. New York: Wiley, 1982

30. Wiggins JS, Pincus AL. Conceptions of personality disorders and dimensions of personality. *Psychol Assess: J Consult Clin Psychol* 1989; **1**:305–16

31. Carson RC. Personality and exchange in developing relationships. In: Burgess RL, Huston TL, eds. *Social exchange in developing relationships*. New York: Academic Press, 1979

32. Kiesler DJ. The 1982 interpersonal circle: a taxonomy for complementarity in human transactions. *Psychol Rev* 1983; **90**:185–214

33. Safran JD. Toward a refinement of cognitive therapy in light of interpersonal theory. *Clin Psychol Rev* 1990; **10**:85–107

8 | Drugs, aggression and violence*

David M. Forshaw
Senior Registrar in General Psychiatry

John Strang
Getty Senior Lecturer in the Addictions, National Addiction Centre, Institute of Psychiatry/Maudsley Hospital, London

---

Introduction

Illicit drugs and violence are so obviously linked—at least in the public eye—that there seems little scope for debate or consideration. Popular and medical reporting of the epidemic spread of crack smoking in the USA takes for granted the association between the drug use and the violent crime. However, more critical scrutiny of the available data does not support the view of a simple relationship between violence and the use of illicit drugs. For what reasons have the drugs been taken? In what ways may the drug use have a relationship with aggression and violence? What other factors, such as perhaps route or dose for example, alter the 'typical' relationship between man and drug to modify the extent of associated violence?

A review of the existing literature, supplemented by clinical experience, highlights the gaps in current knowledge and provides an impetus for more detailed research.

Extent of illicit drug use

Over the last quarter of a century, the use of illicit drugs in the UK has increased at least by an order of magnitude. Not so many years ago, pop stars such as Donovan and Mick Jagger received custodial sentences for possession of cannabis and amphetamines, respectively, yet nowadays it is common practice for police officers merely to caution individuals found in possession of various drugs—not only cannabis but also, more recently, heroin. Since the early 1980s, HM

---

*The relationship between alcohol use and violence is considered in Chapter 9 and is mentioned only briefly here when discussion warrants. The status of research on the possible relationship between violence, drug use and 5-hydroxytryptamine (5HT) metabolism is still unclear, and the reader is referred elsewhere.[1,2]

Customs at Heathrow and elsewhere has operated a system of on-the-spot fines for possession of small quantities of cannabis. Thus, despite the considerable recent attention to extreme calls for legalisation of all drugs, there has quietly been a *de facto* decriminalisation of possession of drugs.[3,4]

Figures from the Home Office Addicts Index offer another perspective on this increased drug use, although these data cover addiction only to the opiates and cocaine (mainly the former). In 1970 there were 2,657 addicts known to the Addicts Index, in 1980 5,107, and in 1990, 17,756. An indicator study using capture-recapture methodology in the early 1980s concluded that these figures probably represented only 20% of the total—thus yielding an estimate of approximately 90,000 opiate addicts in the UK currently. Following similar logic, the Advisory Council on the Misuse of Drugs, in its report, *AIDS and drug misuse*, estimated that in 1986 there may have been between 75,000 and 150,000 opiate users (about half of whom may have been injecting), supplemented by a pool of injectors of other drugs (particularly amphetamines).[5]

Unfortunately, these data provide information only on the extent of contact between these drug users and either the criminal justice or medical system. However, more recent data are also available from (at least small-scale) household surveys. In a MORI poll conducted in April 1989 on a representative sample of 1,079 adults (aged 18 and over) in 108 constituencies, 5% of the sample reported having smoked cannabis, and 1% had taken drugs such as heroin or cocaine, but only 1% had taken cannabis or any other illicit drug in the previous two days compared with 50% who had taken alcohol.[6] The respondents were also asked about the main causes of crime. Interestingly 75% identified lack of parental discipline as a major cause, 71% identified drugs, and 62% alcohol.[7]

Drugs and crime

A strong relationship between unsanctioned drug use and crime in general has been repeatedly demonstrated. Numerous studies of heroin addicts attending hospitals in the late 1960s and early 1970s showed that about 80% of them had at least one criminal conviction. More recent studies have found similar or higher figures in established users.[8] The early British studies noted that the conviction rates before drug use were 30–50% for males and 60% for females, suggesting both that illicit drug use leads to crime and that delinquency, particularly in females, predisposes to drug use.

This difference in pre- and post-addiction convictions is less clear in American studies. Hence the claim that addiction leads an otherwise law-abiding individual to commit crime is challenged. The authors of a recent Scottish survey of clients at walk-in drug centres and individuals detained in penal institutions concluded that their data failed to support the hypothesis that heroin use caused previously honest citizens to take up crime.[9] However, the majority of studies do show that the amount of criminal involvement increases with regular drug use and/or addiction. It should be remembered that the above comments and figures refer to all crimes—not just violent offences.

Drugs and violence

Gordon followed up heroin addicts in London over a 10-year period and noted that, even though drug offences and acquisitive crimes accounted for the majority of convictions, two-thirds of the addicts had received at least one conviction for a violent offence.[10] His data were reliant on official records and the subjects were young, making interpretation and extrapolation difficult. Barton reported on a survey of more than 10,000 prisoners in USA state correctional facilities. A history of using illicit drugs was more prevalent in those convicted of property offences (61%) than violent offences (56%).[11] For this consideration, robbery was treated as a violent offence. The difference was much greater if inmates convicted of robbery were removed from the violent crime category. Seven of 10 of them had ever used drugs, and one in three were using them on a daily basis. A significantly smaller proportion of daily users were incarcerated for violent crimes (47% : 57%), perhaps suggesting that violence committed by drug users tends to be secondary to a primarily acquisitive aim.

Analysis of conviction rates and prison populations may provide some insights into the relationship between unsanctioned drug use and violence, but it is only part of the story. After all, less than 1% of all crimes committed by addicts in Baltimore in the early 1980s had led to an arrest.[12] More direct studies are needed. The results of some self-report studies on involvement in crime, such as the Baltimore study just mentioned, and the addicts' way of life are considered later.

Before considering in detail the ways in which illicit drugs may lead the user to violence, a few preliminary observations are useful to keep in perspective the points raised later.

Roles of drug use in violence

An individual act of aggression or violence will be the result of several complex interactive factors, including personality, social group, opportunity, availability of weapons, likelihood of retaliation or being caught, material or financial gain likely to result, victim's provocative behaviour, increased irritability due to physiological factors such as fatigue, presence of mental disorder and increased disinhibition due to the use of alcohol or drugs.

Drug use could be related to an individual act of violence in one of a number of ways, or through a very complex mix of them. Regular drug use could alter personality; the peer group may be more tolerant of violence (perhaps even prescribe it); the use of drugs also by the victim may make him or her an easier or more provocative victim; lack of sleep may increase the perpetrator's or victim's irritability; the high cost of drugs may make the need for material gain a particularly strong motive. This is by no means an exhaustive list of the possibilities, but gives a flavour of the variety.

Winick has argued that the magnitude of a drug problem in a society is determined by three factors:

- ease of availability of the drug;
- social attitudes towards the drug; and
- conflict and stress associated with social role within society.[13]

The methamphetamine epidemic in Japan following the Second World War, for example, was attributed both to the easy supply of the drug and to the social chaos and upheavals associated with and following the war.[14] Similar explanations were proposed to account for the considerable use of heroin by American soldiers in the Vietnam war.[15,16] Violence on a massive scale would seem to predispose to drug use. A sense of despair with society and the anger and frustration which it engenders may also lead to drug use. In her paper, 'The ideologies of despair', Burr argued that the use of amphetamines by 'Teds' and 'Mods' in the 1960s, and the later use of barbiturates by 'skinheads' and 'punks', reflects a self-destructive use of drugs to blot out awareness, a means of symbolically rejecting the conventions of society, a way of expressing negative attitudes, a demonstration of ideologies of despair.[17]

The mental states induced by drugs may lead the user to be an easier victim for an aggressor. Anecdotal accounts of the use of drugs to pacify victims are well-known. The relationship between drinking alcohol and being a homicide victim is particularly well documented, but recent studies have also confirmed that drug use and being a victim of, for example, homicide is correlated.[18] The relationship was particularly high in Budd's study of homicides in Los Angeles, in which 20% of homicide victims were intoxicated with cocaine at the time of the killing and half of them had also drunk alcohol.[19]

The role of drug use in leading or predisposing an individual to be violent can be very tenuous. Gudjonsson's study of delinquent boys in Reykjavik demonstrated that parental excessive drinking is related to violent offending and persistent recidivism in their offspring.[20] Farrell and Strang have recently expressed concern about the lack of research and information on the effects of drug-using parents on their off-spring.[21] These authors agree with current social policy that parental drug use in itself should never be an adequate reason for removing offspring into care. The result would be to deter drug-using parents from seeking help for their addiction, making the problem even more difficult to manage in the long term. On the other side of the coin, Rounsaville and colleagues found that a third of the addicts whose histories they examined in detail had been victims of some childhood trauma such as physical abuse.[22]

Violence by an individual may be directed to inanimate objects, other people, other living creatures or to the self, as in suicide or self mutilation. It is well documented that there is a higher rate of violence to the self in the form of suicide in those using unsanctioned drugs regularly.[23] It should also be remembered that some suicides may be an expression of hostility to survivors, as shown by Schneidman and Farberrow's classic analysis of suicide letters.[24]

MacDonald reported how abuse of alcohol and cannabis by adolescents was associated with higher mortality, mainly from accidents, suicide and homicide.[25] Hence, it would seem that they are more likely to die by a violent means.

Nature of the relationship between drugs and crime

Unsanctioned drug use and violence may be related in many ways. It may be valuable to consider six main ways in which unsanctioned drug use may lead or predispose the person using the drug to display aggression or to commit an act of violence on another:

- as a direct result of the sought-after effect of the drug;
- intoxication with the drug;
- a mental illness induced by the drug;
- the symptoms of a withdrawal state when neuroadaptation to the drug has occurred;
- any personality changes which may be associated with regular and prolonged use; and
- the life-style often adopted by the regular user as an adjunct to, or to support, his or her use of expensive drugs.

The last relationship is frequently cited to explain the high rates of crimes of acquisition seen in illicit drug users. Inevitably, there is overlap between these causal relations; for example, people may adopt the life-style referred to above in order to avoid the distressing symptoms of withdrawal. Similarly, intoxication may be the sought-after effect. Different classes of drugs have different effects. Not surprisingly, the stimulants, sedatives, opiates, hallucinogens and solvents tend to be related to aggression and violence in different ways. Drugs may be taken by various routes which may themselves be related to violence, the main routes being oral, intravenous or subcutaneous injection, inhaling, sniffing and snorting.

Result of the sought-after effect

A number of national powers, certainly the Axis nations but probably also the Allies, used amphetamines during the Second World War in the combat forces to enhance their performance and hostility.[14,26] The most notable example is surely the regular use of oral and intravenous amphetamine by Adolf Hitler from 1937 onwards.[27] A less extreme example is the use of amphetamines or cocaine by people such as business men, city finance dealers and drug dealers to increase their energy and enhance the aggressive edge on their business styles. Irritability and paranoia are well recognised concomitants of amphetamine and cocaine use and may lead to violence.

The sought-after effects of some drugs, such as LSD and ecstasy, include hallucinations. Violence may result as a direct consequence of the person acting in response to hallucinations. The trial of Lipman (R v. Lipman [1969] 3 WLR 819; [1969] 3 All ER 410; [1970] 1 QB 153) for murder around 1960 highlighted this role of illicit drug use in producing violence. Believing that he was defending himself against attack by snakes, he killed his girl-friend in bed after taking LSD. He was convicted of manslaughter on the grounds that he had lacked the necessary intent for murder.

Secondary to intoxication

Many drugs such as tranquillisers and narcotics are said to reduce hostility and pacify aggression.[27] None the less, many of these same drugs also produce disinhibition with intoxication, and violence may be mediated through this. Lion reported such a disinhibiting effect leading to aggression with barbiturates.[28] Similar effects have been reported for the narcotics and benzodiazepines, and for alcohol.

However, Faulk has suggested that the violence seen in drug use is mainly related to aggression associated with the pattern of life of the user rather than with the disinhibiting effect (as in alcohol).[29] The analysis of the convictions of users as discussed above would seem to support his point.

Solvents produce intoxication. Watson reported that 24 of the 335 young people she studied in Glasgow had threatened someone with a knife while intoxicated by a solvent.[30] Such small numbers are very difficult to interpret, but they do indicate the presence of a problem.

Intoxication may lead to psychological changes other than disinhibition, which may also lead to violence. Keup emphasises symptoms such as depersonalisation and paranoia as well as increased aggression associated with the acute intoxication seen with cannabis.[31]

Secondary to an induced mental disorder

The ways in which mental illness or personality disorders may lead to violence are discussed in other chapters. Mental disorder may be associated with unsanctioned drug use in three main ways.

First, the mental disorder may exist prior to the use of drugs. The use of drugs may be purely coincidental here or may occur as a result of the mental disorder. Anecdotal accounts of individuals with serious mental disorder sedating themselves with unsanctioned drugs are well-known. In these instances, it may well be that the 'abuse' of drugs actually diminishes violence, but this has not been properly studied. There is evidence that drug use is particularly likely in individuals with antisocial personality disorders, where the use may be part of overall delinquency.[32–36]

Secondly, the drug use may cause, precipitate or aggravate a mental disorder. Keup has argued that cannabis can precipitate or aggravate a psychosis in a predisposed individual.[31] These 'cannabis-mobilised' and 'cannabis-aggravated' psychoses are said to be associated with poor prognosis but their status is questioned. The stimulant drugs such as amphetamine and cocaine can induce both acute toxic psychoses and also, more classically, non-toxic psychoses.[37] Violence may arise in this latter disorder from the three symptoms which most characterise it: agitation, irritability and paranoid delusions. Coid and Strang reported a hypomanic-like state from which violence could result, which appeared to be induced by abuse of the anticholinergic drug procyclidine.[38] Abuse of non-psychoactive drugs may also lead to disturbed mental states and consequent violence. Pope and Katz described three cases of previously placid men using anabolic steroids who also developed a hypomanic-like state and then committed homicidal acts.[39]

Thirdly, the mental disorder may be induced during or after withdrawal. Depression following withdrawal from use of stimulants is well-known, and violence in the form of suicide a very real possibility. Ashton described acute psychotic episodes, with paranoia, hallucinations and delusions, occurring during withdrawal from benzodiazepines, and again violence could result.[40]

Secondary to a withdrawal state

Aggression and violence are not features of withdrawal in the same central way that they may be features of intoxication or psychosis. Violence in withdrawal may be linked to the use of force to obtain drugs, should the opportunity arise to stop the symptoms of withdrawal. Avoidance of withdrawal may provide the impetus to adopt a criminal life-style to ensure a regular supply of drugs. Mental disorders occurring as a consequence of withdrawal may lead to violence (see above).

Neuroadaptation, or tolerance, leads the user to need larger doses of the drug to keep withdrawal symptoms at bay. Hence, its contribution to violence may be mediated via the need to obtain more of the drug through such crimes as robbery. Johnson and colleagues demonstrated that more extensive use of heroin was associated not only with more crimes being committed by the user but also with the crimes being more serious.[41]

Secondary to personality changes

Personality factors and violence are considered elsewhere. A major problem with research into the relationship between personality and drug use (and/or drug dependence) is the issue of determining whether any observed personality characteristics were present only before or only after the drug use. Heston and Heston claim that a discernible personality change occurred in Adolf Hitler when he started to use amphetamine regularly in 1937.[41] Statements were collected from numerous individuals who had contact with him both then and subsequently. It seems to be well established that a personality change occurred but whether or not it was due to amphetamine use is another issue. He certainly started to use amphetamine regularly at that time. The change described, with increased irritability, hostility, paranoia, labile affect, is typical of anecdotal accounts of drug-related personality changes.

There is an extensive literature relating personality factors to drug addiction. A common approach has been to compare addicts with normals and/or prison inmates. Three main instruments have been used:

- the Minnesota Multiphasic Personality Inventory (MMPI);
- the Eysenck Personality Inventory (EPI); and
- the Hostility and Direction of Hostility Questionnaire (HDHQ).

Studies using the MMPI have tended to emphasise abnormalities typical of psychopathic and sociopathic profiles, with addicts scoring high on factors such as poor impulse control, low tolerance of frustration, hostility and poor socialisation. Studies using the EPI have revealed that addicts tend to score higher than normals for neuroticism. The neuroticism is said to consist of two main sub-factors: impulse control and socialisation. Gossop and Eysenck found that when profiles of addicts and prisoners were compared, the two groups differed significantly in only four factors, despite the addicts being heavily involved in crime.[42] The addicts tended to see themselves as more 'tense, worried, over-sensitive, depressed and moody' and also more 'socially inhibited' than the prisoners.

Gossop and Roy studied 40 drug-dependent individuals (approximately half inpatients and half outpatients) using the HDHQ.[43] Addicts scored high on extra-punitive hostility, and those who had convictions for violent offences scored the highest on hostility.

Cannabis has been claimed to change personality. Schwartz reported that when cannabis is taken for more than 60 days there are discernible personality changes such as carelessness, lack of motivation and paranoid ideation.[44] There are anecdotal accounts of long-term cannabis users becoming more violent.[45] The status of these reports is difficult to ascertain because detailed studies have failed to confirm the changes.

Use of some non-illicit drugs has also been claimed to be associated with personality changes and aggression. For example, several authors have claimed that regular use or abuse of anabolic steroids by sportsmen and weight-lifters leads to accentuation of the aggressive aspects of their personality.[46]

Secondary to adopted life-style

The addict's life-style, its attractions and problems, have been explored recently by Stephens.[47] Numerous factors, such as unemployment, are associated with the life-style, not just criminality. The need to find a regular supplier of drugs, to 'earn' sufficient money to pay for expensive drugs, and possibly also the desire to mix with like-minded people and take part in a select sub-culture, often leads addicts into the 'junkie' life-style in which criminal involvement is high (for discussion of 'junkie' life-style, see ref. 48). The very high crime rate associated with drug use has already been discussed in relation to analysis of individuals with convictions. Data based on convictions are useful but provide an inadequate picture. Consequently, Ball and colleagues looked at the problem from 'the other end' by studying self-report data from addicts.[12] They used a new measure of 'crime-days per year at risk', and concluded that the following patterns of involvement in crime are discernible, the crimes being involved mainly with:

- theft, 38%;
- drug dealing, 27%;
- pimping and gambling, 26%;
- forgery, 8%;
- violence, 2%.

The same authors demonstrated that, although violent crimes constitute only a small proportion of the total crime committed by addicts,
none the less addicts commit a significant number of violent offences
each year: between 40 and 50 crime-days per year at risk per addict.
Shaffer found similar 'typologies' of crime, although he discriminated
between more groups, again on the basis of degree of involvement in
crime:[49]

- marginals, 34%;
- drug dealers, 20%;
- thieves, 20%;
- gamblers, pimps and receivers, 14%;
- con men, 5%;
- violent, 3.5%;
- super con men, 2%;
- super violent, 1.5%;

Drug groups

Different classes of drugs may have different routes to violence. Some
consideration is required of these routes and how they relate to the
different effects of the various drugs and drug groups.

Stimulants

A common feature of the stimulants such as cocaine, amphetamines
and MDMA (ecstasy) is that, as dose increases, irritability and
paranoia become evident. At higher doses, a drug-induced psychosis
can occur. The aggression can arise out of the irritability or paranoia,
or from the hallucinations or delusions associated with an induced
psychosis.

Sedatives

The sedatives, the barbiturates and benzodiazepines, are most commonly associated with violence due to the effects of disinhibition after
excessive intake, and in this way are like alcohol.

Opiates

The opiates are not typically associated with violence in any of the states (sought-after effect, intoxication or withdrawal), except where secondary gain is involved; for example, where the possibility of a supply of drugs exists if violence is threatened or applied as in robbery.

Hallucinogens

The hallucinogens are typically associated with apparently unprovoked violence when it is mediated through delusions or hallucinations. Hence, the violence may be qualitatively different and require different precautions and management strategies.

Influence of route of drug use

The different possible routes by which drugs may be taken might be expected to influence aggression and violence because of the different absorption rates, timing and magnitudes of peak levels. Thus, the chewing of coca or the snorting of cocaine might be expected to be less associated with aggression or violence than the injection or inhalation of cocaine by smoking (due to the different bioavailabilities and resulting psychoactive effects).

Gossop and Roy studied males attending a London drug-dependence unit and noted that measures of hostility were significantly higher in intravenous opiate addicts.[44] However, it was not clear whether more hostile individuals tend to inject or injectors become more hostile.

Conclusion

Drug use may thus be seen to have a positive, neutral or negative relationship with aggression and violence in different sets of circumstances. However, the variability of this relationship becomes less confusing when consideration is given to the different drug effects, routes of administration and the nature of the relationships which may exist between use of a drug and violence.

Future study of the interplay between drugs and violence would be enhanced by more specific consideration of individual drugs (or drug combinations), the routes of administration and the particular causal relationship between drug and violence. Without such studies, rhetoric and generalisations are likely to go unchallenged.

References

1. van Praag HM. Serotonergic dysfunction and aggression control (editorial). *Psychol Med* 1991; **21**:15–19
2. Fishbein DH, Lozovsky D, Jaffe JH. Impulsivity, aggression, and neuroendocrine responses to serotonergic stimulation in substance abusers. *Biol Psychiatry* 1989; **25**: 1049–66
3. Strang J, Farrell M, Gossop M, Battersby M. Decriminalizing possession of drugs. *Br Med J* 1989; **299**:320
4. Farrell M, Strang J. Confusion between the drug legalisation and the drug prescribing debate. *Drug Alcohol Rev* 1990; **9**:364–8
5. Advisory Council on the Misuse of Drugs (ACMD). *AIDS and drug misuse: Part I Report*. London: HMSO, 1988
6. MORI. *Survey conducted for the News of the World, including questions about drug use*. London: MORI, 1990 (Available from Institute for the Study of Drug Dependence, London)
7. Jacobs E, Worcester R. The British: drinking and drugs. In: Jacobs E, Worcester R, eds. *We British: Britain under the microscope*. London: Weidenfeld and Nicolson, 1991
8. Gordon AM. Drugs and criminal behaviour. In: Bowden P, Bluglass R, eds. *Principles and practice of forensic psychiatry*. London: Churchill Livingstone, 1990
9. Hammersley R, Morrison V, Davies B, Forsyth A. *Heroin use and crime: a comparison of heroin users and non-users in and out of prison*. Edinburgh: Scottish Office, 1990
10. Gordon AM Drugs and delinquency: a ten-year follow-up of drug clinic patients. *Br J Psychiatry* 1983; **142**:169–73
11. Barton WI. Drug histories and criminality: survey of inmates of state correctional facilities, January 1974. *Int J Addiction* 1980; **15**:233–58
12. Ball JC, Shaffer JW, Nurco DN. The day-to-day criminality of heroin addicts in Baltimore—a study in the continuity of offence rates. *Drug Alcohol Dependence* 1983; **12**:119–42
13. Winick C. A theory of drug dependence based on role, access to, and attitudes towards drugs. In: Lettieri DJ, Sayers, M, Pearson HW, eds. *Theories on drug abuse*. Washington DC: National Institute on Drug Abuse (NIDA), 1980: 225–35
14. Brill H, Hirose T. The rise and fall of a methamphetamine epidemic: Japan 1945–55. *Seminar Psychiatry* (vol 1, no. 2), 1969
15. Robins LJ, Davis DH, Goodwin DW. Drug users in Vietnam: a follow-up on return to USA. *Am J Epidemiology* 1974; **99**:235–49
16. Robins LJ, Helzer JE, Davis DH. Narcotic use in South East Asia and afterwards. *Arch Gen Psychiatry* 1975 **32**:955–61
17. Burr A. The ideologies of despair: a symbolic interpretation of punks' and skinheads' usage of barbiturates. *Social Sci Med* 1984; **19**:929–38
18. Lindqvist P. Homicides committed by abusers of alcohol and illicit drugs. *Br J Addiction* 1991; **86**:321–6
19. Budd RD. Cocaine abuse and violent death. *Am J Drug Alcohol Abuse* 1989; **15**: 375–82
20. Gudjonsson GH. Delinquent boys in Reykjavik: a follow-up study of boys sent to an institution. In: Gunn J, Farrington DP, eds. *Abnormal offenders, delinquency, and the criminal justice system*. Chichester: John Wiley and Sons, 1982
21. Farrell M, Strang J. Substance use and misuse in childhood and adolescence. *J Child Psychiatry* 1991; **32**:109–28
22. Rounsaville BJ, Weismann MM, Wilber CH, Kelber H. Pathways to opiate addiction: an evaluation of different antecedents. *Br J Psychiatry* 1982; **141**:437–46
23. Gunn J. *Violence in human society*. Newton Abbot: David and Charles, 1973
24. Schneidman ES, Farberrow NL. Genuine and simulated suicide notes. In: Schneidman ES, Farberrow NL, eds. *Clues to suicide*. New York: McGraw-Hill, 1957

25. MacDonald I. Drugs, drinking and adolescence. *Am J Dis Children* 1984; **1387**: 117–25

26. Ital TM, Wadud A. Treatment of human aggression with major tranquilizers, antidepressants, and newer psychotropic drugs. *J Nerv Ment Dis* 1975; **160**:83–99

27. Heston IL, Heston R. *The medical casebook of Adolf Hitler*. London: William Kimber, 1979

28. Lion JR. Conceptual issues in the use of drugs for the treatment of aggression in man. *J Nerv Ment Dis* 1975; **160**:76–82

29. Faulk M. *Basic forensic psychiatry*. Oxford: Blackwell Scientific Publications, 1988

30. Watson JM. *Solvent abuse: the adolescent epidemic?* London: Croom Helm, 1986

31. Keup W. Psychotic symptoms due to cannabis abuse. *Dis Nerv System* 1970; **31**: 119–26

32. Dackis CA, Gold MS. Psychiatric hospitals for treatment of dual diagnosis. In: Lowinson JH, Ruiz P, Millman RB, eds. *Substance abuse—a comprehensive textbook*, 2nd edn. Baltimore: Williams & Wilkins, 1992

33. Roth M. Psychopathic (sociopathic) personality. In: Bowden P, Bluglass R, eds. *Principles and practice of forensic psychiatry*. London: Churchill Livingstone, 1990

34. Patch IL. Inadequate personality. In: Bowden P, Bluglass R, eds. *Principles and practice of forensic psychiatry*. London: Churchill Livingstone, 1990

35. Ghodse H. *Drugs and addictive behaviour: a guide to treatment*. Oxford: Blackwell Scientific Publications, 1989

36. Kofoed L, Kania J, Walsh T. Outpatient treatment for patients with substance abuse and co-existing psychiatric disorders. *Am J Psychiatry* 1986; **143**:867–72

37. Connell PH. *Amphetamine psychosis*. Maudsley Monograph 5. London: Chapman and Hall, 1958

38. Coid J, Strang J. Mania secondary to procyclidine (Kemadrin). *Br J Psychiatry* 1982; **141**:81–4

39. Pope HG, Katz DL. Homicide and near homicide by anabolic steroids. *J Clin Psychiatry* 1990; **51**:28–31

40. Ashton H. Benzodiazepine withdrawal: outcome in 50 patients. *Br J Addiction* 1987; **82**:665–71

41. Johnson BD, Goldstein PJ, Preble E, Schmeidler J, Lipton DS, Spunt B, Miller T. *Taking care of business; the economics of crime by heroin abusers*. Lexington, MA: Lexington Books, 1985

42. Gossop M, Eysenck SBG. A comparison of the personality of drug addicts in treatment with that of a prison population. *Personality individual differences* 1983; **4**: 207–9

43. Gossop M, Roy A. Hostility, crime and drug dependence. *Br J Psychiatry* 1977; **130**:272–8

44. Schwartz RH. Marijuana: a crude drug with a spectrum of under-appreciated toxicity. *Pediatrics* 1983; **73**:455–8

45. Carney M. The psychiatry of cannabis abuse. In: Bowden P, Bluglass R, eds. *Principles and practice of forensic psychiatry*. London: Churchill Livingstone, 1990

46. Diagel RD. Anabolic steroids. *J Psychoactive Drugs* 1990; **22**:77–80

47. Stephens RC. *The street addict role: a theory of heroin addiction*. Albany, NY: State University of New York Press, 1991

48. Stimson GV. *Heroin and behaviour*. Shannon: Irish University Press, 1973

49. Shaffer JW, Nurco DN, Kinlock TW. A new classification of narcotic addicts based on type and extent of criminal activity. *Comp Psychiatry* 1984; **25**:315–28

9 | Alcohol and violence

John E. Hodge

Rampton Hospital, Retford, Nottinghamshire

Introduction

According to Collins, the relationship between alcohol and violence has been scientifically investigated for about 45 years.[1] The common and widely-held belief that alcohol consumption causes violence does not appear to fit the accumulated evidence. It seems likely that, while it is relatively easy to demonstrate an association between the two, the nature of the relationship is much more complex than a simple causal one. Despite this lengthy history of research, there is still confusion about the exact nature of this relationship.

Before the influence of alcohol on violent incidents can be investigated, it is necessary first to establish that there is some kind of association between them. In the first part of this chapter I will demonstrate that there is adequate evidence of an association between the use of alcohol and incidents of violence. It is when an attempt is made to understand the nature of this association that it becomes less straightforward. One approach might be to establish what kind of relationships might theoretically exist between the use of alcohol and violence. The first possible relationship is the commonly held view that alcohol *causes* violence. However, at least two other relationships are also possible. First, the relationship between the two may be *incidental*: although the use of alcohol and the occurrence of violence may coincide, the two do not interact with each other but may both separately and independently depend on a third (or more) factor(s). Secondly, the relationship may be *complex*, with elements of both these other two relationships in which some direct relationship between alcohol and violence would be expected but mediated by other factors. It is worth bearing these possibilities in mind while reviewing the evidence.

To examine further the nature of the relationship between alcohol and violence, it is important to define the terminology. Collins makes the point that alcohol can be seen to have two types of effect: acute or chronic.[1] *Acute* effects are where the focus is on the immediate consequences of recent drinking, that is, varying degrees of intoxication. *Chronic* effects are concerned with long-term consequences, such as tolerance and the health problems of protracted drinking. In general, the literature examining the relationship between alcohol and violence tends to focus on the acute rather than the chronic effects of drinking. However, long-term effects of alcohol use are also associated in many cases with behavioural changes and should not be entirely discounted. For example, in a study of domestic violence, Leonard *et al.* found that there was a relationship to long-term pathological drinking, but not to the amount of alcohol use in the past month.[2] Pernanen suggests the possibility that long-term drinking may set up new factors, such as cognitive impairment, which may increase the likelihood of alcohol use leading to violence.[3]

It is also important to be clear about what we mean by violence. Collins has differentiated between 'instrumental' violence and 'expressive' violence.[4] He defines instrumental violence as:

> The use of force or threat to achieve a goal, usually an acquisitive one.[4]

Expressive violence, on the other hand, is defined as:

> ...an actual or attempted physical attack by one or more persons on another person(s) for the purpose of inflicting physical abuse, injury or death and where the attack is not related to an instrumental goal.[4]

In examining the relationship between alcohol and violence, most of the literature tends to focus on the relationship of alcohol with expressive rather than instrumental violence. However, statistics presented by McHugh have clearly demonstrated that alcohol use can also be associated with instrumental violence as well as with other crimes in which no violence is involved.[5]

Alcohol and crime

It is also worth putting the research on the involvement of alcohol in crimes of violence into perspective by contemplating its relationship to crime in general. McHugh summarised 34 studies ranging from homicide and rape to property crime and burglary conducted over the previous 30 years.[5] He noted that, although there was a marked variation between studies of the same crime category, alcohol was almost as likely to be implicated in property crimes as it was in crimes of violence. The variation between studies (between 7% and 39% of sample drinking at the time of offence in two studies of robbery) can largely be accounted for by methodological and sampling differences. While McHugh states that, on average, alcohol was involved in about 50% of all crimes of violence studied, his figures make it clear that there was very little difference between crimes where the violence was expressive (for example, assault, homicide) and those involving instrumental violence (for example, robbery, rape).

Alcohol and violent crime

Many studies have found a consistent relationship between alcohol use and violent incidents. The literature demonstrating this relationship is considerable, so several examples of associations have been selected and categorised under the headings of assault, homicide (including murder and manslaughter), rape, domestic violence, and being a victim of violence.

Assault

There is clear evidence of a consistent association with alcohol use in cases of assault. In a review of seven American studies, Collins found that prisoners with drinking problems have higher assault rates than those without drinking problems.[6] Similarly, Meyer et al. found that approximately two-thirds of perpetrators of police assault had been drinking just prior to the assault,[7] while in a large study in which data on over 10,000 inmates of American prisons were reviewed, just under two-thirds of those convicted of assault were found to have been drinking at the time of the offence.[8]

Homicide

This relatively strong association also holds for homicide. In a study in Sweden of 64 offenders and 71 victims, Lindquist found that two-thirds of the offenders and approximately half their victims had been intoxicated at the time of the offence,[9] while Wolfgang found alcohol to have been involved in almost two-thirds of 588 cases of homicide in Philadelphia.[10]

Rape

The use of alcohol by rapists and their victims also seems fairly well established. Shupe found 50% of men arrested for rape had been drinking, and 45% could be described as intoxicated.[11] Johnson et al. found that 72% of their sample of rapes were associated with alcohol use in offender, victim or both.[12] Using questionnaire data, Rada found 49% of child sexual offenders to have been drinking at the time of the offence, one-third of them heavily.[13] A number of studies of rape have found that where alcohol is involved there is usually greater physical injury to the victim compared to those rapes which do not involve alcohol.[12, 14]

Domestic violence

Studies of domestic violence have also found a consistent relationship with alcohol use. Pizzey found that alcohol had been involved in about 40% of cases of battered wives and children seeking refuge from domestic violence.[15] Other studies have tended to find rates of alcohol involvement of about 50%.[16, 17]

Victims of violence

Alcohol is also associated with being a victim of violence. Garriot *et al.* found alcohol present in 63% of 130 homicide victims,[18] while Goodman *et al.* found detectable alcohol in 46% of several thousand homicide victims, above the legal intoxication limit in 30%.[19] Pernanen found that alcohol was more frequently involved in victim-precipitated homicides, in which the victim was the initial aggressor, than in offender-precipitated homicides.[3]

These and other studies demonstrate a clear and consistent association between alcohol and violent crime. However, this apparently clear relationship is complicated both by the finding that alcohol seems also to be involved in crimes against property where no violence ensues and also by the types of association found.

Types of relationship

Statistically, there are three possible direct functional relationships between alcohol and violence:

- a direct linear relationship;
- an inverse linear relationship; or
- a curvilinear relationship.

A search of the current research literature on alcohol and violence can provide examples of all three types. A direct linear relationship between blood alcohol level and the number of victim injuries was found by Tardiff,[20] but Tinklenberg found a curvilinear relationship between alcohol and violence, with less violence at high levels of intake.[21] A different kind of curvilinear relationship was obtained by Coleman and Straus in their 1979 study investigating domestic violence[22] (cited by Collins[1]). They found that the *rate* of violence increased with drunkenness frequency up to moderate frequencies and then tailed off at high levels. To complicate matters further, a direct but inverse relationship was found between problem drinking and violence in a sample of 1,140 prisoners by Bailey and Collins.[23]

Natural experiments

Perhaps some of the most compelling evidence confirming the link between alcohol and violence is from so-called 'natural experiments', which occur when a social change has resulted in a major change to one of the variables under study. In this case, the natural experiments of interest result in reduction of availability of alcohol.

Two classic studies cited by Pernanen[24] are those of Lenke in Sweden,[25] and Takala in Finland,[26] both of which found that events leading to a reduction in alcohol availability resulted in lower rates of violent crime. Olsson and Wikstrom found that a decision to limit alcohol availability on Saturdays in Sweden by closing state-owned retail stores for several months resulted in a reduced rate of outdoor assaults for all days of the week, and of indoor assaults for Saturdays and Sundays.[27] However, they also found an increase in the rate of indoor assaults for Tuesdays, Wednesdays and Thursdays.

Not all 'natural experiments' have resulted in an overall reduction in violent crime, however. Although the prohibition era in America was associated with a reduction in a number of alcohol-related indices, it was also largely responsible for the development of organised violent crime throughout the USA. This perhaps might suggest that where alcohol availability is reduced on a long-term basis other forces come into play to redress the balance of availability.

A study of the occurrence of alcohol use in violent incidents does not therefore significantly clarify the nature of the relationship between the two variables. An alternative approach would be to examine the relationship from the opposite side, and inspect the occurrence of violent incidents in relation to alcohol consumed.

Violent incidents in relation to alcohol consumed

When the relationship is viewed from this opposite perspective it becomes clear that, while alcohol is common in crimes of violence, violence is very rare in relation to the amount of alcohol consumed. Mott estimated that one UK crime is committed for every 500–600 pints of beer consumed.[28] Violent crime is a relatively small pro-portion of the overall number of crimes committed, so it therefore follows that the amount of alcohol consumed per single violent crime is proportionately larger. Unfortunately, very few observational studies have been undertaken on drinkers in their natural environment.[5]

In summary, when the relationship between alcohol and violence is studied by examining violent incidents, there is some evidence that violence is associated with alcohol use—but this evidence includes support for all the possible kinds of relationships. Alcohol is also found to be implicated in non-violent crimes, albeit to a lesser extent. On the other hand, when the relationship is studied by examining the rate of violent incidents associated with alcohol use, violence is found to be an extremely rare outcome of alcohol consumption. As much of the empirical evidence is obtained from arrested and convicted criminals, a number of authors have suggested that the relationship between alcohol and violence may be spurious and merely reflects the possibility that alcohol reduces criminal competence and increases risk of arrest. However, since violence seems to be greater in crimes where alcohol is used than in similar crimes where it is not (for example rape[12,14]), it seems unlikely that the relationship between the two is simply *incidental*.

Theoretical perspectives

Several different theories attempting to establish the causal role of alcohol and violence have developed over the years.

Moral theory

Probably the first was the pre-scientific 'moral theory' which held that drinking loosens moral restraints, with the result that individuals who drink lose personal control and, as a result, engage in immoral behaviours, including violence. While this theory has little scientific validity, it is still popular and its prevalence should not be underestimated, not only in society as a whole but also among social service and health practitioners. Labelling alcohol as the culprit provides a convenient scapegoat for violent acts.

Disinhibition theory

Possibly the most established scientific theory of a causal relationship between alcohol and violence is the 'disinhibition theory'. This states that behavioural constraints are loosened by the pharmacological action of alcohol, and violence then results. However, the theory appears to imply that aggression is a natural state which is normally held in check (possibly by some socialisation process), and which can be released by the pharmacological effects of alcohol. Unfortunately (for the theory), there is little evidence that aggression or violence is a normal human state. Indeed, Blackburn has suggested that aggression is not a biological given (although anger might be).[29]

Sobell and Sobell suggested that alcohol may directly act on the inhibitory control of the cerebral cortex over the lower brain centres and thus disinhibit aggressive urges.[30] However, no empirical evidence has been obtained which either supports or refutes this hypothesis.[24]

Stimulation theory

Brain has suggested that public perception implies a third theory, which might be called 'stimulation theory'.[31] This theory implies that alcohol acts directly to stimulate 'aggression mechanisms'. However, Brain has criticised this model as being physiologically simplistic, pointing out that if the nature of the relationship between alcohol and violence is to be understood, base rates both of alcohol and of violence at the time of the incident must be taken into account. He suggests that if, for example, on a Saturday night a lot of alcohol is consumed by many people, and at the same time violent incidents are perpetrated by a few, the fact that those perpetrators are drunk at the time of those incidents provides little information on the relationship between alcohol and violence.

However, some versions of the stimulation theory have suggested that alcohol may directly stimulate aggression in individuals who may in some way be more biologically sensitive to its effects. A particular example of this is the theory of pathological intoxication, which suggests that a small proportion of individuals are particularly prone to become excessively aggressive under the influence of alcohol. Some research has been undertaken on this condition, particularly by Maletzsky who studied a sample of 22 individuals with a history of violent and bizarre behaviour under the influence of alcohol (but not when sober), and who had no evidence of neurological impairment.[32] An alcohol infusion was given under laboratory conditions. Fifteen of the group became what Maletzsky described as 'psychotic', nine of whom showed inappropriate rage. However, his conclusions have been criticised by Coid, who points out that other studies have failed to replicate Maletzsky's results, thus raising the question of whether there is a genuine syndrome of pathological intoxication.[33]

Another form of stimulation theory was examined by Herman *et al.*[35] They investigated the suggestion that alcohol might provoke aggression through the mechanism of hypoglycaemia, which is occasionally associated with aggression and violence. However, their results offered little support for this idea as they found the overall prevalence of hypoglycaemia in alcoholics is fairly low.

In conclusion, it seems that theories attempting to explain a direct causal relationship between alcohol and violence are generally physiologically simplistic.[31] Few of the theories have any significant empirical support at the present time. It seems unlikely then that there is a simple *causal* relationship between alcohol and violence.

Other factors which may explain the relationship between alcohol and violence

Collins has listed seven factors which may help to account for the observed close relationship in criminal populations between alcohol and violence.[1] The first is the simple physiological effects of alcohol, such as impaired reaction time. It seems unlikely, though, that these effects will lead directly to violence, although it is possible that poor co-ordination may result in a more extreme violent outcome than was perhaps the original intention. Similarly, Pernanen's hypothesis that cognitive impairment may be important in understanding the relationship between alcohol and violence has little supportive evidence.[3] In fact, one study cited earlier suggests that less violence is associated with higher frequencies of drunkenness, at least in the domestic situation.[22] Furthermore, most violence is perpetrated by young male drinkers who are less likely to be suffering from the chronic cognitive impairment more often associated with older drinkers. It is only when he turns to situational and psychological variables that Collins identifies factors which help explain the association between alcohol and violence.[1] One of these is the drinking situation itself. In this case, it is fairly clear that situations do influence the association between violence and alcohol. Alcohol use in some situations (for example, at football matches) is more likely to be associated with violence than in others (for example, party-going). Cultural factors would also appear to be associated with the levels of violence after drinking. After-drinking violence is more common in some cultures, such as the Scottish, Irish and Finnish, than in others. However, there are also many differences in the rules governing permissible behaviour after drinking both between cultures and between different situations within the same culture.

One major factor which may have particularly important implications is the individual's expectancy of the outcome of drinking. If, as seems likely, there is a generally held belief that violence and alcohol are associated, this is likely to affect both the behaviour of the drinker and the interpretations of his/her behaviour by observers. These expectancy factors may lead to a different kind of relationship in which the individual deliberately makes use of alcohol to facilitate either violence or crime. For example, it has been suggested that some football supporters deliberately drink in order to reduce the pain likely to be incurred by fighting, while Cordelia has found that many offenders use alcohol to steady their nerves or to make them more ready to take risks.[35]

Predisposing factors

In summary, to date the nature of the relationship between alcohol and violence is still unclear. While there seems to be a high relationship in criminal populations, this is not reflected when the relationship is considered from the perspective of the amount of alcohol drunk. Furthermore, the type of relationship is uncertain, and theories attempting to explain the relationship are currently generally unsatisfactory. There are other factors which might mediate in the relationship, but few can account for the wide range of research results so far found. At the same time, the general outcome of 'natural experiments' would suggest that a reduction in alcohol availability has the effect, temporarily at least, of reducing violent crime.

Individual differences

So far no particular aspects of the individual perpetrator him/herself have been considered. Many studies have examined personality factors in violent criminals and also in problem drinkers without coming to any firm conclusions. There does seem, however, to be a dearth of studies comparing young people who are violent under the influence of alcohol with those who are not, while controlling for the other effects such as situation and quantity.

One study which throws some light on this relationship is that of Kroll *et al.* They compared the behaviour of adult alcoholic men who were physically abused as children to that of a control sample of alcoholics with no history of abuse and an age-matched sample of non-alcoholics.[36] They found that the abused group demonstrated significantly more legal difficulties (mostly assaults), domestic violence, violence in general and destructiveness compared to both sets of controls. The abused group also had higher levels of serious suicide attempts and high levels of pervasive anxiety. This study is unique in investigating violence while controlling for alcohol intake.

I have argued elsewhere that being traumatised by physical violence may in some circumstances lead to a form of 'addiction' to violence in which individuals may seek out violent experiences.[37] This reaction may be seen in battle-traumatised Vietnam veterans,[38] and may be a cause of criminal violence.[39] Most of Solursh's sample of 100 veterans displayed this reaction and a considerable number (69%) also developed an alcohol problem after returning from Vietnam. In this group, an outsider may well see a close relation between the violence and the alcohol use, although in fact both may be independently related to the experience of violent trauma.

Conclusion

While there is no direct confirmation of the causal relationship between alcohol and violence, it appears very likely that a relationship does exist which is mediated by other variables. There is evidence that situational, cultural and expectancy factors have a strong influence on the association between the two, but it is also possible that individual factors such as the experience of extreme violence, as indicated by other post-trauma symptoms, may also be important or even necessary for this relationship to exist. Considerable further work needs to be done to investigate this kind of mediating variable, and in particular controlled research examining differences in the use of violence in different populations with a high intake of alcohol. On current information, however, it seems probable that the *level* of violence, if not necessarily the *occurrence*, may be increased when alcohol is involved.

References

1. Collins JJ. Alcohol and interpersonal violence: less than meets the eye. In: Weiner NA, Wolfgang ME, eds. *Pathways to criminal violence*. Newbury Park, CA: Sage, 1989
2. Leonard KE, Bromet EJ, Parkinson DK, Day NL, Ryan CM. Patterns of alcohol use and physically aggressive behaviour in men. *J Stud Alcohol* 1985; **46**: 279–82
3. Pernanen K. Alcohol and crimes of violence. In: Kissin B, Begleiter H, eds. *The biology of alcoholism (vol 4: Social aspects)*. New York: Plenum Press, 1976
4. Collins JJ. Alcohol use and expressive interpersonal violence. In: Gottheil E, Druley KA, Skoloda TE, Waxman HM, eds. *Alcohol, drug abuse and aggression*. Springfield, IL: Charles C. Thomas, 1983
5. McHugh MJ. *The role of alcohol in crime—a review of the evidence*. Paper presented at the British Psychological Society annual conference, St Andrews, 1989
6. Collins JJ. The relationship of problem drinking to individual offending sequences. In: Blumstein A, Cohen J, Roth J, Visher CA, eds. *Criminal careers and career criminals (vol 2)*. Washington DC: National Academy Press, 1986
7. Meyer C, Magedanz T, Keiselhorst DS, Chapman SG. *A social psychological analysis of police assailants*. Norman: University of Oklahoma, Bureau of Government Research, 1978
8. US Department of Justice, Bureau of Justice Statistics. *Prisoners and alcohol*. Washington DC: US Department of Justice, 1983 (cited by Collins[1])
9. Lindquist P. Criminal homicide in northern Sweden, 1970–1981—alcohol intoxication, alcohol abuse and mental disease. *Int J Law Psychiatry* 1986; **8**: 19–37
10. Wolfgang ME. *Patterns in criminal homicide*. Montclair NJ: Patterson Smith, 1975
11. Shupe LM. Alcohol and crime. *J Crim Law, Criminol Police Sci* 1954; **44**: 661–4
12. Johnson SD, Gibson L, Linden R. Alcohol and rape in Winnipeg, 1966–1975. *J Stud Alcohol* 1978; **39**:1887–94
13. Rada T. Alcoholism and forcible rape. *Am J Psychiatry* 1975; **132**:444–6
14. Amir M. Alcohol and forcible rape. *Br J Addict* 1967; **62**:219–32
15. Pizzey E. *Scream quietly or the neighbours will hear*. Harmondsworth, Middlesex: Penguin Books, 1974

16. Byles JA. Violence, alcohol problems and other problems in disintegrating families. *J Stud Alcohol* 1978; **39**:551–3

17. Emerson CD. Family violence: a study by the Los Angeles County Sheriff's Department. *Police Chief* 1979; **46**:48–50

18. Garriot JC, DeMaio VJM, Rodriguez RG. Detection of cannabinoids in homicide victims and motor vehicle fatalities. *J Forensic Sci* 1986; **31**:1274–82

19. Goodman, RA, Mercy JA, Loya F *et al*. Alcohol use and interpersonal violence— alcohol detected in homicide victims. *Am J Public Health* 1986; **76**:144–9

20. Tardiff G. *Les Délits de violence à Montreal*. Paper presented at the 5th Research Conference on Criminality and Delinquency. Quebec: Quebec Society of Criminology, 1967 (cited by McHugh[5])

21. Tinklenberg JR. Alcohol and violence. In: Bourne PG, Fox R, eds. *Alcoholism— progress in research and treatment*. New York: Academic Press, 1973

22. Coleman DH, Straus MA. *Alcohol abuse and family violence*. Paper presented at the annual meeting of the American Sociological Association, Boston, 1979 (cited by Collins[1])

23. Bailey SL, Collins JJ. *A refinement of alcohol disorder measures and a test of their relationship to violent behaviour*. Research Triangle Park, NC: Research Triangle Institute, 1987

24. Pernanen K. Theoretical aspects of the relationship between alcohol use and crime. In: Collins JJ, ed. *Drinking and crime: Perspectives on the relationships between alcohol consumption and criminal behaviour*. London: Tavistock Publications, 1982

25. Lenke L. *Violent crime and alcohol: a study of the developments in assaultative crime*. Stockholm: Department of Criminology, University of Stockholm, 1971

26. Takala H. The effect of the alcohol strike on reported crime. *Alkoholpolitik* 1973; **36**:14–16

27. Olsson O, Wikstrom POH. Effects of the experimental Saturday closing of liquor retail stores in Sweden. *Contemp Drug Prob* 1982; 325–53

28. Mott J. *The relationship between alcohol use and crime: a literature review*. Paper presented at the British Criminology Society conference, Sheffield, July 1987

29. Blackburn R. Personality and violence. This publication, Chapter 7

30. Sobell LC, Sobell MB. Drunkenness, a 'special circumstance' in crimes of violence: sometimes. *Int J Addict* 1975; **10**:869–82

31. Brain PF. Multidisciplinary examination of the 'causes' of crime: the case of the link between alcohol and violence. *Alcohol Alcohol* 1986; **21**:237–40

32. Maletzsky BM. The diagnosis of pathological intoxication. *J Stud Alcohol* 1976; **37**: 1215–28

33. Coid J. *Mania à potu*: a critical review of pathological intoxication. *Psychol Med* 1979; **9**:709–19

34. Herman V, Sekso M, Trinajstic M, Vidovic V, Cabrijan T. Hypoglycaemic conditions in the course of chronic alcoholism. *Alcoholism* 1970; **6**:87–90

35. Cordelia A. Alcohol and property crime: explaining the causal nexus. *J Stud Alcohol* 1985; **46**:161–71

36. Kroll PD, Stock DF, James ME. The behaviour of alcoholic men abused as children. *J Nerv Ment Dis* 1985; **173**:689–93

37. Hodge JE. Addiction to violence: a new model of psychotherapy. *Crim Behav Ment Health* 1992; **2**:212–23

38. Solursh L. Combat addiction: overview of implications in symptom maintenance and treatment planning. *J Traum Stress* 1989; **2**:451–62

39. Collins JJ, Bailey SL. Traumatic stress disorder and violent behaviour. *J Traum Stress* 1990; **3**:203–20

Part 3

Victims and survivors: shifting the focus of concern

Pamela J. Taylor

Head of Medical Services, Special Hospitals Service Authority, London

A victim-centred approach to the understanding of violence seems sufficiently important at all levels for it to be almost unbelievable that until the 1980s the caring professions, criminologists, the criminal justice system and society more generally have tended at worst to vilify victims and at best to ignore them. In spite of a recognition over many years that traumatic events cause psychological as well as physical suffering, there has generally been little attempt by doctors or allied professionals to do more than patch up any physical damage, and perhaps later to support or refute claims for compensation.

The concept of a 'compensation neurosis' itself seems to have hostile overtones. It certainly allows doctors to deny the possibility that they may have a role in this field beyond selling reports to lawyers in compensation cases. Kelly described the failure of the medical profession to offer treatment for the psychological problems of accident survivors, coupled with exhortations to the patients to 'pull themselves together'.[1] Terr suggested more positive motives for denying medical attention, but with the same end result of failing to meet need.[2] In seeking to reassure families with children who had been distressed by a school-bus kidnapping, doctors assured them that almost no one would have problems. Unwittingly, they delayed help for the children, because nobody wanted to admit their child was the exception. As recently as 1987, McFarlane *et al.* found their attempts to follow up children involved in an Australian bush fire were blocked because teachers 'could not see the need for such continuing research'.[3] Although the longer-term effects on children of such a disaster are unclear, Terr found that the children had made little progress after four years.[2] There is now good evidence that the untreated effects of sexual or physical assault can put people so abused at substantial long-term risk for serious mental illness (e.g. ref. 4) or behaviour disorder (e.g. ref. 5).

The work of criminologists is generally offender-focused, yet those who have broken free and pursued a victim-centred approach have plainly had an advantage in terms of the completeness of samples for studying the epidemiology and sociology of violence (e.g. ref. 6 and 7). Criminals, by definition, have first to be caught. A victim-centred approach shrinks the impact of the dark figure of unrecorded crime on general prevalence estimates. The privacy of a research interview is more likely to reveal the extensive role of intimates in the perpetration of violence. Such perpetrators are commonly protected by their victim from being reported to police, and thus from official crime statistics, for many and complex reasons, which certainly include a mixture of loyalty and continuing fear. In this section, Elizabeth Stanko's chapter explores these more private areas of danger.

Shapland *et al.* are prominent among those who have not only highlighted the negligible role and resources for victims in the criminal justice system, but also the compounding of distress that this can bring.[8] Since private prosecutions have become unusual, the victim of crime is often deprived of the opportunity to hear of the progress of any enquiry into offence(s) he reports, and is not necessarily called to court in the event of a case coming to trial. If he is, he has no entitlement to legal support or representation, and minimal protection against defamation of character or abilities. The alleged offender, by contrast, is legally entitled to be informed of his rights and of the facts in the case against him. He is entitled to legal representation leading up to and throughout the court hearing. Any disability in relation to the court hearing or the alleged offence is treated sympathetically, while the revelation to the court of antecedent behaviours is barred until the trial is complete and unless a conviction is recorded. Considerable efforts have been made to redress this balance between victim and offender, but the disproportionate power of the perpetrator surfaces even within these efforts. Davis *et al.* showed how readily reparation schemes intended primarily for helping the victim have slipped into services for diverting the offender from custody.[9] The demonstration of the offender's remorse and of sensitivity in his behaviour toward victims—his own or those of others—has become an end in itself.

Although efforts towards change continue, society's essential callousness towards the victim remains demonstrable in many ways. Among them are the almost macabre intensity of curiosity at the fresh scene of any disaster or crime, but the transience of that attention. Perhaps the pain of identification with the injured or bereaved is just too hard to sustain. More difficult to understand is the frequently open spite of some of the general public directed at individual victims, fanned almost by a variant of envy. Woe betide any survivor of a disaster who is honoured for bravery, perhaps saving fellow victims.

Often hounded by some types of journalist for their 'human interest' story, family, friends and neighbours quickly tire of the intrusions and fame alike. Even children at school may find themselves objects of persecution or ridicule because of their father or mother's heroism, a feat which may have somehow disrupted their usual status 'in the pack', so that they 'need bringing down again'. Worse, society as a whole, as well as individuals within it, is content to collude with the continuing victimisation of the exceptionally damaged. Babington recorded how many officers in World War I, who had wandered from their posts in a state of mental abnormality, were shot as deserters.[10] Within the last decade Lewis *et al.*, in the USA, have drawn attention to the depths of physical and emotional damage not infrequently inflicted by their families[11] in young death-row inmates. Those families try to conceal it and, in pursuing the death penalty for these juvenile offenders, society in these states is colluding with that abuse.

Each of the chapters in this section is written by someone who has recognised need in people who have been exceptionally traumatised. After war, natural and man-made disasters have perhaps had the greatest impact on the learning curve of clinicians and non-clinicians alike. Quantity has had an impact where individual distress has gone almost unremarked. Alexander concluded his account of the *Piper Alpha* oil-rig disaster in the North Sea, in which 167 people lost their lives, with a poignant reminder:

> About 4 months before the so-called Piper Alpha disaster, a single worker received fatal injuries on the installation, but few people know ... Certainly she (his widow) was not inundated with offers of help or counselling ...[12]

Barry Webb's account of one of the worst English transport disasters of the 1980s heads the section, not only because of the power of his personal account, but also because it is almost invariably the police who are first on the scene of any disaster, and indeed are immediately looked to for their organisational abilities. (For a description of the medical responses, see Burns and Hollins.[13])

It is apparent from his account that there is growing police recognition of the needs of survivors beyond mere physical rescue, and of the stresses on their own personnel. Sensitivity to the importance of hard, practical measures, such as the rapid and decent return to their families of the bodies of the dead, means that clear outcome criteria for this part of the police operation can be set and tested. The provision of softer necessities including support, explicitly to fill the gap between the disaster and the organisation and provision of professional counsellors, has not been forgotten. The potential toll of disasters on the rescuers as well as on the rescued has been recognised, although the evidence for consequent pathology is mixed and may depend more on research methodology, including duration of follow up, than on reality (e.g. ref. 14, 15 and 16). Possible ways of preparing for such stress have been explored.[17] Police leadership in meeting the needs of victims has not been confined to the scene of multiple victim disasters. Another officer, Ian Blair, pressed the case for a change in police practice in the provision of services for women who have been raped.[18]

Following the spate of disasters in the UK, British health authorities have been forced to start to formulate plans for responding, at least in terms of the treatment of physical injury. As the organisation of health services changes again, it will be important to take full account of the range of need and the lessons learned so far. A full response to large-scale trauma is possible only with extensive inter-service co-operation—within, between and beyond elements of the health service.

Kinston and Rosser formulated a proposal for planning services on the basis that three classes of disorder have to be addressed: disorder caused by the trauma, precipitated by it, *and* disorder that would have occurred at that time anyway.[19] They made specific proposals for appropriate psychiatrist-led evaluation of need at such times—which, indeed, Rosser and colleagues have had subsequent cause to test, since the King's Cross railway station fire occurred within the health district linked to their university department.[20] In a station used by an estimated average of 40,000 people every rush hour, 31 died, seven survivors suffered major injuries, and over 600 people felt themselves close enough to events to make statements to a public enquiry. The department offered pro-active screening and interventions, showing a high rate of probable 'caseness': that is, people with substantial symptoms, requesting services, or both. One of the most revealing comments was, 'The psychological aftermath peaked at the first and second anniversaries but we are still (three years later) receiving seriously ill new referrals'. This is not an unfamiliar experience for those who have worked with similar groups. It was our experience at the Institute of Psychiatry with many of the survivors and bereaved of the *Herald of Free Enterprise* ferry disaster off the coast of Belgium, also in 1987.

Freeman has described the drawing together of the Lothians (Scotland) social work department, mental health unit and voluntary resources together with the emergency services in formulating and implementing a post-disaster counselling service.[21] The planning followed the *Piper Alpha* oil-rig disaster, but again it has, sadly, been amply tested since, with a range of small to large disasters including the Jumbo jet which crashed at Lockerbie.

The impact of interventions remains less clear. Reports of the consequences of victimisation, whether by war, disaster, crime or accident, are depressingly consistent in their repetitive capacity for describing the features of the psychiatric disorders that follow, but light on the delivery and evaluation of treatment. The complexity of achieving the latter, however, should not be underestimated (e.g. ref. 22). Bill Yule's paper in this section thus provides a refreshing difference in highlighting the nature and effects of psychological approaches to management. The use of medication to treat established disorder has been reviewed elsewhere, by Friedman,[23] Kolb,[24] and Silver *et al.*[25] The consensus is that drugs which are effective for both panic disorder *and* depression are likely to be of most value, but in many, perhaps most, cases treatment is unlikely to be satisfactory unless there is sufficient flexibility to combine the use of medication and psychological approaches to treatment. (For a fuller review of current models for understanding post-traumatic mental states, with the range of treatment approaches see also ref. 26.)

It is perhaps worth returning to the earlier point that, whereas the drama of multiple victimisation after a major episode brings at least some attention, singleton victims tend to be more neglected. Bill Yule's chapter highlights important similarities between the two groups, while Elizabeth Stanko's paper focuses firmly on the individual. If disasters threaten to overwhelm rescuers as well as primary victims by the range and quantity of shared damage, many victims of criminal activity, and in particular those offended against by their intimates, are threatened by an overwhelming experience of another kind—the range and duration of the threat. Survivor guilt in one form or another is a well recognised and fairly common phenomenon in relation to almost any major trauma, but becomes very special when compounded by the secrecy often shared with the perpetrator of the abuse as part of the survival mechanism.

Even professional groups can become blinded by the realities of risk to personal safety and integrity, and need reminding that young men are far more vulnerable to physical assault than old women,[6] as are people known to each other rather than strangers. Another reality, however, that Stanko begins to address is the relative poverty of information about the sexual abuse of boys and young men, and its impact on subsequent pathology. Nobody has studied such an association within unbiased samples of men, as now has been done among women (e.g. ref. 4, 27 and 28). Indeed, while it may be an accident of the changing economic climate, it is striking that at least two eminent researchers, with a good track record of such work, have applied unsuccessfully for the necessary financial support to conduct almost identical work among men.

This brief background to the roles for the medical and allied professionals in meeting the needs of victims of any kind would not be complete without a mention of the legal and institutional issues. Reference has already been made to the peripheral role of the victim in criminal cases. Nevertheless, from time to time, there may be a requirement from the courts for medical reports to advise on victim witness competence (see ref. 26). This is particularly likely to arise in relation to those with a mental disorder, or to children. For England and Wales, the Criminal Justice Act 1991 abolished the presumption that children are necessarily not competent as witnesses. It has also allowed them to give evidence on videotape. Few healthy victim witnesses, however, will feel they have sufficient knowledge or experience to handle their court appearance with confidence. In the USA, victim witness schemes—and even victim advocacy schemes—have developed. Such informing and supportive arrangements are much less organised in the UK, but are sometimes available as one of the main services provided by voluntary agencies. Many of the best of them are established under the umbrella of the National Association of Victims Support Schemes (see ref. 29 for an account of their development).

The other major area of medico-legal work in this field relates to compensation.[26,30] A state-funded scheme—the Criminal Injuries Compensation Board (CIB)—makes provision for modest recompense for victims of crime who suffer serious losses or personal injury. There is a lower limit for awards that can be made, which is increased regularly. The criminal courts, however, may order compensation—indeed, since 1988 they have been obliged to consider it. Such awards are generally for lesser amounts, made without reference to the CIB, and often to come from the offender. The victim of crime, as well as of accident or disaster, may also have recourse to the civil court. In disaster cases, procedures have been developed in England to allow for a large number of cases to be dealt with simultaneously, based on test case arbitration. The courts—or arbitrators—generally award higher sums in compensation than the CIB, but monies which none the less seem derisory compared with the sums awarded in libel cases. The preparation of medico-legal reports in these circumstances is the only moderately long established aspect of medical input for victims. While the provision of medical reports in this context is undeniably important work, it is time to recognise that the provision of wider services, and especially treatment services consequent upon appropriate evaluation, has become far more pressing. The Home Office has now published a Victim's Charter which, while naturally emphasising roles for those under its own aegis, makes plain the range of need.[31] The chapters in this section amply illustrate the true justice in this approach.

References

1. Kelly R. The post-traumatic syndrome: an iatrogenic disease. *Forensic Sci* 1975; **6**: 17–24
2. Terr LC. Chowchilla revisited: the effects of psychic trauma four years after a school-bus kidnapping. *Am J Psychiatry* 1983; **140**:1543–50
3. McFarlane AC, Policansky SK, Irwin C. A longitudinal study of the psychological morbidity in children, due to a natural disaster. *Psychol Med* 1987; **17**:727–38
4. Mullen PE, Romans-Clarkson SE, Walton VA, Herbison GP. Impact of sexual and physical abuse on women's mental health. *Lancet* 1988; **ii**:841–5
5. Hodge JE. Addiction to violence: a new model of psychopathy. *Crim Behav Mental Health* 1992; **2**:212–23
6. Hough M, Mayhew P. *The British Crime Survey* (first report). Home Office Research Study No. 76. London: HMSO, 1983
7. Smith DA, Jarjoura GR. Social structure and criminal victimisation. *J Res Crime Deliquency* 1988; **25**:27–52
8. Shapland J, Willmore J, Duff P. *Victims in the criminal justice system.* Cambridge studies in criminology No. 53. London: Gower, 1985
9. Davis G, Boucherat J, Watson D. Reparation in the service of diversion: the subordination of a good idea. *Howard J Crim Justice* 1988; **27**:127–34
10. Babington A. *For the sake of example.* London: Paladin, 1985
11. Lewis DO, Pincus JH, Bard B, *et al.* Neuropsychiatric, psychoeducational, and family characteristics of 14 juveniles condemned to death in the United States. *Am J Psychiatry* 1988; **145**:584–9
12. Alexander DA. Psychiatric intervention after the Piper Alpha disaster. *J Roy Soc Med* 1991; **84**:8–11
13. Burns TP, Hollins SC. Psychiatric response to the Clapham rail crash. *J Roy Soc Med* 1991; **84**:15–9
14. Jones DR. Secondary disaster victims: the emotional effects of recovering and identifying human remains. *Am J Psychiatry* 1985; **142**:303–7
15. McFarlane AC. The longitudinal course of post-traumatic morbidity. The range of outcomes and their predictors. *J Nerv Mental Dis* 1988; **176**:30–9
16. Alexander DA, Wells A. Reactions of police officers to body-handling after a major disaster. A before and after comparison. *Br J Psychiatry* 1991; **159**:547–55
17. Meichenbaum D. *Stress inoculation training.* Oxford: Pergamon Press, 1985
18. Blair I. *Investigating rape.* Beckenham: Croom Helm, 1985
19. Kinston W, Rosser R. Disaster: effects on mental and physical state. *J Psychosom Res* 1974; **18**:437–56
20. Rosser R, Dewar S, Thompson J. Psychological aftermath of the King's Cross fire. *J Roy Soc Med* 1991; **84**:4–8
21. Freeman CP. Lothians post disaster counselling service *Psychiatr Bull* 1992; **16**: 492–5
22. Roth S, Dye E, Lebowitz L. Group therapy for sexual assault victims. *Psychotherapy* 1988; **25**:82–93
23. Friedman MJ. Toward rational pharmacotherapy for post-traumatic stress disorder: an interim report. *Am J Psychiatry* 1988; **145**:281–92
24. Kolb LC. Chronic post-traumatic stress disorder: implications of recent epidemiological and neuropsychological studies. *Psychol Med* 1989; **19**:821–4
25. Silver JM, Sandberg DP, Hales RE. New approaches in the pharmacotherapy of post traumatic stress disorder. *J Clin Psychiatry* 1990; **51**(suppl):33–8
26. Taylor PJ, Gunn J, Mezey G. Victims and survivors. In: Gunn J, Taylor PJ, eds. *Forensic psychiatry: clinical, legal and ethical issues.* Oxford: Butterworth-Heinemann, Ch 23:885–944 1993
27. Harter S, Alexander PC, Neimeyer RA. Long term effects of incestuous child abuse in college women: social adjustment, social cognition and family characteristics. *J Consult Clin Psychol* 1988; **56**:5–8
28. West DJ, ed. *Sexual victimisation.* Aldershot: Gower, 1985

29. Mawby RI, Gill ML. *Crime victims*. London: Tavistock Publications, 1987
30. Gunn J, Briscoe O, Carson D, *et al*. The law, adult mental disorder and the psychiatrist in England and Wales. In: Gunn J, Taylor PJ, eds. *Forensic psychiatry: ethical, clinical and legal issues*. Oxford: Butterworth-Heinemann, Ch 2:21–117 1993
31. Home Office. *Victim's charter*. London: Home Office, 1990

10 | Managing disasters and stress in police officers involved in the aftermath

Barry Webb
Detective Superintendent, Metropolitan Police, London

Introduction

On 12 December 1988 at 8.10 am a rail accident occurred on the British Rail track just outside Clapham Junction railway station when one passenger train collided into the rear of another. It is believed that collectively the two passenger trains were carrying about 1,400 passengers at the time of the collision.

A total of 35 people died (33 at the scene and 2 subsequently in hospital). All the dead were adults, of whom 26 were men and 9 women. One hundred and thirty-two people were taken to hospitals, 31 seriously injured and 101 slightly injured. Many more passengers received minor injuries that did not require immediate hospital treatment.

I attended the scene of the crash about 9 am, and was given responsibility for casualty clearance, identification of the dead, notification to next-of-kin and provision of welfare facilities to the bereaved.

This chapter describes my experiences and those of my colleagues who worked with me during the aftermath of the accident.

Experiences at the crash scene

On arriving at the scene of the crash, my first impression was of 'organised chaos'—everyone seemed to know what they were doing. I felt a need to create an impact by changing things—something that fortunately I resisted.

One of my first actions was to visit the temporary mortuary that had been set up in a servicemen's club about 150 metres away. My initial horror and shock on seeing the extent of the injuries quickly and involuntarily changed to clinical detachment, and I began to see the bodies in terms of the identification numbers they received as they were brought into the mortuary. Several of my colleagues reacted similarly; this will be discussed later.

147

Only people who have witnessed a major disaster can truly appreciate the difficult circumstances in which the rescuers operate. This is illustrated by the several requests I received from people in authority to see the bodies in the temporary mortuary because they suspected a relative may have been on the train, whereas those of us who had seen the state of many of the bodies realised it would be a futile and traumatic exercise.

It is pertinent to mention that the first police response to major disasters is often from young police officers. For three young officers, the Clapham accident happened on their first day of police duty on the street. One of these officers told me two years after the incident that he still has the occasional 'flashback', and also that a certain indiscernible smell instantly reminds him of the appalling scene he was confronted with on his arrival. Of course, officers are helped to overcome the initial shock by having plenty of immediate action to keep them occupied. I was fully committed from the time of my arrival at the crash scene until I returned to the police incident room at 8.30 pm. I found it extremely difficult, if not impossible, to 'switch off' in the next few hours and, after arriving home at about midnight, was unable to sleep. My overriding fear was that I had not done everything that I should have—a fear not based on any disciplinary worry, but on the belief that I had let people down. In subsequent discussions, similar fears have been expressed to me by other officers who have had responsibilities like mine at major disasters.

The need for immediate debriefing of officers

One of the lessons from Clapham is the need for officers involved with the rescue operation, in whatever way, to be debriefed before they go off duty. This did not happen at Clapham, with the result that a number of officers had no opportunity to begin to offload their feelings of frustration, anger and helplessness.

The worst case was a young police constable who did not get near the immediate crash site as he was ordered to divert traffic at a location some distance from the scene. Over the next few days he heard his colleagues talk about their 'hands on' experiences at the scene and saw numerous television reports about the rescue operation. He began to experience a strong sense that he had not done enough. Over a period of weeks his health deteriorated, and it was only his mother seeking medical help that saved him suffering a full mental breakdown.

It is my view that *all* officers should be debriefed before they go off duty and asked to talk through their experiences—a debrief avoids the perceived stigma of counselling for signs of stress. The police service has still not fully accepted that stress is a medical problem and not a sign of weakness. The debrief would be a two-way process, because it is valuable for a police record to be kept of the actions of individual officers at the scene of major disasters.

Involvement in mortuary procedures

About ten officers were engaged in the mortuary procedures over a period of two days, each day consisting of about 13 hours. A conscious decision (which turned out to be correct) was taken not to relieve these officers, but to allow them to complete the task. These officers felt they had made a full contribution to the rescue operation, and were able to provide continuity in the complicated post mortem process.

At the end of this period the temptation was resisted to allow the officers involved to take an extended break from police duties. Instead, during the following three days, they were invited to talk over their experiences both within their own group and with other officers. This provided a forum to talk through their feelings, and an opportunity for the police service to identify signs of stress in individual cases. To my knowledge, none of the officers engaged in the mortuary process has suffered long-term problems as a result of his or her distressing experiences.

Compulsory counselling

A decision was made that all police personnel involved in the rescue operation would receive compulsory counselling by the Metropolitan Police Welfare Branch. This took place about one week after the rail crash. It was confidential, so the success or otherwise of this procedure cannot be assessed. However, I did not derive much benefit from it, a significant reason, among others, being that it was given in the false environment of a police station, with the officers filing in one after the other. I also believe that to achieve success in the counselling process, the individual himself has to want to help—which militates against compulsory counselling.

Support to the bereaved

Although not strictly within my remit, I want to mention some of the ways in which police officers provided support to those who were bereaved as a result of the rail crash. A primary objective I set the police team under my command was to establish a system of identification and welfare support to provide a short-term framework for reducing the trauma suffered by relatives. It was a short-term strategy because I believe that medium- and long-term support of relatives is the responsibility of the appropriate social services department and of specialists in counselling the bereaved.

All the victims were identified by a close relative (in most cases the spouse) on the day following the rail crash. This was usually not done by visual identification, because of the injuries suffered by those who died, but by other methods such as identification of clothing, jewellery and correspondence, and by fingerprints and unusual marks or scars.

Each family attending the incident room to identify a relative was dealt with by a dedicated police officer who, prior to the arrival of the relative(s), would study the information available regarding the dead person. He was instructed to personalise the procedure, and was given only two objectives:

- to obtain a statement of identification from the relative sufficient to satisfy the coroner which, in turn, would allow the early release of the body; and
- to provide whatever immediate welfare support the officer perceived the relative(s) required.

The system worked extremely well, and the help provided to the distraught relatives was both varied and effective. One measure of the success of this aspect of the support programme was that over half the relatives subsequently wrote to the Chief Superintendent thanking his officers for their supportive actions. Another is that the bodies of all those who lost their lives were released to the relatives for burial within 48 hours of the crash.

Dedicated teams of two officers per five to six bereaved families were then formed to become the focal point for the relatives. They were instructed to make at least three visits to each of their assigned families over a two-week period. The objectives were to:

- provide a reference point for the relatives;
- deal with the large number of enquiries; and
- identify welfare support requirements in order that local social services personnel could target the people most in need.

This again proved very effective. The dedicated officers were all invited to, and attended, the funeral services. This personal approach was extended to the full inquest hearings, at which the officers helped relatives through this extremely stressful process.

A 24-hour police helpline was set up for the relatives, a small number of whom made use of this facility in the early stages. Helplines were subsequently set up by all the social services departments who had bereaved families within their geographic area.

Three weeks after the rail crash the decision was made to withdraw the close police support and leave matters in the hands of the professionals. Each bereaved relative was told personally that although the police were moving into the background they could be called upon at any time. A comprehensive list of useful telephone numbers was provided for each family.

Stress suffered by officers engaged in the support process

The level of personal stress suffered by the 12 dedicated officers was brought home to me in a poignant and forceful manner. During the course of giving instruction to the dedicated officers I asked them to obtain, where possible, a recent photograph of each of the persons who had died. A few days after the rail crash one of them handed me a photograph of one of the dead men with his wife and two daughters at what was obviously the birthday party of one of their daughters. This photograph had a powerful emotional effect upon me. Until then, the psychological 'switch off' referred to earlier had been in operation, but this photograph brought home forcefully to me that we were not dealing with 'numbers' but real people and, in this particular case, someone of my own age and similar family circumstances. I related to the person in the photograph in a significant way, and the effect was as dramatic as it was long-lasting. I began to question whether the dedicated officers had suffered similar experiences, and felt that as their line manager I had done little to help them cope with the stressful circumstances they were encountering daily.

I resolved to tackle the problem immediately, and called a meeting of all the personnel involved. When the officers had assembled, I put the photograph in the middle of the group and talked through my earlier experience. This seemed to act as a catalyst for other officers to talk openly, both within the group and privately in my office, about their own emotions and experiences. It became clear that the dedicated relative liaison officers were under substantial and cumulative emotional stress. The experience of moving from one set of grieving relatives to another on a daily basis placed an enormous strain upon them. I decided to hold two meetings each day: a morning meeting to discuss progress on the enquiry and to allocate work, and an evening meeting to provide a forum for officers to talk through their daily experiences. This proved to be therapeutic and, without doubt, helped officers through a most difficult period. I found the evening meetings helped me to cope with the emotional and physical stress. This ongoing opportunity to talk about my experiences in an open and honest way was therapeutic, and helped me to understand the natural processes I was going through.

Conclusion

The main lesson in relation to coping with stress arising out of my experiences at Clapham is that stress has to be recognised and managed. When an organisation has a specialist welfare unit, the temptation as a manager is to leave matters concerning people's well-being to the 'experts', which I recognise now is an abdication of line management responsibilities, and could lead to staff breaking down.

I believe that the line manager is the most crucial individual in the process of trauma reduction and that he or she must create a regular forum where officers feel able to talk through their experiences. This also provides the line manager with an opportunity to assess the well-being of individual members of the team.

A structure needs to be created whereby officers involved in major disasters have easy access to counselling facilities. A monitoring framework needs to be set up to assess their well-being at intervals in the months following the incident. I doubt if anything I have said is original, but if it serves to emphasise the obvious my objective has been achieved. Creating and maintaining the opportunity for personnel involved in traumatic rescue operations to talk openly and freely about their own experiences will greatly reduce their personal stress. Together with an effective monitoring and counselling support structure, this will ensure that even the worst cases are identified and dealt with, and that a cry for help is not recognised too late.

11 | Children as victims and survivors

William Yule
Institute of Psychiatry, Denmark Hill, London

Introduction

Children are both victims and survivors of many violent acts. In this chapter I will briefly summarise issues and findings relating to the direct and indirect effects of violence on children, whether within the family or outside it, and raise the issues of transgenerational continuities in abusive and violent parenting. I will draw attention to a neglected area, that of the effects on children of witnessing violence, and argue that much of the short- and long-term morbidity can helpfully be understood within two conceptual frameworks:

- an interactional, social learning theory of development in general; and
- a model of post-traumatic stress disorder in particular.

The latter will be informed by my recent work with child survivors of disasters.

Violence within the family

Recent studies of violence within the family draw attention to how demanding parenting can be and how dangerous some families can be. Many reviews make the point that serious physical child abuse, even leading to death, has been recognised from time immemorial. Child killing has, at various times and in various cultures, been condoned as a legitimate form of family planning, achieving a desired spacing of children to match perceived resources.[1-3] It was chilling to read that as recently as the 1600s, Massachusetts passed the Stubborn Child Act, '... whereby a rebellious or stubborn child could be petitioned by his or her parents to be put to death'.[3]

Such extreme forms of control were not solely targeted at children. Well into the present century, American courts upheld the 'right' of a husband to '... chastise his wife with a whip or a rattan no bigger than his thumb', from whence the phrase 'rule of thumb' originates.[4] Thus,

153

societies have tolerated and legitimised violence within families—
violence sometimes directed towards children and certainly violence
that children witnessed. Such violence occurred within the relative
privacy of the family home and was largely ignored by society. Where
it was suspected, it was difficult to obtain hard evidence. With the
advent of X-rays in hospital paediatric practice, such evidence became
available, and the incontrovertible evidence of broken limbs and
fractured skulls could eventually no longer be ignored.

Physical abuse

Kempe *et al.* drew attention to the problem in dramatically presenting
their evidence on 'the battered child syndrome'.[5] Twenty years later,
Mrazek and Mrazek concluded that 10% of emergency room visits of
under-fives in the USA are the result of deliberate physical abuse.[6]
They estimate an incidence of 510 new cases of physical abuse per
million children in the USA, leading to over 2,000 deaths, per year.
They advise receiving physicians to treat inconsistencies in parental
accounts of injuries with grave suspicion, particularly when there is a
delay of many hours between the supposed accident and the child
being taken to hospital.

The Mrazeks summarised the short-term effects of physical abuse on
children thus:

- anhedonia;
- poor social interaction;
- poor self-esteem;
- withdrawal;
- oppositionality;
- hypervigilance;
- pseudo-adult behaviour.

Clinicians have often commented on the 'frozen watchfulness' of
abused children.

Recognition of the scale of the problem and the high level of
mortality and morbidity, particularly in terms of head injury in the
under-fives, has led to a great many studies of the characteristics of
abusing parents and the circumstances in which the abuse occurs.

Munchausen syndrome by proxy

A rare, but serious, variant of child physical abuse was recognised by
Meadow in 1977, and termed Munchausen syndrome by proxy.[7]
Here, mothers (usually) present very sick children with falsified
medical histories. The severity of the illness may be out of keeping with

the history, or the problem does not yield to normal interventions. Indeed, treatment may make the child worse, and death has sometimes occurred. At times, careful observation has found the mother administering noxious substances to the child. Once again, physicians should maintain a high degree of suspicion when warning signs are noted.[6]

Child sexual abuse

It took a long time for society and its professionals to recognise the existence of physical abuse directed towards children and to find ways of obtaining hard evidence of that abuse, and even longer to recognise that children were also open to sexual abuse. There is still considerable disagreement among professionals over the definition of sexual abuse, which makes it even more difficult than it is inherently to gather evidence of incidence and prevalence. One of the more useful definitions is that of Schecter and Roberge:

> Child sexual abuse is '. . . the involvement of dependent, developmentally immature children and adolescents in sexual activities that they do not fully comprehend, are unable to give informed consent to, and that violate the social taboos of family roles'.[8]

This definition draws attention to the abuse of power relationships by the perpetrator (and implies a massive breaking of trust) as well as emphasising that the child's developmental level must be taken into consideration. Both the short- and long-term effects of sexual abuse will depend greatly on the child's level of development at the time of the abuse.

Some investigators and clinicians adopt a very loose definition of child sexual abuse, and include non-contact abuse such as witnessing exhibitionism (flashing), seeing pornographic material or hearing sexy talk, while others differentiate non-contact abuse from various degrees of severity of contact from genital fondling to penetration of orifices. It is becoming clearer that severity and frequency of abuse, as well as the context in which it occurs, are important variables in predicting outcome.

Retrospective surveys of adults obtain high estimates (often up to 25–40%) of both intrafamilial and extrafamilial sexual abuse before the age of 18. Only a tiny minority of these incidents was reported to the police.[9] Cross-sectional studies using a definition involving contact obtain much lower estimates, but over the past few years the rates of reporting have increased dramatically.[10] More girls are the victims of sexual abuse than boys. In most cases, the perpetrator is known—either a member of the family or a family acquaintance. Women are the abusers in only 4% of girls, but 20% of boys.[11] Children tend to disclose sexual abuse by a stranger very quickly, but sexual abuse within the family is often a closely guarded secret. When the abuse is eventually disclosed, it is often greeted with disbelief. Pressure may be put on the child to retract the accusation. One study reports that disclosure of sexual abuse was followed by a suicide in 5% of families.[12]

It is increasingly being recognised that child sexual abuse can have very long-lasting consequences.[13] It is implicated in psychiatric problems that manifest well into adulthood, and particular interest is currently focused on the relationship between child sexual abuse and adult dissociative states.

By and large, the closer the relationship of the perpetrator to the child, the greater the subsequent emotional disturbance, with father-daughter incest being the most traumatic.[14-16] The older the perpetrator and the greater the use of force, the worse the outcome. Long-term effects are noted in sexual adjustment and broader inter-personal relationships.[6]

Transgenerational transmission

In a consideration of issues involved in treating children who are the victims of violence, an important issue concerns prevention. It is widely held that abused children grow up to be abusing parents. This message has got through to many child victims of physical and sexual abuse, with the result that many become extremely distressed at what is perceived as the inevitability of the abuse cycle. What is the evidence that such a cycle exists? Is transgenerational transmission of abusive patterns inevitable? If not, are any risk or protective factors known? Can any protective factors point the way to breaking the cycle and so preventing abuse?

Rutter points out that retrospective studies largely confirm that mothers who have experienced *major* difficulties with parenting experience a high degree of parent–child difficulties with their own children.[17] Thus, clinicians who look back from samples of abusing parents may overestimate the strength of the transgenerational connection. The picture, as far as lesser degrees of abuse are concerned, is less pessimistic, with studies such as that of Straus *et al.* of a nationwide sample of 1,146 parents finding that only 15% of those who reported being abused as children themselves became abusive parents.[18]

The picture from prospective studies is markedly different and points to considerable discontinuities in poor parenting. Altemeier *et al.* found that 23 of 1,400 women studied from pregnancy until their children were between 21 and 48 months old seriously abused their children.[19,20] They differed from the others on a number of key variables (Table 1). Although the *proportion* of abusers who had experienced foster care is much higher than the proportion of non-abusers, a higher proportion of abusers had *not* been in foster care and, in *absolute terms*, the number of people in foster care who did not abuse their children is greater than those who did.

Table 1.   Discontinuities in poor parenting

Abusers		Non-abusers		Variable
%	No.	%	No.	
17	4	2	24	Experienced foster care
57	13	25	344	Did not get along with their own parents
57	13	30	412	Received unfair, severe punishment

Prospective studies, such as this and Quinton and Rutter's studies of children raised in care, find some evidence to support the connection between adverse life experiences and later behaviour as parents, but also point to considerable discontinuities.[21] As Rutter concludes:

> ... there are substantial continuities in parenting behaviour. These are stronger looking backward than looking forward. That is to say, it is uncommon for *serious* parenting problems associated with general psycho-social malfunctioning to occur in the absence of important adversities in the upbringing of one or other of the two parents. The experiencing of bad parenting seems to be an almost necessary condition for these widespread severe parenting difficulties, but they are not a sufficient condition. Current marital support and social circumstances generally are also influential. It should be added that intergenerational continuities are *un*important in the genesis of milder, isolated parenting problems that are *un*associated with generally poor psychosocial functioning.[17]

In other words, the experience of abusive parenting is best seen as a high risk factor for later poor or abusive parenting, but the continuity is by no means inevitable. As Wolfe notes, the high risk factor may be activated when the potentially poor parent is put under stress from poverty, unemployment or lack of social support.[1] Where the protective factors of a supportive relationship from an adult or of good self esteem associated with success at school pertain, the risk of continuity is lessened.

Thus, both Rutter[17] and Wolfe[1] conceptualise the issue of transgenerational transmission of violent parenting within the framework of developmental psychopathology, life stressors and broad-based social learning theory. Violence is not seen primarily as a psychiatric or narrowly psychopathological problem qualitatively different from other human behaviour. Rather, it is seen as obeying the same laws of learning and transmission as other aspects of human behaviour.[22] As Gelles and Straus conclude:

> While granting that some instances of intrafamily violence are an out-growth of social or psychological pathology, we maintain that physical violence between family members is a normal part of family life in most societies, and in American society in particular.[23]

Child witnesses of violence

I have highlighted the fact that a high proportion of today's children are the direct victims of physical or sexual abuse, or both, much of which takes place within the family. Having been abused as a child predisposes, but does not inexorably lead, to those victims themselves becoming abusers, and the transmission of violence can be understood in social learning as opposed to qualitatively pathological terms. I now want to focus on indirect violence, in particular the consequences of children witnessing violence.

Two bodies of pioneering work illuminate this neglected topic:

- the studies by Dora Black and her colleagues, at the Royal Free Hospital in London, of children whose fathers have killed their mothers; and
- the studies by Robert Pynoos and his colleagues in Los Angeles, of children who have witnessed a wide range of acts of violence.

Black and Kaplan reported on 28 children of 14 families in which the father had killed the mother, often in front of the children.[24] With their mothers dead and their fathers taken into custody, the children were often placed temporarily with grandparents, themselves shocked and grieving. In most cases, the children's needs were overlooked— they could neither discuss what happened with their new caretakers, nor begin to grieve properly. Issues of custody and access were often not addressed and the children were left in limbo. No one helped the children to make sense of what was witnessed—indeed, too often, no one discussed what had happened at all.

Pynoos and Eth acknowledged how difficult it can be for adults to address these painful issues, let alone help children address them.[25] After witnessing a murder, suicide or rape of a parent, children are often in shock and show many symptoms of acute post-traumatic stress responses. Where a parent has died, they may also be trying to deal with their bereavement. Pynoos and Eth described a technique of interviewing children as soon as practicable after the event to assist them and the remaining family to function more effectively. The main value lies not so much in the specific details of their approach, although the value of this is considerable for anyone forced unexpectedly to deal with such a situation, but rather in emphasising that children want and need to share their thoughts, feelings and fears with an adult outside the immediate social network. Their experience is that most children gain a great sense of relief when taken through the incident in detail.

Pynoos and Nader used a post-traumatic stress disorder (PTSD) reaction index to gather systematic information on children who had witnessed a wide range of injury and death.[26] They showed that children have most of the cardinal features of PTSD as described in the Diagnostic and Statistical Manual, DSM-III and DSM-III-R,[27,28] with:

- re-experiencing of the trauma in intrusive thoughts, dreams and flashbacks;
- feeling detached or having reduced involvement in their world; and
- a range of incident-specific new symptoms and behaviours.

They argued that children of different developmental levels both manifest PTSD in different ways and require age-appropriate treatment approaches. Crisis work can be undertaken in schools, the family and the clinic, but it should all start as soon as practicable after the event.

The recognition that children present with PTSD is very important for a number of reasons:

- it provides a clear framework for professionals in gathering information about the effects of various traumas on children;
- it forces professionals to do what many seem to have forgotten, to ask the child and listen to his or her responses; and
- it points the way to effective treatment.

Wolfe *et al.* were among the first to conceptualise the reactions of children to sexual abuse within a PTSD framework.[29] They showed that careful, sensitive questioning of the children revealed that many of them had intrusive thoughts about the abusive acts and avoidant behaviours; for example, being scared of being left with baby sitters or avoiding the place where the abuse occurred. This way of looking at the problems immediately places the issue within the mainstream of treating adult victims of rape and assault, and forces questions about whether the promising cognitive behavioural therapies described by Kilpatrick *et al.*[30] and Foa and Stekete[31] may be adapted for use with children.

Post-traumatic stress disorder and children

Although PTSD was first defined as such in 1980,[27] it was far from
clear the extent to which such a diagnosis was appropriate for children.
Garmezy and Rutter argued that most serious traumas resulted in only
transient adjustment reactions.[32] However, our studies of children who
survived the capsize of the *Herald of Free Enterprise* at Zeebrugge in 1987
and the sinking of the cruise ship, *Jupiter*, outside Athens harbour in
1988 demonstrated that many children do manifest PTSD.[33-35]

Common stress reactions in children

Sleep disturbance. Almost all children have major sleep problems in the
first few weeks. They reported fears of the dark and of being alone,
intrusive thoughts when things were quiet, bad dreams, nightmares
and waking through the night. Problems persisted over many months.
The use of music to divert thoughts helped.

Separation difficulties. Initially, most children wanted to be physically
close to their surviving parent, often sleeping in the parental bed over
the first few weeks. Some distressed parents found it difficult to cope
with their clinginess.

Concentration difficulties. During the day, children had major problems in
concentrating on school work. When it was silent in the classroom they
had intrusive memories of what had happened to them.

Memory problems. They also had problems remembering new material,
or even some old skills such as reading music.

Intrusive thoughts. All were troubled by repetitive thoughts about the
accident. These occurred at any time, although often triggered by
environmental stimuli: for example movement on a bus, noise of glass
smashing, sound of rushing water, sight of tables laid out like the ship's
cafeteria. Thoughts intruded when they were otherwise quiet.

Talking with parents. Many children did not want to talk about their
feelings with their parents so as not to upset the adults. Thus, parents
were often unaware of the details of the children's suffering, although
they could see they were in difficulty. There was often a great sense of
frustration between parents and children.

Talking with peers. At some points, survivors felt a great need to talk
over their experiences with peers. Unfortunately, the timing was often

wrong. Peers held back from asking in case they upset the survivor further, and the survivor often felt rejected.

Heightened alertness to dangers. Most were wary of all forms of transport, and not willing to put their safety into anyone else's hands. They were more aware of other dangers, and affected by reports of other disasters.

Foreshortened future. Many felt they should live each day to the full and not plan far ahead. They lost trust in long-term planning.

Fears. Most had fears of travelling by sea and air. Many had fears of swimming, and of the sound of rushing water.

Irritability. Many of the children found themselves much more irritable than previously, both with parents and peers. Some found that they got much more angry than before the disaster.

Guilt. 'Survivor guilt' has long been discussed as a paradoxical reaction following a disaster. Inexplicably, this symptom, so characteristic of post-traumatic disorders, is not considered in DSM-III-R although it was regarded as a central feature of the earlier definition. Child and adolescent survivors often feel guilty that they are alive when others have died, and because they feel they might have done more to help others during the disaster. Less frequently discussed, but present nevertheless, they sometimes also feel guilty about things they did during the crisis in order to survive. Guilt has been a particularly strong theme among adolescents surviving the *Jupiter* sinking.

Depression. Adolescent survivors from the *Jupiter* report significantly higher rates of depression than controls of the same age. Whilst these figures refer to self report on questionnaires, similar findings are confirmed on detailed clinical interviews. A small, but significant number of children became clinically depressed, and some had suicidal thoughts and even took overdoses in the year after the accident.

Bereavement. In the *Herald of Free Enterprise* disaster in particular, a number of children were bereaved and no treatment plan could ignore the children's grief. Bereavement reactions complicate the presenting picture of symptoms, but attention must be paid to them.

Anxiety and panic. A significant number of children became very anxious after the accidents, although the impression is that the appearance of panic attacks was sometimes considerably delayed. It is usually possible to identify stimuli in the child's immediate environment that trigger panic attacks, hence the need to get very detailed accounts of the impact of the trauma on all the child's senses.

These commonly occurring symptoms are almost identical with those recognised in DSM-III-R as comprising PTSD. Space does not permit a discussion of individual differences in how children react to major stressors, the role families play in ameliorating or maintaining problems, or the fascinating question of how stress reactions change with age. These topics and the vital one of how to treat the disorders are discussed more fully elsewhere.[36]

Studies on post-traumatic stress disorder

The effects of disasters may be studied systematically. Ten days after the sinking of the *Jupiter*, Dr Udwin and I met with the teachers, 24 teenage girls who survived and their parents. At that meeting, during the debriefing session, all 24 survivors completed three scales:

- the Impact of Events Scale;[37]
- Birleson's Depression Scale;[38,39] and
- the Revised Children's Manifest Anxiety Scale.[40]

On the basis of their scores ten days after the sinking, ten girls aged 14 years were thought to be at high risk of developing problems. When help was offered on an individual or group basis, and without saying which girls were considered to be at high risk, eight of the ten high-risk group came forward for help on the first day. The other two attended the second meeting. Only five others attended any group meeting. This was a highly significant relationship between scores on the screening scales and later help-seeking, and the authors conclude that the battery of tests shows considerable promise in identifying children who most need help after a disaster.[34]

Yule *et al.*[35] asked the same 24 fourth-year girls to complete the Revised Fear Survey Schedule for Children.[41] Effectively, there were three subgroups of girls:

- those who went on the cruise and were traumatised;
- those who had wanted to go but could not get a place; and
- those who showed no interest in going in the first place.

However, this last group could not be considered as an unaffected control group as the whole school was badly affected by the aftermath of the disaster. Accordingly, fourth-year girls in a nearby school also completed the fear schedule, along with the depression and anxiety scales.

Two sets of results should be noted. First, the girls on the cruise were significantly more depressed and anxious than the other groups five months after the disaster. Indeed, there is a strong suggestion of an exposure/effect gradient on these two measures, reminiscent of that reported by Pynoos *et al.*[42] Secondly, the fear survey items were rated as being related to the events on the cruise or not. There was agreement among the authors that 11 items were related and 33 unrelated. There were no differences across the four exposure groups on unrelated fears. By contrast, only the girls who experienced the traumatic events showed a significant increase in reported fears. The authors took the opportunity of the disaster to examine the effects on children's fears, and concluded that the effects are specific to stimuli present, thereby providing more confirmatory evidence of the conditioning theory of fear acquisition.

Later, 334 of the *Jupiter* survivors completed the same self-report battery, and the same findings emerged across the total group. Children showing high scores were assessed individually, and the indications are that approximately half the total group met DSM-III-R criteria for PTSD. Many also showed depression and anxiety. Returning to the early intervention and debriefing, the fact that data were obtained on over 75% of the survivors meant that the ratings of the 24 with whom we worked could be compared with the school that did not accept help and, as far as can be ascertained, provided no systematic help during the first year. Five months post-disaster, the early intervention group scored non-significantly lower on the measures of depression and anxiety, but significantly lower on the Impact of Events Scale (which seems to tap the central feature of PTSD). Thus, there is some slight evidence for the value of early intervention.

Among the other findings that are emerging is the sobering fact that, compared with their pre-cruise examination results over the previous three years, cruise survivors showed a significant drop in their post-cruise examination marks when compared with controls matched for ability level.[43] Our research group has a major interest in the socio-psychological aspects of disasters, and has recently rated the attribution styles of a sub-sample of child survivors. Children who showed a more internal causal attribution style in explaining what happened to them during the disaster had significantly higher levels of post-traumatic psychopathology one year later.[44]

Treatment of post-traumatic stress disorder

There are no systematic trials yet of different treatments for children presenting with PTSD. The multiplicity of problems presented calls for a multi-modal approach, with the child, the family and the school all being targeted. In cases of mild to moderate severity, where avoidant behaviours predominate, it is probably best to focus on anxiety management techniques. Where intrusive thoughts and images predominate, other measures are required.

Yule draws attention to approaches for treating nightmares related to the traumas.[36] It was noted earlier that children can gain a great deal from discussing the trauma in detail with a trusted adult unconnected with the social network. Meeting in groups with others who have survived a disaster also seems right, although it always has to be acknowledged that there are individual differences in the speed with which survivors are ready to accept group treatment.

Kilpatrick *et al.*[30] and Foa and Stekete[31] described more intense, focused exposure treatments for adults who have survived rapes and assault. Richards and Rose described how these techniques have been adapted for treating adult survivors of recent British disasters,[45] and Richards and Lovell reported the preliminary findings of a controlled trial of imaginal exposure for PTSD victims.[46] They argued that merely recounting the experience of the trauma in a detached fashion does nothing to help the anxiety to habituate. Instead, following Rachman[47] and Saigh,[48] they used lengthy exposure sessions where the client has to recount in vivid detail what happened, what he saw, heard, felt, smelt, thought, feared and so on. These narratives are asked for in the first person, present tense to aid reliving them, and each session is recorded on audiotape. The client is asked to listen to the tape for one hour daily, thus potentially increasing the amount of exposure sevenfold in a week. The first results show that high levels of distress as reflected on scores on the Impact of Events Scale, drop dramatically after four sessions, and all but disappear after a further four, with these dramatic improvements holding at one-year follow-up.

Examples of treatment of post-traumatic stress disorder

I have now begun to use these techniques with child and adolescent survivors. A nine-year old boy was held at knife-point when he was six to force his mother to submit to a rapist. He witnessed the bloody rape and experienced recurring nightmares and intrusive thoughts thereafter. Although his mother tried to explain to him the difference between 'good' and 'bad' touching, he remained confused and had not fully discussed what he witnessed. After two sessions, he was able to draw in detail what he witnessed and to share his fears that his mother had been murdered. After four or five sessions, his intrusive thoughts disappeared.

A 16-year-old boy survived the *Jupiter* sinking, but was very guilty about not helping his friends get off the ship. He became extremely anxious, irritable and depressed. He scored near the maximum on the Impact of Events Scale five months after the sinking. Following individual assessment, he was referred to local services. Unfortunately, he did not get any help locally, and was rereferred 20 months later, still scoring near the ceiling on the Impact of Events Scale. He agreed to try the exposure therapy and co-operated well. At each session he was able to recall more relevant, upsetting detail. After four sessions his score dropped from 60 to 40. During the next four sessions he was accompanied on a pleasure boat on the Thames, where he experienced but coped with anxiety. After these sessions, his score further dropped to 22.

These two cases illustrate that techniques which have been shown to work well with adults with PTSD can also be useful with at least some children showing similar problems. Since clinicians are often at a loss to know how best to treat children after a major trauma, these results bring some optimism to an otherwise pessimistic area.

Conclusions

One reason why professionals did not believe that children were subject to physical or sexual abuse, or suffered from PTSD was simply that they never asked them. Children very quickly perceive cues from adults that they do not wish to discuss painful issues. Hence, the great difficulty that many child survivors of disasters have of talking with their parents. Once adults listen, children will tell of their experiences directly and in detail.

Obviously, there are differences between being the subject of abuse and the survivor of a disaster. In the latter case, the trauma is relatively public, a one-off affair, no matter how traumatic. The clinician listening to the child can lead him through what happened as so many details will be in the public domain. In the former case, abuse of all sorts is likely to be within the family, repeated and secret. Clinicians cannot know what went on. Moreover, there are all the complications of children being required to furnish evidence for the prosecution of the perpetrators. This is not the place to discuss the legal issues. Suffice it to say that wherever the abuse is discovered, someone should consider how to talk to the child in such a way as to be therapeutic. Children can be helped to overcome their anxieties. The problem of repairing shattered trust and relationships is another story.

References

1. Wolfe DA. *Child abuse: implications for child development and psychopathology*. New York: Sage, 1987
2. Lystad M, ed. *Violence in the home: interdisciplinary perspectives*. New York: Brunner/Mazel, 1986
3. Cicchetti D, Carlson V, eds. *Child maltreatment: theory and research on the causes and consequences of child abuse and neglect*. New York: Cambridge University Press, 1989

4. Steinmetz SK. The violent family. In: Cicchetti D, Carlson V, eds. *Child maltreatment: theory and research on the causes and consequences of child abuse and neglect.* New York: Cambridge University Press, 1989: 51–67

5. Kempe CH, Silverman FN, Steele BF, Droegemuller W, Silver HK. The battered-child syndrome. *JAMA* 1962; **181**:17–24

6. Mrazek D, Mrazek P. Child maltreatment. In: Rutter M, Hersov L, eds. *Child and adolescent psychiatry, 2nd edn.* Oxford: Blackwell, 1985

7. Meadow R. Munchausen syndrome by proxy: the hinterland of child abuse. *Lancet* 1977; **ii**:343–5

8. Schecter MD, Roberge L. Sexual exploitation. In: Helfer RE, Kempe CH, eds. *Child abuse and neglect: the family and the community.* Cambridge MA: Ballinger, 1976: 127–42

9. Russell D. The incidence and prevalence of intrafamilial and extrafamilial sexual abuse of female children. *Child Abuse Neglect* 1983; **7**:133–46

10. Creighton SJ, Noyes P. *Child abuse trends in England and Wales 1983–87.* London: NSPCC, 1989

11. Glaser D, Frosh S. *Child sexual abuse.* London: Macmillan Educational, 1988

12. Goodwin J. Suicide attempts in sexual abuse victims and their mothers. *Child Abuse Neglect* 1981; **5**: 217–21

13. Jehu D. Beyond sexual abuse: therapy with women who were victims in child-hood. Chichester: Wiley, 1988

14. Landis JT. Experiences of 500 children with adult sexual deviation. *Psychiat Quart* (suppl) 1956; **30**:91–109

15. Gibbens TCN, Prince J. *Child victims of sex offences.* London: Institute for the Study and Treatment of Delinquency, 1963

16. Finkelhor D. *Sexually victimised children.* New York: Free Press, 1979

17. Rutter M. Intergenerational continuities and discontinuities in serious parenting difficulties. In: Cicchetti D, Carlson V, eds. *Child maltreatment: theory and research on the causes and consequences of child abuse and neglect.* New York: Cambridge University Press, 1989

18. Straus MA, Gelles RJ, Steinmetz S. *Behind closed doors: violence in the American family.* Garden City NY: Doubleday/Anchor, 1980

19. Altemeier WA, O'Connor S, Vietze P, Sandler H, Sherrod K. Antecedents of child abuse. *J. Paediatr* 1982; **100**:823–9

20. Altemeier WA, O'Connor S, Vietze P, Sandler H, Sherrod K. Prediction of child abuse: a prospective study of feasibility. *Child Abuse Neglect* 1984; **8**:393–400

21. Quinton D, Rutter M. *Parenting breakdown.* Aldershot: Gower, 1988

22. Yule W. Behavioural treatment of children and adolescents with conduct dis-orders. In: Hersov LA, Berger M, eds. *Aggression and anti-social behaviour in childhood and adolescence.* Oxford: Pergamon, 1978: 115–41

23. Gelles RJ, Straus MA. Determinants of violence in the family: toward a theoreti-cal integration. In: Burr WR, Hill R, Nye FI, Reiss IL, eds. *Contemporary theories about the family.* New York: Free Press, 1979:549–81

24. Black D, Kaplan T. Father kills mother: issues and problems encountered by a child psychiatric team. *Br J Psychiatry* 1988; **153**:624–30

25. Pynoos RS, Eth S. Witness to violence: the child interview. *J Am Acad Child Psychiatry* 1986; **25**:306–19

26. Pynoos RS, Nader K. Psychological first aid and treatment approach for children exposed to community violence: research implications. *J Traum Stress* 1988; **1**: 243–67

27. American Psychiatric Association. *Diagnostic and Statistical Manual of Mental Disorders, 3rd edn.* Washington DC: American Psychiatric Association, 1980

28. American Psychiatric Association. *Diagnostic and Statistical Manual of Mental Disorders, 3rd edn (revised).* Washington DC: American Psychiatric Association, 1987

29. Wolfe VV, Gentile C, Wolfe DA. The impact of sexual abuse on children: a PTSD formulation. *Behav Therap* 1989; **20**:215–28

30. Kilpatrick DG, Saunders BE, Amick-McMullan A, Best CL, Veronen LJ, Resnick HS. Victim and crime factors associated with the development of crime-related post-traumatic stress disorder. *Behav Therap* 1989; **20**:199–214

31. Foa E, Steketee G, Olasov Rothbaum B. Behavioral/cognitive conceptualizations of post-traumatic stress disorder. *Behav Therap* 1989; **20**:155–76

32. Garmezy N, Rutter M. Acute reactions to stress. In: Rutter M, Hersov L, eds. *Child and adolescent psychiatry: modern approaches, 2nd edn.* Oxford: Blackwell, 1985: 152–76

33. Yule W, Williams R. Post-traumatic stress reactions in children. *J Traum Stress* 1990; **3**: 279–95

34. Yule W, Udwin O. Screening child survivors for post-traumatic stress disorders: experiences from the Jupiter sinking. *Br J Clin Psychol* 1991; **30**:131–8

35. Yule W, Udwin O, Murdoch K. The Jupiter sinking: effects on children's fears, depression and anxiety. *J. Child Psychol Psychiatry* 1990; **31**:1051–61

36. Yule W. Work with children following disasters. In: Herbert M, ed. *Clinical child psychology: social learning, development and behaviour.* Chichester: Wiley, 1991

37. Horowitz MJ, Wilner N, Alvarez W. Impact of event scale: a measure of subjective stress *Psychosom Med* 1979; **41**:209–18

38. Birleson P. The validity of depressive disorder in childhood and the development of a self-rating scale: a research report. *J. Child Psychol Psychiatry* 1981; **22**:73–88

39. Birleson P, Hudson I, Buchanan DG, Wolff S. Clinical evaluation of a self-rating scale for depressive disorder in childhood (depression self-rating scale). *J. Child Psychol Psychiatry* 1987; **28**:43–60

40. Reynolds CR, Richmond BO. What I think and feel: a revised measure of children's manifest anxiety. *J Abnormal Child Psychol* 1978; **6**:271–80

41. Ollendick TH, Yule W, Ollier K. Fears in British children and their relationship to manifest anxiety and depression. *J Child Psychol Psychiatry* 1991; **32**:321–31

42. Pynoos RS, Frederick C, Nader K *et al.* Life threat and post-traumatic stress in school-age children. *Arch Gen Psychiatry* 1987; **44**:1057–63

43. Tsui E. University of London, unpublished MSc dissertation, 1990

44. Joseph SA, Brewin CR, Yule W, Williams RM. Causal attributions and post-traumatic stress in adolescents. *J Child Psychol Psychiatry* 1992 (in press)

45. Richards D, Rose J. Exposure therapy for post-traumatic stress disorder: four case studies. *Br J Psychiatry* 1991 **158**:836–40

46. Richards D, Lovell K. *Exposure treatment for PTSD.* Paper presented at 20th meeting of British Association for Behavioural Psychotherapy, Oxford, July 1991

47. Rachman S. Emotional processing. *Behav Res Therap* 1980; **18**:51–60

48. Saigh PA. *In vitro* flooding in the treatment of a 6-year-old boy's post-traumatic stress disorder. *Behav Res Therap* 1986; **24**:685–8

12 | Everyday violence and experience of crime

Elizabeth A. Stanko
Department of Law, Brunel University

Defining public violence

Broadly speaking, violence involves the infliction of emotional, psychological, physical and/or material damage.[1,2] The harm felt by the recipient varies, as well as the long-term impact on his or her everyday life. A recent experience of violence or its threat may have significant effects, altering an individual's routines and personal life-style or it may have little noticeable influence on daily life (see, for example, references 3 and 4).

Violent crime continues to capture the imagination of the public and is the chosen fodder of the media. Despite their seemingly rare occurrence, violent incidents are 'good' news.[5] Perhaps because they portray life as 'precarious' or indeed as 'exciting', the love affair of the media sensationalises violence and distorts its typical form.[6] The wanton, brutal attack by a stranger on an elderly person provides the 'best' example for the media's picture of violence.[7] This idealised image is not only accepted by the public and the media, but it also influences how physicians, police, social workers and other professionals deal with victims of violence. By far the most typical forms of violence and threat in adult life arise from the daily interactions of lovers, friends, acquaintances, neighbours, partners and ex-partners.[8-10] As others have observed, offenders and victims are sometimes one and the same.[11]

Public violence is usually characterised as that violence which takes place outside the home. There is a strong assumption that violence is most likely to occur at the hands of faceless assailants usually in public streets, isolated one-off events and difficult to anticipate. Certainly, when crime statistics are released by the Home Office or police, the rise in reported and recorded violent crime is used as a barometer of the safety of the street both by politicians and by the media. As the Working Group on the Fear of Crime pointed out, this reaction fuels the fear of crime.[7]

According to conventional criminological thinking, people fear
personal violence more than other forms of criminal behaviour. Fear of
crime is associated with people's concern for personal safety and is
reported more by women than by men,[12-15] by those who live in less
well-off areas, and by those who reside in inner city areas.[16,17]
Personal crime, which is the most feared, includes crime categories of
murder and manslaughter, assault, robbery and rape. Crimes of theft,
especially theft from the person, motor vehicle crime and burglary are
excluded from the kinds of crime which are felt to threaten the
individual personally.[18] However, evidence suggests that these crimes
induce anxiety and fear,[12,15,19,20] especially if they happen in nearby
shopping areas or supposedly safe havens, such as the home.[15]

Public violence, which is assumed to threaten all equally, is not
randomly distributed throughout the population. Criminological evidence strongly suggests that there are patterns of multiple victimisation, consistent across studies and national jurisdictions (see references
11 and 21 for a review). These studies show that individual risk of
violence increases with age, with the under-25s at most risk,[22,23] and
race, with non-whites disproportionately represented.[24] Sex and marital status significantly affect risk, with single men and separated and
divorced women most likely to be victims of violent crime.[23,25] The
qualitative aspects of violence also differ by gender. Women are more
at risk from sexual assault and serial violence (assaults) from intimates[8]
and predatory violence (such as purse snatch),[12] whereas men are
more at risk from robbery by strangers and assaults by friends and
acquaintances. Those who are poor, moreover, are most at risk for all
forms of crime, especially violent crime.[26,27]

Crime does not impact evenly upon different segments of the
population, nor is it any more equal at the individual level. Gottfredson's analysis of the 1982 British Crime Survey notes that 28% of
victims of personal crime were multiple victims and account for 44% of
all crimes in the survey.[23] The work of Genn,[28] Pease[29] and others
illuminates the importance of multiple victimisation for the understanding of victim risk. Research leading to the Kirkholt Project found
that burglars, for example, are likely to strike a once-burgled house
again.[30] Such houses have a four times greater chance of another
burglary within four weeks of the first.[30,31] Serial violence, characteristic of racial and domestic attacks, accounts for a small but significant
proportion of victims. As repeated violence escalates—which it often
does—these victims no doubt constitute a substantial proportion of
those who request the assistance of medical personnel. Sheperd has
reported the impact of multi-victimisation on the work of casualty
departments in Bristol.[32]

The danger

Summarised below are the findings from a study I conducted exploring adult women's and men's experiences and understandings of violence and personal danger.[15] Through a series of focused interviews in London and the Eastern seaboard of the USA, I argue that an understanding of violence and danger is very much a part of everyday life. This is not to say that violence should be accepted as good or even natural, but simply that social conditions make danger a reality. It is not to suggest either that everybody experiences violence on a daily basis. Most people have learned to manage violence and to cope with experiences and memories of danger, but this ability to manage violence is not without cost. Research indicates that a variety of precautionary strategies are used to avoid violence, which restricts many people's mobility and quality of life. In particular, the lives of women, non-whites and the poor are most likely to be affected.

Individuals gather information about potential personal danger and violence throughout their lifetimes. Direct involvement, observation and the shared knowledge of family, peers, acquaintances and co-workers all contribute to assessments of risk and strategies for safety. In my study, people reported various exposure to frightening situations and violent encounters as children. Those who met dangerous and scary predicaments did so in many circumstances and places—within or near the child's own home or elsewhere—and the threatening person was often known to the child, either as a family member, family friend or acquaintance. There were also situations involving danger perpetrated by individuals completely unknown to the child or young adult. As children, these individuals were often taught about potential danger from strangers, but their memories of unsafety point out the contradiction of this advice, for the danger arose from parents, relatives or friends of the family, schoolmates, neighbours or even a local shopkeeper, and especially peers.

A recently published study of the prevalence of physical and sexual abuse of UK children suggests that many children experience something they remember from their childhood as frightening.[33] From a detailed questionnaire completed by 1,244 young women and men, one in two girls and one in four boys reported some form of sexually intrusive experience. Sexual abuse, defined broadly in the study, includes being touched, being pressured to have sex, 'flashing' and attempted and actual assaults/rapes. Whilst some would argue that many of these experiences are not 'serious' (see, for example, reference 34), they left lasting memories in the minds of young people taking part in the study. What is important here is that memories of childhood danger stemming from personal violence are by no means uncommon. Violence and danger have a familiar face, yet we are taught as children a recipe for safety which assists children's avoidance of danger only from unknown adults.

Many learn as children to cope with potential violence and danger by developing strategies to maximise personal safety, often with those familiar to them. Some use avoidance, like Mike, sexually threatened by a strange man in a park:

> I just started staying away from the park and I think that being scared of gay men who look like they may be gay or look like they may look at my body.

Some, like Sylvia, keep others around for protection, even in her own home. A girl-friend kept her company after school to stop her uncle from making sexual advances.

Many children cope with aggression and danger close to home because it seems part of growing up. For example, Gordon reflects:

> There were a lot of children [in my neighbourhood]. ... And when you have that many kids, there's always going to be a lot of competition— who's better than who, who's bigger than who, who's stronger than who and the way people usually figure that out is by proving it. I'm not bemoaning some of the shit that I went through as a kid 'cause it toughened me in ways now that might not have if I hadn't gone through that. And I wouldn't go through that again for all the tea in China, no way.

Attendance at school also puts some children at risk to bullies and harassment, some of it racial, sexual and homophobic, teaching them that they are targets because of who they are. Ricardo bitterly recalls his childhood:

> When I was 11 years old we moved to [this city] and I was beat up because I didn't know the language and that put fear in me.

And Deborah reports:

> I rarely went out in the playground. I only had one or two friends. I basically avoided people in my first secondary school. Everybody hated me there. They ripped my clothes off at PE lessons. [They] did it to humiliate me.

At the very least, the recalled incidents were experienced as distressing and violating; at worst, they were dangerous, and left indelible memories. Only a few of these incidents were considered crimes, and even fewer reported to the police, yet the situations involved assaults, sexual indecency, damage to property, theft and threatening behaviour.

Personal danger and violence experienced during childhood is similar to that experienced as adults. Exposure to danger is experienced as a private event and, if it is shared with others, it is usually sorted out without involving official agencies such as the police. Crucial to the understanding about danger, moreover, is how the meaning of danger differs according to gender. Whilst some boys and men encounter distressing and damaging unwanted sexual abuse, by and large, girls and women endure sexual intrusions and the potential for sexual intrusions as an everyday feature of their lives as females.[15,35-37] It is during childhood that the orientation to physical and sexual safety develops, and this carries on into adulthood. Exploration of the relationship between gender and violence, and its implications for the treatment of anxiety and distress, which sometimes appear long after the physical wounds have healed, are now discussed, with particular advice for physicians.

Women, violence and danger

When women are asked about their experiences of physical and sexual intrusion, they reveal a range of sexually frightening incidents. In this study, women revealed sexual danger from uncles, fathers, neighbours, family friends, authority figures such as lawyers, school companions, and strangers. For a number of reasons—embarrassment, humiliation, self blame or self denial—the women rarely told anyone else about what had happened.

Women's lives rest upon a continuum of unsafety. This does not mean that all women occupy the same position in relation to safety and violence. Many other features of their lives, such as direct experience, class, race, sexual orientation or physical abilities, will mean that their circumstances differ. Not only do some women feel vulnerable because they are female, but because they are, for instance, Afro-Caribbean, Asian, or Irish and female. Somehow, though, as all women reach adulthood they share a common awareness of their particular vulnerability. Learning the strategies for maintaining sexual integrity is a continuous lesson about what it means to be female.

For the most part, women find that they must constantly negotiate their safety with men—those with whom they live, work and socialise, as well as those they have never met. As men are likely to be women's intimate companions and colleagues and bosses at work, the very people women turn to for protection are the ones who pose the greatest danger.

By and large, women take more precautions for safety in their everyday lives than do men (see also reference 38), and are more likely to limit their movements in public or isolate themselves in order to avoid danger. They are also surrounded by advice about sensible precaution. An example of this special advice is the Home Office's own crime prevention leaflet, *Practical ways to crack crime,* now in its fourth edition[39] (for a critique, see reference 40).

Women's precautionary behaviour occurs both in public and in private. Maria states:

> I don't go out at night unless it's with someone. If I'm going out with friends, they will always pick me up at my door. When I come back they'll walk me to my apartment and make sure everything is OK.

Jane, too, reports:

> When I get into the car, I always check the back seat, to make sure that there is no one lurking around. I always have my keys in my hand, so that when I get to the car, I could stick the key into the door . . . And I lock the doors right away.

Linda, who was raped in her own home by an unknown man who crawled into her first-storey bedroom, actually had security built into her new home:

> We built this house because I had been raped. . . . I think everybody thinks we're crazy . . . Our doors are really good. We have grates on the basement windows, that sort of thing. Very small windows at the top.

And Bea, threatened by her first husband and sexually abused by her father, told her second husband before she married him:

> If you ever, ever, ever touch me I will call the police. I've never known if this man would have thought on these lines.

—but she made certain that he knew that he would not get away with being abusive, a strategy for her own peace of mind.

Despite all the best strategies, the growing body of feminist research indicates that women's actual experiences of sexual assault and perceived sexual danger are so widespread that they should be considered as endemic (see also references 35–37, 40). This means that all women's precautions do not protect them. Avoidance of the street for potential danger, the advice issued by police and Home Office alike, places women at risk to the danger from known men. The limited evidence from police statistics and Home Office research suggests that it is heterosexual intimacies and friendships which lead to physical and sexual assault of women.[8–10] As Eileen learned, her common sense about safety did not help her:

> If I went out to a pub or disco, wherever, at night, I drove back and didn't drink. Or I arranged that I could get there and back or knew I was with people I could get home with or get back to their place and stay [there overnight]. I have never been [in the situation] where I have been out and not known I could get home. I took all the general precautions, like not opening the door, always knowing who was on the other side of the door before opening it, especially at night when there's no people around. All those precautions I took. I didn't expect that somebody I had met two or

three times would . . . who had been in my home, who had been invited
into my home, would do this [rape] me, after having known him.

Research indicates that women's overall experience of violent crime
differs significantly from men's. In a recent Home Office study of 2,839
murders committed between 1984 and 1988, 43% of those killed were
women.[41] Of those killed, 44% were killed by husbands or lovers (1 in
10 men were killed by a wife or lover), 18% by other relatives and a
further 18% by friends or acquaintances. Other research indicates that
women also perceive any criminal encounter or potential criminal
encounter as sexually threatening. Maguire's study of victims of
burglary, for instance, found women felt sexually violated and threatened by a burglary.[19] Davidoff and Dowds in their analysis of recent
trends in crimes of violence in England and Wales note that more than
half the assaults against women (56%) reported in the 1988 British
Crime Survey were 'domestic' compared with only 8% of the assaults
against men.[8] Davidoff and Greenhorn's analysis of violent crime
reveals that just over half of all offences of violence and three-quarters
of attacks on women occurred indoors in either the victim's or the
suspect's home.[42]

Women's safety is therefore not just a matter of avoiding the
potentially dangerous stranger. Their relationships with known men
should be grounds for greater precaution. My research, despite its non-
random sample and qualitative analysis, illustrates the growing statistical evidence that women's understanding of safety means sexual *and*
physical safety.

Men, violence and danger

Men have not benefited from any advice concerning safety issues in
crime prevention campaigns, which is curious given the consistent
findings that young men report the highest levels of personal violence
to crime survey researchers.[12,16,17,24] It is assumed that young men
can protect themselves, but they do not seem to do so very successfully.

It seems to be a universal assumption of crime prevention that men
do not need safety advice. Yet men do take precautions for their own
safety (see also reference 38). They may be loath to admit it, but they
do manage danger in their everyday lives. One significant difference is
that for the most part they learn to negotiate physical danger and
violence in the company of other men. In contrast to women, who
concentrate their strategies for safety by monitoring men's behaviour,
men look to their own gender for signs of potential danger.

When men express concern about safety, it is largely an unease
about physical safety, their wariness directed towards groups of young

men. La Grange and Ferraro have recently found that one in 10 men express concern about sexual safety.[43] Interestingly, this finding coincides with the aggregate evidence of the proportion of young men who report being victims of sexual abuse during childhood.[44] Whilst some of the men interviewed for my study reported experiences of sexual abuse during their childhood, they conceptualised safety in adulthood as revolving around physical, not sexual safety.

Seidler suggests that:

> as boys, we have to be constantly on the alert to either confront or avoid physical violence. We have to be alert to defend ourselves. . . . Masculinity is never something we can feel at ease with. It is always something we have to be ready to prove and defend.[45]

Most of the men recalled incidents of fighting while growing up. Their stories, however, varied a great deal. Not all physical confrontations were the 'usual' boys' spats and disagreements, as many boys' battles are characterised. Some boys were clearly victims, others victimisers. Many, at some point, used fights to resolve arguments, establish territory or display the fact that they were 'real' men, while a few succeeded in steering clear of physical altercations altogether.

One important function of learning physical defensiveness is negotiating forms of acceptable heterosexual masculinity, which may mean that men are more willing to settle disputes through physical force. The 1988 British Crime Survey for example found that 57% of all assaults are suffered by young men aged 16–24, of which approximately 60% are assaults arising from street brawls and pub fights.[8]

Homophobia, and the potential violence experienced by a boy or man seen to be homosexual, are natural extensions of negotiating heterosexual masculinity. Fred describes one such situation:

> I was assaulted on Main Street about five years ago. Someone came up behind me and started screaming 'faggot' and punched me on the side of the head. I fell unconscious. . .

So, too, may racism be used as a way to denigrate other men and justify violence. The non-white men interviewed were clearly aware of the potential danger of being a target for racial violence. The 1988 British Crime Survey indicates that non-whites tend to be more at risk than whites for many types of crime, and that being threatened and assaulted because of race is common.[24]

Men name prison as the place where they would fear sexual violence. Rape and other forms of sexual exploitation serve to 'feminise' and degrade inmates. Male rape, still a hidden phenomenon, may serve more to enhance heterosexual masculinity, for its victims question their own identity as *men*, whether they themselves are heterosexual or homosexual.[46] Moreover, the rapists, inside and outside prison, may feel that they have enhanced their own image of themselves as men because they have raped.[47,48]

By and large, the men who avoid sexual exploitation—and, unlike women, most of them do—speak of their lives in terms of less restriction and greater mobility. When men experience a life-threatening or potentially life-threatening situation not only do they re-evaluate their relationship to personal safety and criminal violence, but they also feel that the assault is as much an affront to their masculinity as it is to their physical well-being.[15,49]

Physicians' work and everyday violence

There are a number of implications for physicians' work when consideration is given to the above patterns of violence. The following is a personal list of some points felt to be the most important.

Sexually intrusive situations

Women experience a variety of situations as sexually intrusive. They may also have past experiences of violence they have repressed or tried to forget. Feelings of helplessness, anxiety, depression, sleeplessness, change of eating habits and so forth may be symptomatic of anxiety caused by past victimisation or linked to an overall feeling about unsafety. While some of the conditions may reach acute levels, many of these situations are normal reactions of women living in contemporary society. They indicate that women are much more likely than men to be targets of sexual abuse, exploitation and harassment. Studies of crime victims also suggest that sexual offences have the greatest impact upon victims.[50] Speaking to women about the impact of abuse on their lives—either as experience or as potential—may encourage them to talk about their fears rather than allow them to continue unrecognised.

Physical danger within the home

Women experience the greatest physical danger within their own homes. Treating the wounds will not cure the problem of domestic violence. Literature and information should be available for women in surgeries, listing advice services, refuges, victim support and help lines. Whilst some women may leave violent men after the first punch, many more will put up with it for years. Information about alternatives, speaking to women in similar situations, and not hiding the violence from the general practitioner or psychiatrist is a step towards getting out of violence.

Violence against men

Men are reluctant to seek help after violence or to admit fear because it would not appear 'manly' to do so (see Chapter 9). Asking direct questions to men, without attributing blame, about violence encountered is the most straightforward way to confront the problem. It must not be assumed that all fights are 'fair' fights.

Racial or homophobic violence

Attacks motivated by racial or homophobic hatred also have special dimensions and should be recognised.

Post-traumatic stress disorder

The experience of disasters such as Hillsborough and Bradford indicate that the experience of sudden violence is extremely traumatic. Moreover, women and men who confront violence at work may exhibit problems and anxiety about returning to work. An awareness of post-traumatic stress disorder and of its patterns in relation to crime is needed. Some people will experience acute symptoms even when no actual physical or sexual attack has occurred. Although related to a different kind of stressor, the description in Chapter 9 of the problems of the policeman on point duty away from the scene of a disaster are broadly illustrative of this point.

Conclusions

Women's and men's experience of danger is a part of their everyday lives, and all of us take some precautions in our routines to avoid violence. Research in the USA—always assumed to be a more violent country than the UK—now indicates that as many as 9 out of 10 Americans suffer some serious violence in their lifetimes. Even if the UK figures are half those of the USA, as a guessing exercise this still means that almost one in 5 people in this country will experience some serious violence. Assistance for people to come to terms with violence and develop healthy mechanisms for dealing with its aftermath is essential.

References

1. Greenberg MS, Rubak RB, Westcott DR. Seeking help from the police: the victim's perspective. In: *New directions in helping (3)*. New York: Academic Press, 1983
2. Torrance J. *Public violence in Canada*. Kingston, Canada: McGill, Queen's University Press, 1986

3. Janoff-Bulman R, Frieze I. A theoretical perspective for understanding reactions to victimisation. *J Social Issues* 1983; **39**:1–17
4. Wortman C. Coping with victimisation: conclusions and implications for future research. *J Social Issues* 1983; **39**:195–221
5. Chibnall JS. *Law and order news*. London: Tavistock, 1977
6. Soothill K, Walby S. *Sex crime in the news*. London: Routledge, 1990
7. Grade M. *Fear of crime*. Report of a Working Group. London: HMSO, 1989
8. Davidoff L, Dowds L. Recent trends in crimes of violence against the person in England and Wales. *Res Bull*, no. 27:11–17
9. Smith L. *Domestic violence*. London: HMSO, 1989
10. Smith L. *Concerns about rape*. London: HMSO, 1989
11. Sampson R, Lauritsen J. *Violent victimisation and offending: individual, situational and community-level risk factors* (in press)
12. Maxfield M. *Fear of crime in England and Wales*. London: HMSO, 1984
13. Maxfield M. *Explaining fear of crime: evidence from the 1984 British Crime Survey*. London: Research and Planning Unit, 1987
14. Stanko EA. Typical violence, normal precaution: women, men and interpersonal violence in England, Wales, Scotland and the USA. In: Hanmer J, Maynard M, eds. *Women, violence and social control*. London: Macmillan, 1987
15. Stanko EA. *Everyday violence*. London: Pandora, 1990
16. Hough M, Mayhew P. *The British Crime Survey*. London: HMSO, 1983
17. Hough M, Mayhew P. *Taking account of crime: key findings from the 1984 British Crime Survey*. London: HMSO, 1985
18. Walmsley R. *Personal violence*. London: HMSO, 1986
19. Maguire M. *Burglary in a dwelling*. London: Heinemann, 1982
20. Shapland J, Willmore J, Duff P. *Victims in the criminal justice system*. Aldershot: Gower, 1985
21. Farrell G. *Multiple victimisation: its extent and significance*. Manchester: Department of Social Policy, Manchester University, 1991
22. Hindelang M, Gottfredson M, Garofalo J. *Victims of personal crime: an empirical foundation for a theory of personal victimisation*. Cambridge, MA: Ballinger, 1978
23. Gottfredson M. *Victims of crime: dimensions of risk*. London: HMSO, 1984
24. Mayhew P, Dowds L, Elliot D. *The 1988 British Crime Survey*. London: HMSO, 1989
25. Harlow C. *Female victims of violent crime*. Washington, DC: Bureau of Justice Statistics, 1991
26. Jones T, McLean B, Young J. *The Islington Crime Survey*. Aldershot: Gower, 1986
27. Crawford A, Jones T, Woodhouse T, Young J. *The Second Islington Crime Survey*. Middlesex Polytechnic, 1990
28. Genn H. Multiple victimisation. In: Maguire M, Pointing J, eds. *Victims of crime: a new deal?* Milton Keynes: Open University Press, 1988
29. Pease K. The Kirkholt project: preventing burglary on a British public housing estate. *Security J* 1991; **2**:71–103
30. Forrester D, Chatterton M, Pease K. *The Kirkholt burglary prevention project, Rochdale*. Home Office CPU, paper no. 13. London: HMSO, 1988
31. Polvi N, Looman T, Humphries C, Pease K. Repeat break and enter victimisation: time course and crime prevention opportunity. *J Police Sci Admin* 1990; **17**: 8–11
32. Sheperd J. Violent crime in Bristol: an accident and emergency department perspective. *Br J Criminol* 1990; **30**:289–305
33. Kelly L, Regan L, Burton S. *An exploratory study of the prevalence of sexual abuse in a sample of 16–21 year olds*. North London Polytechnic: Child Abuse Students Unit, 1991
34. Markowe HLJ. The frequency of childhood sexual abuse in the UK. *Health Trends* 1988; **20**:2–6
35. Stanko EA. *Intimate intrusions*. London: Routledge, 1985

36. MacKinnon C. *Feminism unidentified.* Cambridge, MA: Harvard University Press, 1989
37. Kelly L. *Surviving sexual violence.* Oxford: Polity, 1988
38. Gordon M, Riger S. *The female fear.* New York: Free Press, 1988
39. Home Office. *Practical ways to crack crime.* London: HMSO, 1989
40. Stanko EA. When precaution is normal: a feminist critique of crime prevention. In: Gelsthrope L, Morris A, eds. *Feminist perspectives in criminology.* Milton Keynes: Open University Press, 1990
41. Chowdry Q. Husbands or lovers kill half of women murder victims. *The Times*, 14 April 1990
42. Davidoff L, Greenhorn M. *Violent crime.* Paper presented to British Criminology Conference, York, 1991
43. LaGrange RL, Ferraro KF. Assessing age and gender differences in perceived risk and fear of crime. *Criminol* 1989; **27**:697–719
44. Finkelhor D. *Sexually victimised children.* New York: Free Press, 1979
45. Seidler V. Raging bull. *Achilles heel* 1980; no. 5:9
46. Seabrook J. Male rape. *New Statesman Soc*, 5 October 1990:19–22
47. Wooden NS, Parker J. *Men behind bars: sexual exploitation in prison.* New York: Da Capo Press, 1980
48. Scully D, Marolla J. Riding the bull at Gilley's: convicted rapists describe the rewards of rape. *Social Problems* 1985; **32**:20–2
49. Hobdell K. *Men talk.* London: Islington Victim Support, 1989
50. Maguire M, Corbett C. *The effects of crime and the work of victim support schemes.* Aldershot: Gower

Part 4
Evaluation of the clinician's role

Pamela J. Taylor
Head of Medical Services, Special Hospitals Service Authority, London

The preceding chapters in this book have demonstrated that the medical profession, clinical psychologists and colleagues from allied disciplines have much to contribute to limiting some violence and containing the effects of still more. However, three notes of caution are worth emphasising. The first is that there are and always will be substantial areas in the management of violence in which the clinician is just a layman and, whilst his intervention should not necessarily be discouraged, all parties should recognise the limits to his expertise. Secondly, wherever a clinician's role is theoretically valid, the exercise of that role must be subject to continuous evaluation, and thus to informed improvement. In Chapter 13 Graham Robertson demonstrates that, as yet, methods for evaluation have been simplistic, perhaps even inept. More reliable and valid measures of risk, and in turn of the impact of clinical interventions and predicted risk, are essential in individual case work. Such measures are also vital for the furthering of medical and psychological understanding, and relate to the third caution—that there remains so much that is not known.

13 | Reconviction: a measure of psychiatric efficacy?

Graham Robertson
Department of Forensic Psychiatry, Institute of Psychiatry, Denmark Hill, London

Introduction

Although it may be legitimate for a psychiatrist to be interested in the re-offending of a particular patient, for the most part reconviction and reconviction studies are of no relevance when considering the efficacy of psychiatric treatments. The first part of this chapter is concerned with reconviction in relation to studies of mentally ill and mentally handicapped people, and the second with reconviction as a measure of psychiatric efficacy among other groups of people with whom psychiatrists have to deal—namely, the psychopathic or personality disordered. The issues raised by the two types of patient in the matter of reconviction seem to be very different.

The mentally ill and mentally handicapped

In the UK, dating from the end of the Second World War, changes began to take place in the amount of freedom allowed to psychiatric patients. The introduction of phenothiazine medication in the early to mid-1950s speeded up this process dramatically. The Mental Health Act 1959 (MHA 1959) may be taken as a marker for this gradual change, a by-product of which was increasing concern about public safety. Put in its crudest form, would we be able to sleep easily in our beds if all these mad people were let out of the asylums? The sanitised, academic version of the question took the following form: do mentally ill and mentally handicapped people commit more offences, and are they liable to commit offences of serious violence more often than would be predicted, given their numbers in the population?

Expressed in this form, neither question deserves to be answered. The end-product of all investigations initiated by this type of thinking is bound to produce the response: what if mentally ill people *do* commit more offences than other people? Should they all be locked up, the just with the unjust, because of some statistical association? Of course not.

There would be as much reason to lock up all the so-called sane if the opposite conclusion was taken.

Probably the largest group of mentally ill and mentally handicapped offenders to be studied in England and Wales was collected by Walker and McCabe in the early 1960s.[1] They examined the effect of the then newly introduced MHA 1959 by seeking information about all the people given hospital orders by courts over a 12-month period. This population was followed up 15 years later by the present author and Gibbens, a large part of our work being concerned with obtaining information on their subsequent offending.[2,3]

The mentally ill offender

The pattern of offending by mentally ill people (almost all of them suffering from a psychosis, usually schizophrenia) differed from the typical criminal pattern in a number of respects:

1. Notably, the average age at first conviction for this group of people was different from that normally found among criminal populations. Typically, many first came to the attention of the police in their mid- to late 20s after the onset of illness. For such people their entry into the criminal justice system may be regarded as a function of the deterioration in their mental health. However, this central tendency statistic should not hide the fact that many also come into the criminal justice system along the more conventional route of juvenile delinquency.
2. As with crime in general, offences involving serious violence are rare. When they do occur, they can be terrible of course and headline-grabbing—but they are infrequent. For example, only 7 of the 268 mentally ill men sent to a local hospital under a hospital order in the Walker and McCabe study were reconvicted of an offence of serious violence in the following 15 years.
3. Offenders who suffered from a psychotic illness were more likely to have been found guilty of an acquisitive offence than of any other type of offence, an overall pattern of offending similar to that of the general population. They probably differ both in their vulnerability to detection and in their propensity for committing public order offences of various types, such as criminal damage, threatening behaviour and police assaults. All these can vary in seriousness from the trivial to the potentially fatal. The person with schizophrenia who is homeless and/or a heavy drinker may be especially liable to commit and be arrested for this type of disorderly behaviour.

The mentally handicapped offender

There was a major difference between the mentally handicapped and mentally ill groups in that the average age at first conviction of the former was much closer to that of the general population. Once again though, the types of offence for which most handicapped people were convicted were acquisitive. Within the population of mentally disordered offenders there was a statistical association with sexual offending and, to a lesser extent, with the offence of arson—but it has to be remembered that the great majority of offenders in both categories were (and are) not people with mental handicap. Offences of serious violence are rare, but they do sometimes occur in that most tragic of circumstances involving the sexual murder of children.

Follow-up study of mentally disordered offenders

There were about 1,200 people in the original study by Walker and McCabe. A study population of this size followed up over 15 years provided an excellent opportunity to examine the question of dangerous re-offending. What characterised those people among this population who went on to commit serious life-threatening offences, and could the perpetrators of such offences be predicted?

The 15-year follow-up study included data on 887 of the people who had entered hospital via the courts or the prison system in 1963 and were still alive in 1978.[2,3]

A majority of these people (63%) had obtained at least one conviction during that period, but the most interesting finding concerns the pattern of reconvictions, which was very intermittent. When the criminal records of what might be called 'normal criminals' are examined, they present, in general, a steady decline in the frequency of offending with age. This is not the pattern among the mentally disordered. In this sample, often many years would pass without any involvement with the courts, and the fall off with increasing age was not nearly so marked. The picture presented is one of long-term vulnerability to trouble, as might be expected, given the lifelong nature of psychotic illness. In the 15-year period involved, 52 (6%) of the 887 on whom adequate information was available had subsequently been convicted of what was considered to be a very serious offence, specifically, homicide, grievous bodily harm (GBH), arson and rape. An attempt was made to see whether any characteristic or group of characteristics distinguished these offenders from their contemporaries.

Table 1. Variables which discriminated 'dangerous' re-offenders

	People reconvicted of a 'dangerous offence'	Others	*p*
Age at entry to study	25	30	0.001
Age at 1st conviction	19	23	0.001
Arson offence as index offence	12%	3%	0.001
Mean number of juvenile offences	2	0.9	0.024

Table 2. Age distribution of 'dangerous' re-offenders and others

Age distribution	'Dangerous' re-offenders		Others	
(years)	(no.)	(%)	(no.)	(%)
10–19	19	37	154	18
20–29	16	31	283	34
30–39	12	24	220	27
40+	4	8	175	19

The details summarised in Table 1 show that criminological, not psychiatric, variables predominate. This information is of little practical use, however, which is well illustrated with reference to the most statistically discriminatory variable, age at entry into the original study. Details of the distribution of this variable are presented in Table 2. Using central tendency statistics, it is evident that the difference observed is due to the fact that the so-called dangerous re-offender group contains proportionately more teenagers. A third of this group were under 20 in 1963 compared to less than one-fifth of the other group. On the other hand, only 11% of the 173 teenagers in the population came into our dangerous re-offender category, and 89% did not. The more sophisticated statistical device of multiple regression analysis, using dangerous re-offending as the criterion variable, revealed that only age made a significant independent contribution to the prediction of the distribution of the dependent variables and, as already shown, the relationship was weak (correlation coefficient 0.13).

Eight of the 887 people for whom information was available had killed or attempted to kill someone. Details for three of these cases are provided below to help illustrate some of the reasons why the statistical approach is of such limited value.

Case histories

Case 1

The first man was 14 when he was convicted for theft and, judging from his record, he fell into the habit of stealing, and the courts certainly developed the habit of sending him to prison. At the age of 23, he was admitted for the first time to a mental hospital, with the diagnosis of schizophrenia and a secondary diagnosis of psychopathic disorder. He was 32 when he came into the Walker and McCabe study, having been convicted of fraud. For this acquisitive offence, he was given a hospital order with a restriction order of five years' duration. He was admitted to a local hospital. (This order was made in the early years of the operation of the MHA 1959 when judges were still inclined to regard mental hospitals as secure and therefore the equivalent of prison.) He absconded from the hospital to which he had been admitted, and on the same day attacked two strangers in the street with a broken bottle. For this apparently motiveless offence, which may well have been caused by an abnormal mental state, he was sentenced to seven years in prison, although he was soon transferred to a special hospital, from which he was discharged $4\frac{1}{2}$ years later. Eighteen months after this he was convicted of attempted murder, having stabbed a stranger in the street. A life sentence was awarded, but he was once again transferred to a special hospital. In the follow-up study he was placed in the category of mentally ill and violent offenders, but the nature of any relationship between his criminal acts and his mental abnormalities was far from clear, at least in the material available to us.

Case 2

The second case concerns a mentally handicapped man who was only 18 when he was convicted of his index offence. In trouble from the age of 9, he had six convictions, including two for indecent assault, before he was convicted for homicide in 1960 and sent to a secure hospital under the provisions of the Mental Deficiency Act 1913 which then operated. The offence which brought him into the Walker and McCabe study was the attempted murder of a nurse in a hospital. In

1974, he was again brought before a court and found guilty of attempted murder, this time of a fellow patient. He was again returned to special hospital under a hospital order, this time with restrictions without limit of time. He was still there when the follow-up study ended. Never at liberty in the community, he was none the less one of the most serious of the serious re-offenders.

Case 3

The only woman in this group of eight homicidal people had not been convicted of an offence until 1963 (her index offence), when she was found guilty of assaulting one of her neighbours. Diagnosed as having paranoid schizophrenia she was in hospital for four months before being discharged. Within a year she had been returned to court charged, on this occasion, with murder. She was found unfit to plead and was sent to a special hospital. She was still there some 13 years later when the study ended.

Value of reconviction data to the clinician

It is difficult to know how these three people, or indeed all eight who formed the homicide re-offender group, can be regarded as having anything in common other than the type of offence of which they were (re)convicted. No other single factor united them. If, however, it is assumed that early and persistent delinquency reflects social and personal disadvantage,[4] it might be noted that most of the men in the group came from such a background, and were doubly disadvantaged in that they also suffered from some terrible mental illness such as schizophrenia, or were mentally handicapped to some degree.

The collection of reconviction data on people who suffer from a major mental illness can be of little use to the clinician. This question has recently been reviewed for the Home Office by Murray, who concluded that the actuarial approach has potential to aid prediction.[5] However, the model he advocates is so dependent on the clinical one that it is difficult to see what incremental value it might have.

No one can predict what another person will do over the long term. In any case, those who have the care of this type of patient are required to have the ability to recognise and take action in respect of likely violence in the short term. This is important. There is no need to read many special hospital case notes before appreciating that trage-dies can and do happen when psychiatric emergencies are not recog-nised and treated appropriately by the relevant local psychiatric services.

Comparison of people with psychosis and people with personality disorder

Psychotic disorders

The parameters for judging whether or not psychiatric treatment of psychotic people is being effective are well defined and apply regardless of whether or not they come into treatment consequent to a criminal conviction. Several years ago consultants at Broadmoor hospital were interviewed about the admission, treatment and discharge of their patients.[6] With the psychotic patients, in almost every case the doctor had a good understanding of the nature of the relationship between the illness process and the violent action which had resulted in admission to hospital. Such patients were given the same type of treatment as they would have received in any psychiatric hospital, with the aim of restoring the person's thinking to some sort of order. This was not always possible, of course, and the net effect of medication was often simply to sedate.

Suitability for discharge of psychotic patients was judged on the basis of how well they were. Obviously, a psychotic patient who had committed a homicide would be required to show stability over a long period of time, and the consultant would have to be convinced that the person concerned would co-operate with treatment after discharge, which was unusual, or transfer to a hospital with less security nearer to their home community. None the less, the basic criteria for fitness were determined with reference to those factors which pertain in general psychiatric practice.

Psychopathic disorders

This was not the case with the treatment and discharge of those men detained in Broadmoor under the legal category of psychopathic disorder. I suggest that it is because of their involvement with this group that psychiatrists, especially those working in forensic psychiatry, have come to regard post-treatment offending as a legitimate measure of their work. As things stand at present, it is not. The way in which attempts have been made to link treatment and re-offending are methodological and statistical nonsense. This is as true in the prison system as in the health service.

Psychotherapy and Grendon Prison

A study in which I was involved a number of years ago was designed to examine the therapeutic effectiveness of Grendon Underwood Prison.[7]

This prison, opened in July 1962, was the Prison Department's first attempt to put into practice the recommendations of two psychiatrists, East and Hubert, who published a report for the Home Office in 1939 on their experiences of treating prisoners with psychotherapy.[8] The type of treatment on offer had been either the supportive/directive kind or a much more intensive form of psychoanalysis.

East and Hubert were very concerned to point out the likely limitations of psychotherapy for prisoners, but none the less their report recommended that a penal institution of a special kind should be built to house and treat suitable offenders. Neither psychotic men nor men who were mentally handicapped were accepted into Grendon prison. Treatment consisted of fairly intensive group therapy and, insofar as possible within a prison setting, the regime operated as a therapeutic community. The prison's first governor was a psychiatrist, it was staffed by five doctors, three or four psychologists, and it had a high ratio of prison officers to prisoners. Needless to say, it cost a lot of money to run and, inevitably, the question to which everyone wanted to know the answer was whether it worked. By this they meant not whether it made ill people better, but rather whether it affected the criminality of people who went there—a question which, of course, assumes a causal link between treatment and criminal behaviour. It crystallises the confusion which has arisen because the term 'better', meaning the relief of symptoms, has often been used interchangeably with 'better', meaning improved behaviour and, in this case, specifically, a reduction in reconviction.

The prison was examined and the effect of the treatment on its inmates evaluated. An important aspect of the work was a follow-up study of men once they had completed their sentences.

Follow-up study of reconviction: experimental design

Figure 1 presents the basic detail of the design used for this part of the project. There were two groups: one had experienced the treatment regime in Grendon, the other had not. By using the parole index, Grendon men could be matched with men in other prisons. Once the groups were matched, we examined their criminal records over 2 and 10 years.[7,9] The model employed is common in the social sciences. It is widely used in medicine, and is fundamental to the physical sciences from which it emanates. But in the way in which it is often used within the social sciences, and certainly as it was used here, it is so much nonsense. An example of the type of experimental set-up on which the model used in the Grendon study was based is the following: equivalent pieces of metal are studied, one of which is treated with a special compound and the other left untreated; both pieces are then exposed

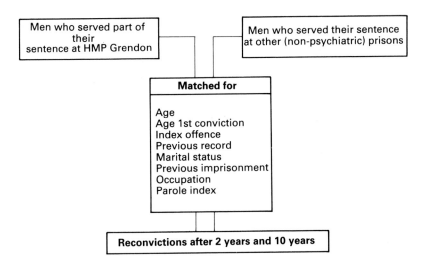

Fig. 1. *The Grendon reconviction study.*

to the atmosphere, to heat or whatever, and then examined to determine whether there is a differential effect. At first sight, the same type of process seems to have been undertaken in the Grendon study but, in fact, so many assumptions had to be made that the integrity of the model breaks down:

1. The *level of control* that can be exerted over the raw material in the experimental situation: for the metal experiment, it is possible to exercise control over almost all the potentially confounding variables, but at Grendon it was impossible to control in any way for the previous experience of the men in either the Grendon or control groups.
2. The *experimental condition*: whereas in the metal experiment there is almost complete control quantitatively over the measurement of the treatment condition, this was not the case in the Grendon situation, and it must be assumed that the men who came to Grendon were affected by the place in a variety of qualitative ways, many of which were dependent upon what they brought to the institution. For example, some people will have been truly motivated, others not; some will have been intelligent and articulate, able to make good use of the group treatment which is the hallmark of the place, whereas other men would not have been in this position.
3. The *post-experimental condition*: whereas in the metal experiment it is possible to assume adequate control over what is done to the metal plates, in the Grendon so-called experiment it must be assumed that the men in both the Grendon and the control groups were subject to a wide variety of post-discharge experiences.

4. The *criterion measure of reconviction*: the treatment effect was time
   spent in Grendon as opposed to time spent in another type of
   prison, but the treatment effect must be a very small part of the
   variance which contributes to the criterion measure—the theoretical contribution must be minute.

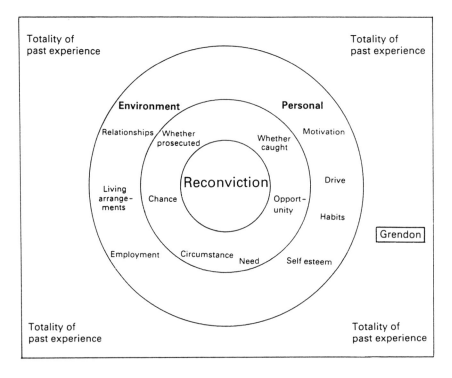

Fig. 2. *Relationship with criterion measure of reconviction.*

The criterion measure of reconviction

Looking closer at the criterion measure of reconviction (Fig. 2), the
size of the contribution made by error or random variance is almost
impossible to estimate, a prerequisite for any experiment within the
physical sciences. However, it is known that many offences, particularly the less serious type of offence, are not reported. Most offending
which *is* reported does not result in someone being charged with that
offence, and many of the people charged with an offence are not
eventually convicted—our criterion measure of 'success' or 'failure'.
These factors are placed close to the criterion measure of reconviction
in the figure because they affect it in a major way. Next to these are
placed items such as the man's circumstances immediately before the
offence was committed, his living arrangements, for example, and also

his habits—he may after all make a living from theft of various kinds. Outside this boundary can be placed all that he is and all that he has experienced, part of which is whether or not he was ever in Grendon Underwood Prison.

It might be thought that 10 years would be a long enough period for many chance or random effects to be 'ironed out', especially if only serious re-offending is of interest, but this is not so, for which there was ample evidence in the 10-year follow-up study. Once again, three case histories are presented.

Case histories from Grendon Prison

Case 1

A man had been admitted to Grendon in his late 30s in the course of serving a long sentence for armed robbery. He had a very long record and was realistic about his chances of going straight after his release. However, he was pleased that he had been sent to Grendon where, for the first time in his life, he had felt able to contribute to other people, in this case the younger men on his wing. He received his first post-discharge conviction (for stealing) within a few months of leaving the prison. This was followed over the years by convictions for burglary, drunkenness and drug-taking, a total of four convictions, none of which resulted in further imprisonment. In comparison with his pre-Grendon career his post-Grendon record might have been viewed as a considerable improvement, but it could also have been due to ageing or to changes in the sentencing habits of the courts.

Shortly before the end of the 10-year follow-up period he was involved in a drunken fight in a public house. The fight continued on to the street, and ended in his opponent being killed. This offence did not, and never will, appear on his criminal record. When he was remanded in custody, medical examination revealed that he was suffering from a cancer which was fairly well advanced and prosecution was not pressed. These circumstances are known to us only because I was carrying out some research in Brixton when the man was remanded there and saw him in the hospital wing of that prison. Had he not been terminally ill, he would have appeared as a homicide offender in the Grendon group, causing a 100% increase in this particular type of offence.

Case 2

A man in his early 20s who came from a criminal family had his first offence recorded before he was a teenager. His record was notable for its variety, and included offences for living off immoral earnings. He had, incidentally, requested his own transfer to Grendon because he wanted to do something about his feelings of depression. When interviewed shortly before he left the prison he said that he had benefited from his stay. He felt he had come to terms with what he called his inferiority complex and was more confident in himself. His complaints were of psychological problems and he had obtained help from his experience of Grendon. In the same interview, he said that he would probably return to stealing once released. It was possible to keep in touch with him by post for 12 months after his release, and he said that he had been stealing but had not been caught. At least the second part of this statement could be confirmed from his criminal record.

When the 10-year follow-up period ended, no further convictions had been recorded against him. Compared to his pre-Grendon record, this might have been hailed as little short of a miracle. However, several months later he was convicted of a firearms offence and given a 10-year prison sentence. The severity of the sentence may have been a function of crimes he was suspected of having committed but with which he had never been charged. Rather than representing a radical change in his criminal behaviour, his clean record may simply have reflected an improvement in his ability to avoid arrest. In following the model he had to be included in the non-offender population. Again, the point is simply that the random or error variance makes statistical examination of the treatment effect totally inappropriate.

Case 3

The third man was in his mid-20s when first seen in Grendon. His first recorded conviction was when aged 11, and he had a long record of offences, including several for serious violence. On release from Grendon, he quickly returned to drug-taking and petty theft which took the form of stealing from meters. This was known because he told us, but he was not caught and convicted. Within a year, he met a woman, they settled down together and he obtained a job in the civil service. It was some time before his employers discovered he had a record, by which time he had proved himself in his work and he was kept on. This was his first period of settled employment. This situation continued for some years, but when his relationship with his girl-friend broke down, he became depressed, left his job and there was a general deterioration in his behaviour. Eventually, he was convicted for theft and sought psychiatric help. The variable which probably had most influence over his early 'success' and later deterioration was his relationship with his girl-friend an event over which Grendon had no control, and for the effects of which it could not be held responsible.

Reconviction as a criterion of therapeutic success

What has been criticised so far is the way reconviction has been used to measure group differences, but criticism can also be made of the use of the criterion at the individual level. In order to support the view that reconviction reflects on the efficacy of psychiatric treatment for an individual, a number of conditions must apply. It must be shown that a particular offence is caused by something which can be called a symptom of something that can be called an illness. If this is possible, it is then necessary to have a treatment or course of treatments which can be applied to the person who is suffering from this illness, and which is designed to make the illness better by removing or ameliorating the symptom. How often does this situation hold good in the field of personality disorder?

One reason why reconviction has become an issue for psychiatry is because some psychiatrists find themselves detaining under secure conditions people who are not suffering from a major mental illness. In ordinary life, people present to doctors in order to seek expert advice, usually to be relieved of some pain or discomfort. In two types of medical practice, emergency work and psychiatry, this paradigm may not hold good and the patient may be an unwilling or unconscious participant in the exchange which takes place with the doctor. In psychiatry, this situation arises when the patient is so mentally disordered and his powers of reason so impaired by psychotic illness that he is regarded as being 'out of his mind'. In such conditions, responsibility for treatment may be taken out of his control.

Men detained in conditions of security under the label of psychopathic disorder are not, in my view, 'out of their minds', yet are subjected to compulsory medical treatment. The official reason for their detention is their supposed need to be made better in the medical sense, but what is desired as a rule is that they should be made to behave better and not re-offend: to be made less dangerous to others to a significant degree. Morality and mental health have become hopelessly confused in the conceptual porridge of legal psychopathy. The use of reconviction as a criterion for measuring treatment efficacy is a by-product of this. Concern with post-discharge behaviour very often represents not so much concern about treatment efficacy as with the correctness of the discharge decision itself. In other words, people are not asking whether their treatment was correct, did it work, but rather whether they did the right thing when the patient was discharged.

This tends to be an emotionally loaded question, rather than one which is amenable to scientific evaluation.

Conclusion

Responsibility may be defined as that which is demanded of an individual by virtue of his position. Psychiatrists and other doctors have responsibility to and for the care of patients and to work conscientiously for the authority which employs them. This is true whether the fashion is for therapeutic optimism or nihilism. They can only do what they consider to be best for their patients. Sometimes they do not know whether they have done any good at all, especially in those cases where the patient is not suffering from a major mental illness. What is certain is that they are not responsible for their patients' behaviour, providing they have followed the tenets of good clinical practice. For this reason, and for all the other reasons outlined in this chapter, their work—their therapeutic effectiveness—cannot be judged by whether or not their patients are ever reconvicted.

References

1. Walker N, McCabe S. *Crime and insanity in England* (vol 2). Edinburgh: Edinburgh University Press, 1973
2. Robertson G, Gibbens TCN. *The criminal careers of mentally disordered offenders.* Unpublished report to Home Office, 1979
3. Gibbens TCN, Robertson G. A survey of the criminal careers of hospital order patients. A survey of the criminal careers of restriction order patients. *Br J Psychiatry* 1983; **143**:362–9, 370–5
4. Farrington DP. Antisocial personality from childhood to adulthood. *Psychologist* 1991; **4**:389–94
5. Murray DJ. *Review of research on re-offending of mentally disordered offenders.* Research and Planning Unit, paper 55. London: Home Office, 1989
6. Dell S, Robertson G. *Sentenced to hospital.* Oxford: Oxford University Press, 1988
7. Gunn J, Robertson G, Dell S, Way C. *Psychiatric aspects of imprisonment.* London: Academic Press, 1978
8. East WN, Hubert WHdeB. *The psychological treatment of crime.* London: HMSO, 1939
9. Robertson G, Gunn J. A ten-year follow-up of men discharged from Grendon Prison. *Br J Psychiatry* 1987; **151**:674–8

14 | Furthering medical and psychological understanding of violence

Pamela J. Taylor

Head of Medical Services, Special Hospitals Service Authority, London

Violence is not unique to humans, nor to a particular period in time. It seems so intrinsic to society that it perhaps has to be regarded as a normal phenomenon. The harm that can ensue both to the aggressor and to the aggressed against is, however, undeniable. With the help of the conference delegates, as well as the main speakers, this book has attempted to show some of what is known about the genesis of violence, when it might be regarded as pathological, and when and how doctors and their non-medical colleagues might be expected to exert some influence on the limitation of harm. The potential for intervention has been considered particularly with three perspectives in mind:

- where it might be possible to prevent violence, because that violence may arise from a developmental or disease process;
- where it might be possible to limit pain and suffering for those who have suffered violence; and
- how it might be possible to identify those who become trapped in cycles of violence, and how to break those cycles.

Much is known but, for those who are familiar with the field, that knowledge tends to highlight gaps both in basic information and in its interpretation. For those not so familiar, there is the problem of how to convey to them the sort of knowledge and spirit of enquiry that would lead to more informed and effective practice. Violence may or may not be increasing, but there is little evidence to suggest that society generally, or 'the experts' more specifically, are yet dealing with it more effectively. The reason for this, in part, undoubtedly relates to a lack of motivation and real commitment—as much by the peaceful, law-abiding and healthy as by the violent or diseased. Resources are made available on a massive scale to ensure the potential for a level of violence that few clinicians will ever experience at first hand, on the presumption that it has potential as a preventive measure. Chemical, biological and nuclear weaponry research, development and mainten-

197

ance are not underfunded from the perspective of the average worker in health or social services! Resources are less readily committed to the promotion of harmony in society, the restoration of those harmed by violence, and the development of those highly special skills and skill mixes needed to prevent occurrence and recurrence of that part of the violence spectrum that is generally accepted as pathological or driven by pathological states.

Reiss and Roth have also put the research commitment into its health service perspective.[1] They reported on the work of the Panel on the Understanding and Control of Violent Behavior, set up by the Commission on Behavioral and Social Sciences and Education of the National Research Council for the USA. After conducting a census of federal agencies thought to be sponsoring research, they found that federal expenditure for the fiscal year of 1989 was around \$18–20 million. 'In human terms', as they put it, this amounts to just \$3.41 per violent victimisation in 1988. Estimates of the cost to society of each violent event (e.g. money spent within the criminal justice system or on direct hospital costs) include \$54,000 per rape, \$19,200 per robbery and \$16,500 per aggravated assault. As a medical research topic, the level of commitment to advancing knowledge and containing the problem is even more shocking. The research expenditure per year of potential life lost is \$794 for cancer, \$441 for heart, lung and blood conditions, and \$697 for acquired immune deficiency syndrome (AIDS). It is just \$31 for violence. Comparable UK figures are not available, but it is unlikely that they are proportionately very different. Realistically, with minimal resourcing, advances will be proportionately tiny.

If \$500 million were released in the USA to bring federal support for violence research into line with federal support for cancer research, *and* equivalent amounts were also made available in the UK, other European countries, Commonwealth countries and other comparatively wealthy nations, how should or could that money be spent? With difficulty, is the partial answer, because in such a resource-starved field the pool of expertise is small and a considerable amount of time and resource would have to be spent in developing essential skills. For England and Wales, this was one of the key issues addressed in more than one of the advisory committees to the Review of Health and Social Services for Mentally Disordered Offenders and others Requiring Similar Services (known as the Reed Report).[2] Fantasising, however, about the availability of expertise as well as money, where should the great investment be made?

Accurate, reliable and valid measurement of criterion variables and risk factors must form the foundation of advancement. Graham Robertson (Chapter 13) illustrated well how convictions and reconvictions for violent offending are so seductively simple as measures of violence, and yet how misleading they can be in any clinical context—and indeed probably also in the criminal justice system. They have been allowed to stand for far too long as substitutes for comprehensive data that will better reflect both the details and complexity of reality.

At the conference, we were privileged to hear from Henry Steadman of his work, with John Monahan and others, supported by the MacArthur Foundation in the USA. The impressively thoughtful and scientific backgrounds of the two men (e.g. ref. 3–6) convinced the Foundation that support for no less than a seven-year basic, multi-centre programme would be essential for the promotion of knowledge in just the one area of the association between mental disorder and violence. The first two years were to be spent on planning and the development, revision and consolidation of assessment packages.[7] The risk assessment packages will be published in book form in late 1993.[8]

Although Monahan and colleagues will focus on the development of informed risk assessment among the mentally disordered, many of the same principles apply to work with offenders without obvious mental disorder, to perpetrators of harmful violence who never become, for one reason or another, technical criminals, and to work with those who find themselves suffering or coping with the effects of violence.

This means in part abandoning treasured all-or-nothing concepts such as dangerousness—whether to self or others—accepting the multi-plicity and variety of risks and their interrelationships, and matching these with correspondently pragmatic variety in intervention. The evaluation of risk of violence is best viewed as a continuum with prediction, counteractions and monitoring taking place within recog-nised limits of confidence, time-scale and circumstance. Thus, in a clinical situation, answers to key questions about risk can be given a value—even a numerical value:

- What is the seriousness of the risk identified?
- What is the imminence of the risk?
- What is the probability of the risk becoming actuality?

The answers may be specified as valid for the next 24 hours, four weeks or other interval, taking account also of the clinical and other social contexts. The matter might include a note of compliance with relevant treatment, any threat of the prospect of significant loss or, by contrast, the existence of a stable, supportive domestic and employment situ-ation. The appropriateness and reliability of the factors can be monitored, the accuracy of judgements checked, and the effectiveness of interventions tested as easily in the day-to-day clinical situation with individual patients as in major research projects. Members of each group of violent offenders or those offended against, and indeed every affected individual, can thus be treated as ordinary people with problems that can be addressed scientifically and professionally, rather than, as too often at present, as objects of fear, disgust or failure and weakness.

References

1. Reiss AJ, Roth JA, eds. *Understanding and preventing violence.* Washington, DC: National Academy Press, 1993
2. Department of Health, Home Office. *Review of health and social services for mentally disordered offenders and others requiring similar services.* Final summary report. Cmnd 2088. London: HMSO, 1992
3. Monahan J. The prediction of violent behaviour: toward a second generation of theory and policy. *Am J Psychiatry* 1984; **141**:10–5
4. Monahan J. Risk assessment of violence among the mentally disordered: generating useful knowledge. *Int J Law Psychiatry* 1988; **11**:149–57
5. Steadman H, Cocozza J. *Careers of the criminally insane.* Lexington, MA: Lexington Books, 1974
6. Steadman HJ. A situational approach to violence. *Int J Law Psychiatry* 1982; **5**: 171–86
7. Steadman HJ, Monahan J, Robbins PC, *et al.* From dangerousness to risk assessment: implications for appropriate research strategies. In: Hodgins S, ed. *Mental disorder and crime.* Newbury Park, CA: Sage, 1983:39–62
8. Monahan J, Steadman HJ. *Violence and mental disorder: developments in risk assessment.* Chicago: Chicago University Press (in press)